THE ELUSIVE CHILD

Winnicott Studies Monograph Series

The Person Who Is Me:
Contemporary Perspectives on the True and False Self
  edited by Val Richards

Fathers, Families, and the Outside World
  edited by Val Richards

André Green at The *Squiggle* Foundation
  edited by Jan Abram

Art, Creativity, Living
  edited by Lesley Caldwell

The *Squiggle* Foundation is a registered charity
set up in 1981 to study and cultivate the tradition
of D. W. Winnicott. For further information, contact
The Administrator, 33 Amberley Road, London N13 4BH.
Tel: 020 8882 9744; Fax: 020 8886 2418

Winnicott Studies Monograph Series

THE ELUSIVE CHILD

edited by
Lesley Caldwell

KARNAC
LONDON   NEW YORK

for
The *Squiggle* Foundation

First published in 2002 by
H. Karnac (Books) Ltd., 6 Pembroke Buildings, London NW10 6RE

A subsidiary of Other Press LLC, New York

Copyright © 2002 The *Squiggle* Foundation

Introduction © 2002 Lesley Caldwell; chapter 1 © 2002 Pierre Drapeau; chapter 2 © 2002 Margaret Tonnesmann; chapter 3 © 2002 Abe Brafman; chapter 4 © 2002 Catherine Mathelin; chapter 5 © 2002 Monica Lanyado; chapter 6 © 2002 Angela Joyce; chapter 7 © 2002 Alain Vanier; chapter 8 © 2002 Richard Frankel; chapter 9 © 2002 Amal Treacher; chapter 10 © 2002 Nicholas Spice

The rights of the contributors to be identified as the authors of this work have been asserted in accordance with §§ 77 and 78 of the Copyright Design and Patents Act 1988.

All rights reserved. No part of this publication may be reproduced, stored in a retrieval system, or transmitted, in any form or by any means, electronic, mechanical, photocopying, recording, or otherwise, without the prior written permission of the publisher.

British Library Cataloguing in Publication Data

A C.I.P. for this book is available from the British Library

ISBN 1 85575 296 4

10 9 8 7 6 5 4 3 2 1

Edited, designed, and produced by The Studio Publishing Services Ltd, Exeter EX4 8JN

Printed in Great Britain

www.karnacbooks.com

CONTENTS

CONTRIBUTORS   vii

Introduction
Lesley Caldwell   1

CHAPTER ONE
From Freud to Winnicott: an encounter between mythical children
Pierre Drapeau   15

CHAPTER TWO
Early emotional development: Ferenczi to Winnicott
Margret Tonnesmann   45

CHAPTER THREE
Infant observation: what **do** you see?
Abe Brafman   59

CHAPTER FOUR
Defects of inscription in language: Anne and Anna
Catherine Mathelin   71

CHAPTER FIVE
Creating transitions in the lives of children suffering from
    "multiple traumatic loss"
    Monica Lanyado 93

CHAPTER SIX
Prince Blackthorn and the Wizard: fantasying and thinking
    in the psychoanalysis of a ten-year-old boy
    Angela Joyce 113

CHAPTER SEVEN
Some remarks on adolescence with Winnicott and Lacan
    Alain Vanier 133

CHAPTER EIGHT
A Winnicottian view of an American tragedy
    Richard Frankel 153

CHAPTER NINE
"I like my life, I just like my life": narratives of children
    of latency years
    Amal Treacher 177

CHAPTER TEN
Winnicott and music
    Nicholas Spice 193

REFERENCES 205

INDEX 215

CONTRIBUTORS

Dr A H BRAFMAN is a psychoanalyst of adults and children. He worked in the NHS as a child and adolescent psychiatrist. He has been involved in teaching programmes for psychotherapists and he is now an Honorary Senior Lecturer at the Psychotherapy Department of University College Hospital. Dr Brafman has run seminars on Infant Observation and his work seeing children and parents together has now been published by Karnac as *Untying the Knot*.

LESLEY CALDWELL, PhD is the Director of the Squiggle Foundation and the editor of *Winnicott Studies*. She is an associate member of the Lincoln Clinic and Institute, a psychoanalytic psychotherapist in private practice and a University lecturer. She is writing a book on family constellations in Italian cinema.

JENNY DAVIDS is a child and adolescent psychotherapist and a member of the British Association of Psychotherapists. She teaches and supervises at the Anna Freud Centre and she has a long-term interest in adoption and fostering.

PIERRE DRAPEAU is a psychoanalyst and child psychoanalyst, a member of the Société Psychanalytique de Montréal and of the Canadian Psychoanalytical Society, a member of the Institut Psychanalytique de Montréal and of the Canadian Psychoanalytical Institute, a child psychiatrist at the Hôpital Ste Justine, Montréal, and Associate Professor of Psychiatry, Université de Montréal.

RICHARD FRANKEL is a psychotherapist in private practice in Boston, USA. He is the author of *The Adolescent Psyche: Jungian and Winnicottian Perspectives* (Routledge, 1998) and is completing his PhD at the University of Essex.

ANGELA JOYCE worked as a psychiatric social worker in the ILEA Child Guidance Service before training with the Guild of Psychotherapists. After having children, she trained as an adult psychoanalyst at the British Psycho-Analytical Society and then in child analysis at the Anna Freud Centre. She works in private practice and in the Parent Infant Project (infant mental health) at the AFC.

MONICA LANYADO helped found the Child and Adolescent Psychotherapy training in Scotland. She is a training supervisor at the British Association of Psychotherapy, and she consults to therapeutic communities in the Peper Harrow Foundation. She has a special interest in children suffering from multiple traumatic loss and carried out clinical research on sexually abusive behaviour in young adolescent boys at Great Ormond Street Hospital. She has published widely, and is former co-editor of the *Journal of Child Psychotherapy*. With Anne Horne she is joint editor of the *Handbook of Child and Adolescent Psychotherapy: Psychoanalytic Approaches* (Routledge, 1999). She works in private practice.

CATHERINE MATHELIN, PhD, is a training analyst of *Espace Analytique*. She is the author of *Le sourire de la joconde* (Denoël), *Qu'est ce qu'on a fait à Freud pour avoir des enfants pareils* (Denoël), *Raisins verts et dents agacées* (Denoel). The latter is published by Other Press as *Lacanian Psychotherapy with Children* (2001). She has written the prefaces for the French editions of the Tavistock series, "Comprendre votre enfant de la naissance à l'adolescence", "Les Guides du Centre Tavistock", Albin Michel.

NICHOLAS SPICE contributes essays on music and literature to the *London Review of Books*, where he has been publisher since 1982. He is currently working on a short book about the Polish American pianist Artur Balsam.

MARGRET TONNESMANN MD, is a psychoanalyst of the British Psycho-Analytical Society, and a member of the British Association of Psychotherapists. She was a consultant psychotherapist (now retired) in the NHS and she is a lecturer and seminar leader on Freud and object-relations theorists to various Institutions in London, Germany, Switzerland and the USA. She is in private practice.

AMAL TREACHER, PhD is a lecturer in the Centre for Psychosocial Studies at Birkbeck College. She has written on ethnicity, children and the family romance, and adoption.

ALAIN VANIER is a practising psychoanalyst and President of *Espace Analytique* (France). He has doctorates in medicine, with a specialization in psychiatry, and in psychopathology and psychoanalysis. He is now Professor of Psychopathology and Psychoanalysis at the University of Paris VII. One of his books, *Lacan*, has been translated into English (New York: Other Press, 2000).

THE ELUSIVE CHILD

Introduction

Lesley Caldwell

Fuelled by agitation and panic about paedophilia, child abuse, violence and neglect on the one side, and by children as violent murderers and killers on the other, there has been an explosion of concern regarding the place, care, treatment and life of children in Europe and beyond. The frequency of current debate about children may attest to their centrality and importance. However, the places they are described as occupying, and the arenas evoked by their representations, speak of a disturbing, conflictual account. The preoccupation extends from the documented failures of care within any particular country, to the fate of those children throughout the world who do not share even the rudiments of what has come to be regarded as the basis of childhood in late modern societies. In the gap between rhetorical flourish and lived experience, in the division between what is said and claimed, and what is done and lived, a sense of unease and of disquiet is evident. This divergence, in practice and possibility, testifies to the cultural specificity of notions of childhood and its place in the wider culture. That very cultural specificity is increasingly held up for scrutiny and found wanting. Perhaps the constant engagement with children, that is such a distinguishing feature of contemporary life, may be a way of displaying those very uncertainties and anxieties that a stereotype of centrality seeks to efface.

But what may be at stake in all this talk about children? What are the frameworks that have put in place such a cultural arena? How have they emerged and how are they sustained? What are the effects of what is said and said with increasing frequency and, specifically relevant to our purposes here, what is the place of psychoanalysis in this confusion of voices?

In her account of children's fiction and the notion of a universal (imaginary) child, Jacqueline Rose identifies a strong tradition of thought about childhood. For instance, she links Locke's view of education as grounded in direct access to the objects of the world, with Rousseau's conception of sexuality as that which interferes with the child's use of language and direct knowledge of that world. Rose sees these philosophical perspectives as expressing "both sexuality and social inequality as realities that the child somehow be used to circumvent. The child is rendered innocent of all the contradictions which flaw our interaction with the world" (1984, p. 8). This traceable line of thought in which a chronological unknowing and access to "a primary state of language" are seen as interdependent, is a version of the primitivism described by Boas in *The Cult of Childhood* (1966). In his review of a series of significant western texts from the Greeks onwards, Boas attributes the current status of the child above all to the influence of the nineteenth century and especially to the development of the Human Sciences. He suggests that it was the rejection of an earlier anthropological assumption concerning the parallels between chronological and cultural primitivism—the binding together of the notion of the primitive as both prior and ignorant—that produced the wish for an alternative exemplar of that cultural state. "Together with the woman, the folk (rural) and later, the irrational or neurotic and the collective unconscious, the child is one of modernity's figures of the primitive" (p. 3).

The tradition that ascribes primitiveness to the child, as untamed/savage, or as innocent, or both, is one that predates the rise of the Human Sciences. But it is their ongoing concern with the management of populations and with the increasing regulation of personal life, whether through sociological, legal, historical, economic, or psychological accounts, that identifies the figure of the child as the fulcrum of the aspirations of modern states and their citizens. In its attention to childhood, psychoanalysis has been perhaps the most insistent of the psychologies. Its practitioners, beginning with Freud and Klein, who took their own children as objects of investigation, were only continuing the work of nineteenth century psychological experimentation, where the father, as both investigator-scientist and author, explored the child's development and acquisition of social skills in and through family relations. The child, first an object of interest in itself, always contained implications for its "management" in the family by both parents, but especially by the mother. These perspectives became increasingly concerned with the relation first, between mother and child, then with familial relationships more generally: psychology, education, health and welfare offered increasingly comprehensive accounts of the child and society. Winnicott's insistence on the mother as *environment and as ego* for the neonate represents a particular psychoanalytic development of this tradition.

If, before Freud, the notion of the child contained ideas of the untamed and the primitive alongside those of innocence, since Freud childhood innocence has been difficult, if not impossible, to sustain. *The Three Essays* may occupy a pre-eminent place in the texture of modernity (Marcus, 1984) but their controversial reputation is especially linked to the continuing challenge of the second Essay, (on infantile sexuality), which has extended the understanding of the human being in a way that is still resisted. Despite the widespread sense in which later psychoanalytic thinkers, notably Klein and Winnicott, appeared to shift the debate away from the force of Freud's position on sexuality and the drives, contemporary psychoanalysis does insist upon the *passionate* relation of the child with his/her internalized objects: parental imagos in some relation, more or less obvious, with real parents. Lacan and Laplanche go further in emphasizing the desire of the other and the logic of seduction by the other at issue in relations between child and mother. The contribution of psychoanalysis to the modern concern with the child provides one of the cultural frameworks through which humans now come to understand themselves as human. It proposes an account in which the adult mind and personality have their roots in, and are emergent from, a childhood consciousness; and it asserts that this is consistently demonstrated by the examination of the adult in analysis. The contemporary account of the adult requires the contemporary account of the child. This is, however, no mere consigning of conflict to the past, nor is it the assertion of a trouble-free adulthood for those who have resolved a conflictual past. Although psychoanalysis does not put forward a very decisive account of the adult, it does insist upon the presence, in fantasy and in the internal patterning of the mind, of the conflicts of the past and their ongoing resonance in the present. In fantasy the child of the past is integral to the adult of the present, but both the boundaries that separate child and adult and the continuities in what is shared and what is not shared are considered important. Pierre Drapeau's exposition of the development of Freud's thinking links the evolution of the metapsychology precisely to an evolution in Freud's ideas about the child, and the relation between child and adult. Their interdependence supplies the means by which the topographical model of the 1890s was transformed into the structural model of the 1920s. Its object of investigation for both adult and child patients remains the unconscious and its effects.

But psychoanalysis itself forms part of that same historical interest in the regulation of human beings, as individuals and in groups, that distinguishes all the Human Sciences. Arguably, it provides the most sustained investigation of this through a form of treatment that seeks to interrogate the continuing effects of childhood for mental health. In so doing, it further contributes to the constitution of the category of the child and the arena demarcated by it. The myth of childhood may now be regarded as one of the primary myths that actively shape our epoch and ways of thinking, and it is a myth that psychoanalysis has helped to consolidate.

To ask what a child is, or how children are thought of, or what a child means, or what images of children signify, directs attention to many registers—personal, social and discursive. These questions, in their very asking, simultaneously extend and negate the cultural assumptions that see the idea of the child as self-evident. It is, amongst other things, to invoke a series of legal prescriptions—the provision of guarantees, the existence of prohibitions—through which certain rights and duties established by the law, regulate the providers of care, usually, but not exclusively, the biological parents themselves. The twentieth century, especially the post-1945 period, saw increased external attention to the care and control of children in families whose inter-generational responsibilities and expectations were laid down, kept in place and, where necessary, acted upon, to demand the assumption and maintenance of obligations decided elsewhere.

Accompanying these legal prescriptions are sets of cultural expectations, assumptions, norms, and beliefs. All turn upon a similar, if contradictory, understanding: the child as a somehow natural status, a taken for granted entity and the child as a subject, constituted legally and socially as of a particular age, and possessed of certain rights, denied access to others. The child's caretakers are expected to fulfil certain duties and, up to a certain point, and a certain point only, have rights over, and access to that same child. What is experienced as private, personal, and natural is (and always has been) legally, socially, religiously, and culturally inscribed.

Although these developments are not confined to the last two centuries, the contemporary concern with children and with childhood, with the child as both object and subject of increased public and private, collective and individual concern, is essentially a modern phenomenon of the west. That childhood and family life and relations form part of both private and public concerns is one significant factor that makes it so contested an arena. In particular it has accompanied the parallel attention to the individual, individuality, and an apparent polarization between public and private worlds. How this concern is deployed, disseminated, routinized and internalized, is the result of an array of specialist forms of knowledge that have taken the family and its members as their focus, and have emphasized the psychologization of human relations in every sphere. The obligation to send the child to school, for instance, may first have occurred through external imposition derived from philanthropic and liberal notions of proper education in the so-called best interests of the child. However, it also formed part of an array of complex debates about the nature of the social and about increasing state responsibility. At the same time the ever-widening arena of potential for state intervention has been accompanied by extensive practices of self-regulation whereby citizens, as parents, on the basis of the widespread dissemination of a variety of forms of psychological knowledge, actively assume personal responsibility for the health and welfare of their children, or evince their guilt about their failure to have done so (Rose, 1996). The health of the adult has increasingly been understood as deriving from the adequate provision of care in childhood. As a consequence, the association of adult neurosis, dissatisfaction, madness and criminality with childhood and family experience, far from being confined to specialists, has become a more general concern.

In all these debates, the family is given a central status, both pragmatic and symbolic. The responsible state's pursuit of the appropriate organizational and institutional forms for the perfect family, as well as the responsible citizen's hunt for the perfect prescription for family life, are now social mirrorings of the individual's own wishes for the "right" kind of family, the "right" kind of childhood and the "right" kind of children. These are widespread concerns in the west. The grind of poverty and the terror of war in other parts of the world ensure that what have become expected aspects of western childhood are rendered meaningless. In the face of such conditions of life, the social indicators that ascribe the status of child to those of a certain age become irrelevant and their participation in the grim necessities of adult life is equalized. The optimum conditions of protection and love in which a child is assumed to flourish mirror current adult preconceptions and wishes, but have never been universally available. Even in those countries where a significant shift in the parameters and expectations about childhood has developed, the discrepancy between the rhetoric of the child and the reality of the lives of vast numbers of children continues to be reported daily. The means for tackling the social and psychological issues that impinge upon millions of children in the west remain underdeveloped in comparison to the insistence upon the importance of children and their often idealized place.

Images of children

In her examinations of the representational forms of the Christian tradition, particularly the recurring image of mother and child, so central a part of its religious iconography, Julia Kristeva suggests that, faced with this image of motherhood, a commonality of the sexes is set up. The mother-child couple recalls "the fantasy of a lost territory", so that children carry the adult's own fantasized younger selves, an idealized relation, bond, or longing for a fantasized, unattainable younger self. For Kristeva this is the unlocalized place of primary narcissism. The wish of the adult to be in the place of the child has little or nothing to do with the place of real children in real life families

Why it takes the image of a child to wake the world is the caption for a piece, "A Child in Time" (7 September 2001, G2, p. 2). The photograph used is a recent image of a crying girl, framed by leather gauntleted, beshielded police. It is an already much travelled image, as powerful, according to the journalist, as any image to emerge from thirty years of Anglo-Irish bloodshed. There are five other photographs of children in catastrophic situations: a young Jewish boy from the Warsaw ghetto surrendering to the Nazis in 1943; nine-year-old Kim Phuc, having torn off her burning clothes, running with her brothers and sisters from an aerial napalm attack in 1972; a bombed baby in Oklahoma in 1995; a Palestinian in 2000 sheltering his son, who was shot minutes later by Israeli fire; a newborn baby airlifted from a treetop during floods in Mozambique in the same year.

The journalist begins "we don't bomb babies. You don't shoot children. You don't single them out for hatred". He then immediately revises his own statement: "this is a sentimental delusion; babies are bombed, children are shot, children are waged war upon, and wage war themselves. They starve to death in African famines, they lose limbs in Angolan landmines, and they die of neglect in Romanian orphanages". Commenting on a recent exhibition of photographs of Cambodia (*Reporting the World*), Jeremy Harding makes the observation that "the powerful animating presence of children as victims and survivors" is a "recurring motif of war reporting" (*London Review Books*, 23.8.01. p. 31).

Harding's starting point, the power of *images* of children, inscribes the indignation and helplessness of the adult world in its encounter with events of the kind he lists.

Perhaps the child in the picture haunts us so powerfully because what it speaks about is adult cruelty. We know how children suffer when we see it played out in children. When the image pierces, it is because it makes us dimly remember, imagine, feel again, how we would have felt when we were as small. What the pictures we cannot forget do is to expose the fact that hope has been betrayed; again and again they make us remember how we would have felt. After all, we were children once. They make us remember a time when we expected better of people just like us.

In such an account the image of the child in trouble is enough, it provides an immediate response: the response of the helpless and *not* responsible adult faced with the devastation produced by other adults; a sort of passive, somewhat simplistic acknowledgement of resignation at the failures of society, and of human possibility. Such images have not only been a recurrent feature in the work of photographers, but also of film makers like the Italian neo-realists of the immediate post-war period, who frequently took the image of the child as the means for an examination of the adult conflicts of post-war Europe. Recently, it has been a strong presence in contemporary Iranian cinema. Images of children may trigger the emotional response of adults or gesture at social concern, but the emotionality of the image only serves to emphasize the rhetorical possibilities produced by it. The instant response and the sense of indignation or distress it encourages, underline the ongoing confusion and guilt about children that surface in adult memory, hope or desire, when confronted with the child's difference, and the child's desire. Cultural representations of children are embedded in and contribute to a web of significations through which adults seek to know and not to know, to make sense and not make sense of themselves and their world.

The representation of the child in these accounts is the obverse of the fury and rage visited upon those children vilified as dangerous killers and murderers. In this case adult rage and the desire for vengeance obliterate any idea of the child as different in the demand that the murderous child, exemplified as evil, be held responsible for his or her actions, as if he or she were an adult. Children who do not fit the desired image of the child are made to pay dearly for this through the sadism they provoke in the adult population. In the name of justice, calls for vengeance towards children who betray adult ideals are similar in tone to the witch hunts for paedophiles and child killers as the real threat to "proper" children and to "proper" families.

The interchangeability of child and adult, and of parent and child, in the currency of fantasy, and the capacity of representations of the child to encode a weight of signification, always suggesting a potential excess of meaning, has made the resort to images of children a commonplace in the late modern visual repertoire. In such a context the problem may be to envisage images where the resonance can be read in a less determined way, and where the child's life may be acknowledged as precisely that, his or her life, a separate, if related entity to the adult projections visited upon it.

The papers

In the articles discussed in this collection, a general category, "the child" gives way to detailed studies of different children of different ages. Psychoanalysis, together with more socially based approaches, shares an awareness of the need for attention to the specific ways in which differently aged children may be recognized and investigated. The papers by Drapeau and Tonnesmann are theoretical accounts of Freud, and how Ferenczi and Winnicott develop his insights. Both see the infant coming to assume the capacities of a human subject through the encounter with others, and with a self that emerges through those encounters and their internalization. Drapeau traces a comparison between mythical children utilized in the Freudian account, and the no less mythical child who is the focus in the evolution of Winnicott's thought. Drapeau argues that Winnicott's ongoing concern with issues of being and feeling real is a continuation of Freud's earliest discussions of the origins and the nature of the ego.

Both he and Tonnesmann make the link between Winnicott and Ferenczi via Ferenczi's remarkable 1913 paper. As Drapeau says, "It is as though, thirty years in advance, Freud had had access to Winnicott's first writings on the illusion of the creation of the object". Tonnesmann stresses Ferenczi's similarities to Winnicott in his emphasis on both the importance of the mother's adaptation to the infant's needs as the means of continuation of the illusion of omnipotence, and the mother's presentation of the breast at the right moment as proposing a creative hallucination for the baby. This echoes Ferenczi's stage of hallucinatory magic omnipotence.

The work of Winnicott develops the insights of the first generation of psychoanalytic thinkers through close consideration of the essential relation of child and adult as the condition of the child's relation with itself. The very different ways the child, at different stages, encounters the social world and its demands and pleasures, and the different psychological dispositions associated with these encounters, are judged by Winnicott to emerge from the relationship with the significant carer, the mother.

Exploring the central place of infant observation in the training of psychoanalytic practitioners, Brafman acknowledges its utility for the student while questioning the feasibility of just what can be observed and how it can be conceptualized. The different psychoanalytic approaches identify and depend upon very different accounts of the evolution of the human being and of how the baby exemplifies them, but all are united in ascribing a centrality to the beginnings of infant life. The centrality of infant observation in training courses resides in its use in assessing the capacities of candidates. Brafman draws attention to the variability in observations and how dependent these are upon the mind of the observer. Winnicott's own account of the observation of infants (1941) focused on the physiological changes that accompanied the infant's impulse to motility, and proffered a view of what this revealed about infant development. He believed his interpretation of the relation between these processes contributed to understanding how particular cognitive and psychological processes are laid down and imprinted upon the neonate.

The papers by Mathelin, Lanyado and Vanier, together with the responses of Joyce and Davids, were presented at a symposium on British and Lacanian approaches to child analysis organized by the Squiggle foundation with the support of Karnac books. In her description of her work in a neo-natal unit, Mathelin gives a moving account of the fates of two premature babies born an hour apart. She touches upon the implications of the triangular situation established between mother, baby and the staff of the unit as an extra dimension in the histories of these little girls. Together with the vital importance of the mother's own history this contributes to her possible response to her baby and to the baby's possible survival. History, both in its uterine and post-uterine sense, is fundamental as part of the processes shaping the present. The child who arrives in the adults' fantasies and family history, becomes part of the mechanisms by which those trans-generational imprints are transmitted. "For a neonatal unit, the only way to love a baby is to want it to live at any cost", says Mathelin, but what is involved in keeping alive the premature baby also involves a meeting between the desire of the workers and the parents', in this case mother's desire, as formed through that family history and its unconscious registration. The difficulty for the unit workers in allowing the mother her defences and her ambivalence were underscored by the discussion.

Mathelin's second focus concerns the impact of adoption and the potential threat contained in the permanence of the written word for three adopted children, among whose primary symptoms was an inability to write. For these children, symbolizing the place of the birth parents as a place of absence, produces added complexity for their recognition of their own place, a complexity that is compounded by their unease with their own absence in the fantasized primal scene of the adoptive parents. For Mathelin the drive to know the desire of these different sets of parents makes the psychical difficulties attendant upon adoption particularly confusing for the child.

Lanyado's paper is a sensitive account of painstaking work with two little boys facing the dislocation involved in moving from fostering to adoption. The fears and anxieties attendant upon such a move for children with such devastating histories, and the issue of origins so poignantly present for the adopted child, is present here as multiple losses of different parents and parental figures. These children require the active intervention of external experts who try to establish the conditions to offset earlier deprivations. Lanyado describes the ongoing work of the consulting room as it is linked to the practicalities of local state intervention, and the work of the team in finding a new family for each child. Without these interventions, and the sensitive recognition of the difficulties these children face when the new family is found, life for these children would be bleak indeed. Lanyado provides a sober acknowledgement of the limits of what can be done, even for those children, still a very small percentage, who gain the kind of support given by Lanyado and her colleagues. We are reminded of the numbers of such children for whom nothing is done, or for whom too little is done far too late.

Angela Joyce uses Winnicott's distinction between fantasying and dreaming to chart the shifts in the analysis of a nine-year-old boy's capacity to relate. She links this capacity to his age and family history. She identifies a problem in paternal function that uses a strong trans-generational understanding in her exploration of the boy's problems. The place or absence of a paternal function in the preceding generations' psychical structure has contributed to a similar, potentially serious absence in that of her patient. Here again the histories and the fantasies of the parents are shown to be a crucial part of the inheritance of the child.

Joyce and Lanyado use Winnicott as a basis for their work with children of latency age in the consulting room. Treacher describes a set of interviews carried out in a school with children of a similar age, and argues for the centrality of their wish to tell stories about their lives as part of the business of how they make sense of those lives. She draws attention to the need and the desire to communicate oneself to another, revealing, from a different approach, the necessity of the other as the basis of the constitution of the self.

Alain Vanier's paper comments upon the notion of adolescence as a recent category before undertaking a re-reading of Winnicott's classic paper (1961). He offers some thoughts on the place of time in accounts of adolescence that describe it as return, stressing that the return is not a return to the same thing. With Winnicott, he underlines the enormity for the adolescent of the shift from the former biological impotence in regard to both sexuality and to aggression, to the possibility of their being enacted. He draws attention to Winnicott's statement that adolescents do not wish to be understood as helpful to those who treat them, and notes Winnicott's lack of emphasis on puberty's genital and sexual transformations. His greater interest in the power to destroy forms part of his own reading of adolescence. Vanier describes the tasks of adolescence as more about the acceptance of prohibition and the engagement with the idea of the father. He recognizes that the real task is to come to terms with the self and the strength of the death drive. His clinical vignettes cautiously endorse a treatment frame that accepts the inevitability of acting out and thinks of analysis as "a place where conflict can be resolved in the subject's own terms". Richard Frankel also employs a close reading of Winnicott's paper. He discusses the murderous actions of two American child killers, and the additional difficulties posed for contemporary adolescents by virtual reality. He offers an interesting analysis of the potential it may represent for the confusion of imaginative elaboration, fantasy and play for Winnicott, and the deadliness of "fantasying" and the emptiness underlying it. Is this one of the possible consequences of interaction with the web?

Finally, in his piece on knowing and not knowing about music, Nicholas Spice tackles the traditional way music is introduced to the child, and how frequently a child's apprenticeship replicates that of the parents and their desire. He points to the stark difference between Winnicott's ideas on how to use and play with an object, and the form taken by the music lesson with its hierarchical structure and its focus around performance. Spice's imaginative account of a Winnicottian music lesson shows, by contrast, just what can be lost in the insistence upon a particular rigidity when making "sacred" the canon of western music. Spice demonstrates the way that changing notions of childhood and the child gain their potency from the wishes and concerns of adults as individuals, citizens and group members within larger populations. His article hints at the dangers of such rigidity for professional practice more generally.

Restraint in interpretation, the imposition of too rigid a technique, together with an openness to the pace of the patient in the session, are issues adverted to in both the theoretical and the clinical pieces, written from a broadly Winnicottian approach. The patient finds his or her way in the space opened up between the clear boundaries provided by the frame. The space within that frame offers the opportunity, in what occurs between patient and analyst, for the exploration and encounter with the self in all its manifestations. Psychoanalysis's recognition of the continuing importance of childhood and the child, and its central place in the lives of adults, is a continuing challenge to adults' claims to know themselves and the world. The recognition of the interdependence of adult and child involves the stubborn intractability of the unconscious and the ongoing centrality of fantasy. This constitutes one arena of investigation. Another concerns the increased knowledge about what is required for a good enough childhood, and how it can be made more available to the large numbers of children for whom such a possibility is as remote from reality as the idealizations that form the backbone of so much contemporary writing about children.

CHAPTER ONE

From Freud to Winnicott: an encounter between mythical children

Pierre Drapeau

On November 5, 1952, Winnicott gave a lecture to the British Psycho-Analytical Society during which he elaborated at length on the link between anxiety and insecurity. He was misunderstood and challenged. A few days later, in a letter (Rodman, 1987, p. 34) to Melanie Klein, he recognized that in developing his "own language", he had made the understanding of his practice and theory more difficult. Elsewhere, he describes his approach:

> I shall not give an historical survey and show the development of my ideas from the theories of others, because my mind does not work that way. What happens is that I gather this and that, here and there, settle down to clinical experience, form my own theories and then, last of all, interest myself in looking to see where I stole what. Perhaps this is as good a method as any. [Winnicott, 1945, p. 145]

Coupled with a very individual language however, this method has led to many different interpretations of his thought. For some, Winnicott made a radical departure from Freud, despite claiming that the latter was a source of inspiration (Greenberg & Mitchell, 1983). Others see in him a representative, albeit unique, of Ego psychology (Fromm, 1989, pp. 3–26), or associate him with self psychology (Fromm, 1989, pp. 52–87). André Green considers him to be one of the greatest analysts in the history of psychoanalysis, Jean Pontalis, while underscoring certain theoretical impasses, nonetheless praises the richness and creativity of his work. Without naming him specifically, Jean Laplanche criticizes him for reducing psychoanalysis to a general psychology of development, thus creating confusion and losing the vital thread (*le "fil rouge"*) of sexuality.

How then may we situate Winnicott, without idealizing him, entrenching him determinedly in a rigorous Freudian filiation, viewing him as an outsider to a certain psychoanalytic orthodoxy, or supporting, in his name, practices which have nothing to do with psychoanalysis, while allowing ourselves the renewed vitality and creativity he brought to analytical thought?

In January 1967, a group of senior analysts invited Winnicott to give an informal lecture on the connections between his theories and other models of early development. He titled his paper: "D.W.W. on D.W.W.". To guide his audience, he distributed a concise plan listing Freud, Klein, Anna Freud, Hartmann, Greenacre, Bowlby, Little and Erickson. While he did not compare his theories with theirs, he did provide much information about his own history and his relationships to Freud, Klein and other thinkers of the same period. "I've realised more and more as time went on what a tremendous lot I've lost from not properly correlating my work with the work of others" (Winnicott, 1967b, p. 573), he began, apologizing for the task thereby imposed on those who would seek to understand him. Recognizing this failing, he maintained, nonetheless, that his temperament would not have allowed him to do otherwise.

Winnicott reiterated his loyalty to Freud or, more specifically, to the method of exploration that is his legacy. He denied having done anything un-Freudian, "I just feel that Freud gave us this method which we can use, and it doesn't matter what it leads us to. The point is, it does lead us to things; it's an objective way of looking at things and it's for people who can go to something without preconceived notions, which in a sense, is science" (Winnicott, 1967b, p. 574).

In Winnicott's view, it is the method that is essential, the method that enables us to advance, so that should new discoveries question certain established theoretical points, progress should not be hindered by conflicts of loyalties. He acknowledged his debt to Klein, explaining that while Freud helped us to discover psychic reality, it was her descriptions of the internal world that made possible the analysis of children. He also acknowledged the profound influence of Fairbairn's work, particularly with respect to the notion of "object-seeking" and the importance Fairbairn gave to the fact of feeling real or unreal.

In the letter to Klein quoted above, Winnicott reveals two elements that are crucial to the present discussion.

> I personally think it is very important that your work should be restated by people discovering in their own way and presenting what they discover in their own language. If you make the stipulation that in future only your language shall be used for the statement of other people's discoveries then the language becomes a dead language. Your ideas will only live in so far as they are rediscovered and reformulated by original people. [Rodman, 1987, p. 35]

A living language, "ideas which will live only in so far as they are rediscovered", creativity, these are the essential elements of Winnicott's thinking permeating his attitude towards Freud and his work.

In "The Use of an Object and Relating through Identifications" (1968b), Winnicott suggests that the object becomes real only by being resilient to aggression: the infant can only substantiate the external world through ultimately fruitless attempts to destroy it. This theory of the "destroyed-found object" is the key to understanding how Winnicott came to develop his own language and his own relationship to the theoretical corpus of psychoanalysis. In developing new concepts based on his clinical work, Winnicott put the "foundations" of psychoanalytic theory to the test.

Winnicott and Freud

"I have never been able to follow anyone, not even Freud", Winnicott (1962b, p. 177) tells us. And yet, in "The Location of Cultural Experience", Winnicott clarifies the essential dialectic between being true to one's self and respecting tradition: "it is not possible to be original except on a basis of traditions. The interplay between originality and the acceptance of tradition as the basis for inventiveness seems to me to be just one more example, and a very exciting one, of the interplay between separateness and union" (Winnicott, 1967a, p. 99).

To situate Winnicott, we must therefore return to tradition and find the theoretical sources from which he drew his inspiration. The roots of his thought are, above all, Freudian. From 1923 to 1933, he pursued a lengthy analysis with Strachey, an analyst impassioned by the writings of Freud. His training in the 1930s also centred on Freud, although he writes of his reluctance to read Freud then (Rodman, 1987, p. 33) and admits not knowing him as well as he should, yet describes himself as "having Freud in my bones" (Grosskurth, 1986, p. 401). Time and again, Winnicott asserts this direct filiation: "From my point of view any theories that I may have which are original are only valuable as a growth of ordinary Freudian psychoanalytic theory" (Rodman, 1987, p. 75). Or, "[This] theory does not affect what we have come to believe in respect of the aetiology of psychoneurosis, or the treatment of patients who are psychoneurotic; nor does it clash with Freud's structural theory of the mind in terms of Ego, id, Superego". He explains that his propositions concern an entirely different question: "What is life about? Psychotic patients who are all the time hovering between living and not living force us to look at this problem, one that really belongs "not to psychotics but to all human beings" (Winnicott, 1967a, p. 99).

Who was the Freud of Winnicott? Or, more specifically, what are the Freudian concepts that Winnicott subjects to destruction in order to reassemble them into a language where they could find new life? Freud, first and foremost, sought to develop a "scientific" psychology based on the model of the natural sciences. To describe the soul's apparatus and its functioning and to build his metapsychology, Freud first resorts to key concepts in the physical sciences: forces (dynamics), quantities (economics) and locations (topographical structures). But he was also profoundly influenced by the type of causality that forms the basis of evolutionary Darwinism. He describes the stages of psychosexual development and uses concepts of fixation and regression to explain different types of pathologies. To illustrate the origin of the psychic apparatus, Freud builds what he refers to as "fictional constructs", mythical children, who develop according to a logical sequence that follows the theoretical demands of his models, but have nothing to do with the infant who can be observed from without, during "real time" development. Freud began by using materials discovered in his study of dreams and neurosis, then drew upon his understanding of psychosis and narcissism, eventually arriving at a model of primitive man that mirrors the development of the very young child.

Above all a clinician of great genius, Winnicott had little interest in metapsychological construction or in precise "scientific" definitions. But he associates the wonder he experienced on discovering Freud with that he felt as a student upon first reading Darwin. He tells us that in the encounter with a new case, which is always an exploration of unknown territories, his sole companion is his own theory of affective development: to understand a clinical phenomenon is to situate it in relation to a sequence of development in time and relational space (Winnicott, 1971c, p. 6). But, in responding to the comments on his discussion of the splitting-off of male and female elements, he stressed his difference: "I found myself greatly enriched by this way of thinking which was somewhat new to me. I discovered myself looking at an essential conflict of human beings, one which must be operative at a very early date" (Winnicott, 1968–1969, p. 191). He described two basic principles at the root of development: "I allowed my thoughts to carry me to the concept of male and female elements" (Winnicott, 1968–1969, p. 190). In the beginning, there is, in both boys and girls, the pure female element, which Winnicott associates with "being", that is, a "primary" identification to the breast which "is", an identification from which first emerges the sense of being, and then a particular type of non-instinctual object relation. Winnicott associates the pure male element, which corresponds to "doing", with instinct and drive. This essential distinction reveals that while the Freudian child is described from the point of view of drives, the Winnicottian child is primarily described on the basis of the sense of being, and of the experience of the "real".

Winnicott's theoretical model of first beginnings invokes a child no less mythical than that of Freud. In centring on the dimension of being, it echoes his experience of the emptiness encountered in psychotics and of the deficiencies in the mother–child relationship. This child will oscillate between being and not-being (continuity and non-continuity of existence), being real, inhabiting his body, being dependent, being independent, being alive and creative, being in his mother's gaze, being true, being false, being able to be alone. The Winnicottian child passes from the subjective created-found object to the objective destroyed-found object; it will possess a transitional object with a paradoxical status as a being of both fantasy and reality, and it plays in a potential space where the issue of being real or being a fantasy is irrelevant.

Of course, "being" and "the instinctual" are profoundly interlinked. Freud, speaking of the sexual, continually refers to "being", and Winnicott, focusing on "being", does not exclude impulses. To link the two theoretical frameworks, an imaginary encounter between apparently different mythical children is proposed.

The cornerstone of Freudian theory is the hallucinatory realization of desire which inaugurates fantasy life. Winnicott's starting point focuses on the feeling of continuity of existence and presents us with a being in perpetual danger of falling into emptiness and losing itself in nothingness. Freud is interested, above all, in the destinies of sexual impulses; Winnicott ignores libido and focuses on the ego and its creativity. The Freudian child emerges from the play of impulses; the Winnicottian child develops mainly during moments of calm, sheltered from instinctual storms.

This paper recognizes these differences in perspective, but its concern is to establish theoretical continuities and complementarity. In elaborating the topographical frame of reference, Freud had attached great importance to the development of the ego, but he was hindered because the in-depth study of the narcissistic neuroses he considered essential to proceed was unavailable to him. Thus he initially left aside a whole series of ideas on the role of the ego in pathology and development. The thesis developed here is that Winnicott develops the ego aspect of the first theory of drives by enriching and transforming it. He does not take up Freud's ideas systematically, but, from a different clinical experience he does ask himself the same questions about the beginnings of psychic life: the relation between fantasies and reality, investment and perception of the "ego-subject" and the object, the elaboration of fantasy life.

From 1910 to 1920, Freud gradually elaborated five models of mythical children. The first, born of the encounter between sexual drives and ego drives, is the child of neurosis and dreams. The second is the child of psychosis and narcissism: charged with libido, the ego changes status, allowing the addition of a narcissistic object-choice to the former anaclitic object-choice. The third child is the child of prehistory, philogenesis, identification and religious illusion. The fourth emerges from the metapsychological synthesis of 1915. Finally, a fifth child, the child of trauma and its mastery appears rather suddenly in *Beyond the Pleasure Principle* (1920). These children intertwine and eventually merge, only to resurface in more abstract forms in the elaboration of the structural model. It is they, in their primitive form, who provide the most interesting links with the Winnicottian child.

The child of dreams and neurosis

In his article on psychogenic disturbances of vision, (1910) Freud proposed the notions of the ego instinct, responsible for self-preservation, and of the sexual instinct, essential to the survival of the species. In 1911, he explored the relationship between these types of instincts through his description of the two modes of mental functioning identified through his work with patients: a part of their psyche which seeks help, co-operates in treatment, and functions according to the reality principle, and another part of their psyche, stranger to consciousness, that functions solely according to the pleasure principle and expresses itself in dreams and pathology. For Freud, the functioning processes of the unconscious mind are the most ancient and the most primary: "We consider these to be the older, primary processes, the residues of a phase of development in which they were the only kind of mental process" (Freud, 1911a, p. 219). In a lengthy footnote, he defends this proposition, recognizing that "An organisation which was a slave to the pleasure principle and neglected the reality of the external world could not maintain itself alive for the shortest time" and that such a fiction is justified "provided one includes with it the care it [the infant] receives from its mother".

In presenting his theory of the parent–infant relationship,

Winnicott relies on the first part of this note to reassert that "There is no such thing as an infant (alone)" and that in the early stages of life "the infant and maternal care together form a unit" (Winnicott, 1960b, p. 39). Freud employs another fiction to describe what happens to the infant who faces being deprived of food. To do so, he returns to his earlier account of the experiencing of satisfaction. At first, satisfaction is linked with the image of the object which provided it, but, as the state of tension reappears, the image of the object is reinvested: "[The infant] probably hallucinates the fulfilment of its internal needs; it betrays its displeasure, when there is an increase of stimulus and an absence of satisfaction by the motor discharge of screaming and beating about with its arms and legs, and it then experiences the satisfaction it has hallucinated" (Freud, 1911a, p. 220).

When the object corresponds to the needs of the ego instincts, the hallucination brings nothing, "the psychical apparatus had to decide to form a conception of the real circumstances in the external world and to endeavour to make a real alteration in them" (Freud, 1911a, p. 219). The reality principle must then be applied. On the other hand, when the hallucinated object corresponds to the object of the sexual instinct which can be satisfied in an auto-erotic manner, "one species of thought-activity was split off; it was kept free from reality-testing and remained subordinated to the pleasure principle alone. This activity is phantasying, which begins already in children's play, and later, continued as day-dreaming, abandons dependence on real objects" (Freud, 1911a, p. 222). Freud adds, "Art brings about a reconciliation between the two principles in a peculiar way" as the artist makes "use of special gifts to mould his phantasies into truths of a new kind" (Freud, 1911a, p. 224).

Although Winnicott elaborates on Freud through his concepts of transitional phenomena and potential space, he remains dissatisfied with Freudian theory as an explanation of the beginnings of psychic life. Those elements that Freud considers as being established are precisely the object of Winnicott's research. Freud describes the beginning of psychic life as corresponding to the beginning of object relations, but Winnicott returns to the moment where there is no permanently existing object, the moment where "the object behaves according to magical laws, i.e. it exists when desired. It vanishes when not wanted" (Winnicott, 1945, p. 153). He redefines the experience of satisfaction in relation to the existence or non-existence of the object, rather than in relation to the satisfaction of a need or the fulfilment of a wish. If the mother presents the breast to the child at the precise moment when it is hallucinated, there is an illusion of the creation of the breast: this is the created-found object. Where Freud attributes the beginnings of fantasy to the possibility of auto-erotic satisfaction of the sexual instincts, Winnicott adds the illusion of a magical satisfaction of the ego instincts because of the mother's perfect holding.

In Freud's view, experiencing reality is an act of thought, an act of judgement. For Winnicott, subjective objects appear in reality through the omnipotence of thought and acquire real existence as the first objects from their resistance to magical destruction through thought. Two developmental lines are described by Freud: "While the ego goes through its transformation from a pleasure-ego into a reality-ego, the sexual instincts undergo the changes that lead them from their original auto-eroticism through various intermediate phases to object-love in the service of procreation" (Freud, 1911a, p. 224). Within his understanding of psychopathologies, Freud centres mostly on fixations in the development of the sexual instincts and on their encroachment upon the ego, but he also attaches much importance to the effect of abnormalities in the development of the ego. He hypothesized that in obsessional neurosis, the ego instincts have developed too rapidly, and in psychosis,

> We can no more dismiss the possibility that disturbances of the libido may react upon the ego-cathexes than we can overlook the converse possibility—namely, that a secondary or induced disturbance of the libidinal process may result from abnormal changes in the ego. Indeed, it is probable that processes of this kind constitute the distinctive characteristic of psychoses. [Freud, 1911b, p. 75]

Freud further develops the *"théorie de l'étayage"* to elucidate the original relation between the two main instincts: "the sexual instincts find their first objects by attaching themselves to the valuations made by the ego-instincts, precisely in the way in which the first sexual satisfactions are experienced in attachment to the bodily functions necessary for the preservation of life" (Freud, 1912, p. 80). In applying this theory of early infancy, Freud distinguishes the affectionate current and the sensual current, specifying the former, linked to ego and self-preservation, as the most ancient. The mother–child relation therefore first finds its origin in a relationship of tenderness upon which an instinctual relationship is later built.

Winnicott adopts the binary structure of the topographical model as the foundation of his entire theory. The instinctual component to which he refers closely corresponds to the sexual component of Freud's first theory of the instincts, which includes the aggressive dimension as "a universal and indispensable attribute of all instincts" (Freud, 1909, p. 141), that ruthlessness which is truly a part of primitive oral love. As in Freud's theory, Winnicott's ego does not emerge out of the instinctual or from what would later be referred to as the Id. Rather, it is a structure that develops in parallel with the instinctual, in the real or logical time that precedes it.

Winnicott generally speaks of ego needs rather than ego instincts. For him, the innate potentialities of the ego absolutely require an external catalyst to actualize themselves, so dependency on the mother is essential to his understanding of the formation of the ego. In addition to the processes of maturation, Winnicott also describes a creative instinct at the foundation of the ego, which has nothing to do with sublimation, and which enables him to go beyond the concept of self-preservation. In its development, the ego does not merely react and adapt; it is animated by a creative instinct in the construction of self and in the discovery of the object. Prior to becoming, much later, scenarios of wish fulfilment, the first fantasies are indeed the result of an imaginative and creative elaboration of portions of sensations or of somatic functions. Initially felt as external phenomena, the ego must recognize that these instinctual experiences come from the soma and progressively appropriate them as subjective.

Both founding currents described by Freud appear in Winnicott's work: the environment mother who cares for the needs of the ego: holding, handling, object-presenting and mirroring; and the instinctual mother, exciting, seductive, who also corresponds to the instinctual projections of the child. As the child develops new capacities to synthesize, these two mothers merge, leading to a stage of concern: can the ruthlessness of instinctual excitements annihilate the environment mother?

Although both types of relation overlap and are dependent on one another, the relation with the environment mother, during moments of calm, will produce trust, the capacity to be alone in the presence of another, ego relatedness and even the possibility of ego orgasm in its creative dimension. Moreover, a successful relation to the mother at the moment of instinctual excitement will result in normal psychosexual development, free of devastating conflicts or paralyzing fixations. Here Winnicott reaffirms his utmost respect for Freud's contribution.

The child of psychosis and narcissism

At this time Freud was also working on the autobiography of President Schreber. The study of psychosis soon after that of homosexuality (Leonardo da Vinci) enabled him to perceive the passage from auto-eroticism to object-love from a different angle, that of narcissism. In the following years, he further developed this train of thought (1911, 1914).

At the culminating point of his illness, two themes dominated Schreber's delirium: a feeling of the imminence of a terrible catastrophe, of the end of the world, and a sense of omnipotence which gave him divine powers. Freud explains this delirium as caused by a movement of the libido quite different from anaclisis. On the one hand, the libido has withdrawn from the exterior world, and on the other hand, there has been an over-cathexis of sexual energy in the ego. There was thus in Schreber a regression of homosexual love sublimated to narcissism, that is, an over-cathexis of the libido in the ego.

In Freud's view, this regressive movement illustrates the child's development in reverse. Thus, he describes the following sequence: auto-eroticism, narcissism, homosexual object, heterosexual object of love. He explains the passage from auto-eroticism to narcissism,

> There comes a time in the development of the individual at which he unifies his sexual instincts (which have hitherto been engaged in auto-erotic activities) in order to obtain a love-object; and he begins by taking himself, his own body, as his love-object, and only subsequently proceeds from this to the choice of some person other than himself as his object. [Freud, 1911b, p. 60]

Here is the evocation of the unifying psychic moment and of the amoebic interplay of the libido that is expanded upon in *On Narcissism: An Introduction*.

In conclusion, Freud asks whether the regression of libido alone can explain the loss of contact with reality. Without providing an answer, he hypothesizes that libidinal disorders may be secondary to abnormal modifications of the ego. He further adds, "Indeed, it is probable that processes of this kind constitute the distinctive characteristics of psychoses". Finally, he proposes to distinguish paranoia from paraphrenia by considering the degree of regression. Paranoia is associated to narcissism, paraphrenia to auto-eroticism (Freud, 1911b, p. 75).

Winnicott's work displays the same awareness of the movements towards integration and the same recognition of the dangers of regression towards disintegration, but they are not movements of the libido, they relate to the ego, the self and the continuity of being. Rather than a movement back to auto-eroticism, there is a return to the moment where the unification of the ego and the sense of the continuity of existence is still unstable, and when, at any moment, traumas can lead to a fall into the void. Applying this theory to the story of president Schreber, the fantasies of the end of the world can be seen as attempts to symbolize the fear of collapse, while the delusion of divine power can be interpreted as an echo of the feeling of omnipotence necessary to cope with a terrifying anxiety.

In *On Narcissism: An Introduction*, Freud expanded his theory of the evolution of libido by adding his "observations and views on the mental life of children and primitive peoples" (Freud, 1914, p. 75) to his clinical studies. Narcissism is no longer a mere stage of development but acquires a structural definition involving a condition of stasis of the libido that no object-cathexis can completely eradicate. He refers to a crucial passage from auto-eroticism to narcissism: "we are bound to suppose that a unity comparable to the ego cannot exist in the individual from the start; the ego has to be developed. The auto-erotic instincts, however, are there from the very first, so there must be something added to auto-eroticism—a new psychical action—in order to bring about narcissism" (Freud, 1914, p. 77).

Three phenomena occur with this new action: a movement of synthesis which brings together erotic instincts, the appearance of a new ego dimension which self-recognizes and a new form of cathexis of the ego and of objects. Although Freud does not explicitly say so, it appears that in a first logical time, synthesis occurs at the level of the ego, "the ego cannot exist in the individual from the start; the ego has to be developed" (*ibid.*). In his text, Freud vigorously defends his theory of ego instincts and sexual instincts as the two principal lines of development, and states that narcissism is "the libidinal complement to the egoism of the instinct of preservation" (Freud, 1914, p. 74) and that narcissism and egoism coincide perfectly. As such, anaclisis of the sexual instincts to the selfish ego results in narcissism. A capacity for self-recognition and self-investment arrive at this moment of synthesis, adding a new dimension to the ego apparatus, a new dimension which many authors have defined as the self, but which Freud refused to name. Finally, there is much more than mere anaclisis of the libido, the ego becomes the reservoir of libido that it can invest in itself or in objects. There is, in addition to the anaclitic type of object choice, a narcissistic choice based on the search for one's own image. Two ways of being in the world flow from this new power of the ego, a balancing between two types of investment, investment in oneself or in an object that represents oneself, and investment in a real object. On the basis of this new vision, the instinct for self-preservation is doubled up with, or strengthened by, the investment of the libido in the ego, and, by the same token, loses some of its importance in the understanding of psychic conflict. Winnicott says, "I have never been satisfied with the use of the word 'narcissistic' in this connection because the whole concept of narcissism leaves out the tremendous differences that result from the general attitude and behaviour of the mother. I was therefore left with an attempt to state in extreme form the contrast between being and doing" (Winnicott, 1968–1969, p. 191).

In this period Freud mostly centred on the libidinal and energetic dimension of narcissism, but Winnicott was concerned with the dimension of "being", the feeling of continuity and existence, of self-recognition of the ego. Freud studied the transformations that follow the appearance of narcissism, but Winnicott went deeper into the time preceding this mutation and the conditions without which it cannot appear.

For Winnicott, the founding moment is the end result of a long progression from a state of unintegration to a state of integration. This is a cognitive, experienced-based phenomenon: there will be a transition from a weak and fragmentary ego to a consciousness of oneself. Primary narcissism is a state where the "me" and the "not-me" are not yet differentiated. This is a time of absolute dependence, where the mother is not recognized as existing outside the self, and yet, what is felt and experienced during this period is extremely important for psychic development; it is the cornerstone upon which the whole edifice rests.

In "The capacity to be alone" (Winnicott, 1958a, pp. 29–36) he submits that, after having thought in terms of three- and two-body relationships, it may seem natural to think in terms of a one-body relationship which may seem to correspond to narcissism. But things are not so simple. In making the leap from the two-body relationship to the one-body relationship, it is necessary to take into account the lessons derived from both analytical work and the observation of the mother–child relationship. Winnicott describes "ego-relatedness", a relationship to the ego which, in his view, neatly contrasts with "id-relatedness", the instinctual relationship. He draws attention to the emergence of this relationship that the individual has with himself as occurring precisely at the time when the relationship to the other has not yet become conscious. He brings us back to "a very early stage, when the ego immaturity is naturally balanced by ego-support from the mother". If this support is adequate, there will be a feeling of omnipotence. If it does not satisfy these needs, there will be a fall into the void.

Taking up the subject from a different angle, Winnicott describes the following progression: First there is the word "I", implying much emotional growth. The individual is established as a unit. Integration is a fact. The external world is repudiated and an internal world has become possible. This is simply a topographical statement of the personality as a thing, as an organization of ego-nuclei. At this point no reference is being made to living. Next come the words "I am", representing a stage in individual growth. By these words the individual not only has shape but also life. In the beginnings of "I am" the individual is (so to speak) raw, is undefended, vulnerable, potentially paranoid. The individual can only achieve the "I am" stage because there exists an environment which is protective (Winnicott, 1958a, p. 33).

Winnicott adds that at this stage it is not necessary to assume an infant who is aware of the mother's existence. Only when the mother has acquired a continuity of existence in the child's mind will there be a passage to "I am alone in the presence of another", and only when the infant internalizes the mother will it be possible for the infant to be truly alone. The turning point of interest is the moment of "I am alive", which is analogous to Freud's description of the mutation of the ego which follows "a new psychic action" and which consists of a first crystallization of the self. For Winnicott, however, the self represents much more than mere self-recognition or self-investment, and the distinction between self and ego is often difficult to explain.

In a letter to his French translator in response to her questions regarding the difference between ego and self and the translation of the latter, Winnicott recognized the meaning he gave to the word "self" was rather ambiguous, even in his own mind:

> For me the self, which is not the ego, is the person who is me, who is only me, who has a totality based on the operation of the maturational process. At the same time, the self has parts, and in fact is constituted of these parts. These parts agglutinate from a direction interior-exterior in the course of the operation of the maturational process, aided as it must be (maximally at the beginning) by the human environment which holds and handles and in a live way facilitates. The self finds itself naturally placed in the body, but may in certain circumstances become dissociated from the body or the body from it. The self essentially recognizes itself in the eyes and facial expression of the mother and in the mirror which can come to represent the mother's face. Eventually the self arrives at a significant relationship between the child and the sum of the identifications which (after enough of incorporation and introjection of mental representations) become organised in the shape of an internal psychic living reality. [Winnicott, 1971a, p. 47]

This did not solve the problem for the translator, who was seeking a French word different from *"moi"* or *"moi corporel"* to translate "self". Indeed, terms such as maturity, identification, support of the environment, recognition by the other, could all just as well serve as a description of the ego. Ego-nuclei, self-nuclei, primary identification, identification of the ego, protective role of the mother, support of the ego, support of the self. Ego and self relate to each other like the two sides of Moebius' band which correspond to the same continuous surface. Winnicott adds, "I think that the user of the term self is on a different platform from the user of the term ego. The first platform has to do with life and living in a direct way; the second, where the word *le moi* is used, the speaker or writer is more detached, less involved, perhaps clearer because of being able to use all that there is of the intellectual approach" (Winnicott, 1971, p. 48). Commenting on Winnicott's theory, Pontalis wrote: "An ego is never more than a sum, more or less integrated, of identifications, a more or less disparate group of functions: an amalgam of odds and ends and of a computer. What animates the ego is not within it. The ego, we have stated, represents the organism as a form, while the self is not the élan vital but, in psychic space, the representative of that which is alive" (Pontalis, 1977, p. 159).

In "Creativity and its origins" (1971e) Winnicott reintroduces his account of the splitting-off of pure male and female elements in a discussion of how he had situated the roots of the self in being and in primary identification. We can thus see how the concepts of being, life, creativity and self come to be articulated in Winnicott's thought.

If we now come back to the play of comparing mythical children, the analogies and essential differences that, in a complementary fashion, reflect clinical phenomena regularly encountered in our practice become clear. The Freudian child whose libidinal evolution is emphasized manages to balance investments of sexual energy in oneself or in the external world. Because of this balance, a stable structure of functioning organizes itself and is expressed in a characteristic form of object-choice and object-relation. The Winnicottian child, centred on the ego and the self, oscillates between two different poles: the pole of being, life, creativity, authenticity; and the pole of withdrawal, submission, and false self. As a result of this oscillation, two fundamental ways of being in the world are revealed, two ways of perceiving and animating reality. For Winnicott, this split is less about mental health or illness, and more about being gifted or impoverished as an individual, "we are poor indeed if we are only sane" (Winnicott, 1945, p. 150).

Freud discovers the structuring effects of the illusion of the parents in their narcissistic identification with the child. Winnicott, for whom the parents' contribution is so fundamental, focuses mostly on the traumas which result from the parents' narcissistic illusions. The non-recognition of oneself in the parental gaze can completely arrest and divert the child's progress towards development and the conquest of his or her own identity.

Finally, Freud finds in the adult individual the heirs of infantile narcissism with the ideal ego drawing one back and the ego ideal pushing one forward. He is already describing the guardian of such an ideal, a structure not yet referred to as the superego but which corresponds to the incarnation, in the ego, of the relation to the parents. "Originally, this sense of guilt was a fear of punishment by the parents, or, more correctly, the fear of losing their love" (Freud, 1914, p. 102). The residues of infantile experience that Winnicott encounters are on the side of the "negative", of the emptiness that so often occupies such a large portion of psychic space, on the side of the fear of collapse, and of the false self.

Freud develops his theory of narcissism further in *Instincts and their Vicissitudes* (1915a), but before tackling this very complex work we turn to the child of prehistory.

The child of prehistory

In the concluding statements of his study of Schreber, Freud opens up a new path of reflection and research:

> In dreams and in neuroses, so our thesis has run, "we come once more upon the child and the peculiarities which characterize his modes of thought and his emotional life. And we come upon the savage too", we may now add, "upon the primitive man, as he stands revealed to us in the light of the researches of archaeology and of ethnology". [Freud, 1911b, p. 82]

From now on Freud, who had relied on the physical sciences to develop a scientific psychology, began to use models inspired by the social sciences to travel the roads of prehistory. With the legend of the primal horde in *Totem and Taboo* (1913b), he confirms the central role of the father, of oedipal conflict and of castration anxiety; with the "totemic feast", he brings to light a new form of primitive identification which foreshadows *Mourning and Melancholia* (1917) and newly establishes the role of identification in the development of the child. He reiterates his theory of narcissism as a stage in development between auto-eroticism and object-relating, but no longer speaks of a phase of homosexual object choice. He employs a model of animistic thinking, the "conceptions of the world" in the history of primitive peoples, to detail the steps between a narcissistic conception of the world and the objective conception of external reality. He describes three phases: animist, religious, scientific:

> At the animistic stage men ascribe omnipotence to themselves. At the religious stage they transfer it to the gods but do not seriously abandon it themselves, for they reserve the power of influencing the gods in a variety of ways according to their wishes. The scientific view of the universe no longer affords any room for human omnipotence: men have acknowledged their smallness and submitted resignedly to death and to the other necessities of nature. [Freud, 1913a, p. 88]

The child first believes in his omnipotence and a part of him will never relinquish this belief. He then attributes this power to gods, that is, to his parents, while trying to retain a part of it. Finally, he recognizes the reality of his weakness and smallness before the world, and the reality of certain painful losses against which he is powerless.

Freud was particularly interested in the belief in the omnipotence of thought he described in President Schreber. He attributes this belief to a sexualization of thought, to an anaclisis of sexual instincts upon this thinking activity of the ego. He also introduces differences in the exercise of narcissistic omnipotence by distinguishing magic and sorcery. Magic is the absolute exercise of omnipotence: all that matters is the direct satisfaction of need, solely through the will of the subject. In magic, there is no mechanical or logical cause. Elements are united by their similarity or their contiguity: if I pierce the leg of a doll who represents my enemy, he will no longer be able to walk; if I burn objects belonging to him, I destroy him entirely. It is the contact between the two phenomena that provokes their association, magic is but an illusion. Sorcery, on the other hand, consists essentially of the art of influencing spirits through magical means; it can bring about the enchantment of the world, but it acknowledges the presence of the gods and of external reality. The work of an intermediary is recognized without, however, forsaking the dream of absolute power.

In Winnicottian terms, magic is that which enables the creation of the world, the created-found object, while play in the transitional space corresponds to the casting of a spell upon the world through sorcery. The object's survival of the child's fantasized destruction, the failure of magic and sorcery, bring about the scientific phase, where functioning according to the reality principle imposes itself and where the use of an object becomes possible.

Illusion has a different origin and role in Freudian and Winnicottian thought. At the beginning of life, Freud attributes illusion to narcissism, to the sexualization of thought at the moment where all love is directed toward the ego. Here, illusion may be attributed to an economic factor, it is the image of the earthly paradise which has not yet been lost. When the libido is invested in the object, the illusion will result from a conflict between the fulfilment of desire and the perception of reality; it is the denial of the loss of paradise. Within this viewpoint, "institutionalized" illusion, as in religion and neurosis, can only imprison and have a pejorative meaning.

Winnicott places himself on the side of the Ego. At first, illusion is due to a cognitive error provoked by the perfect holding of the mother. Subsequently, at the moment of object-relating, when the child has acquired the capacity to be alone in the presence of his mother, the space of illusion enables the gap between fantasy and reality to be bridged. Illusion thus becomes a source of creation, it enables play and has an eminently positive value.

Despite these apparently opposite perspectives, Freud, in underscoring the development of culture in the evolution of humanity, recognizes the beneficial and necessary historic role of religious illusion that has to be transcended. Winnicott, while emphasizing the constructive role of illusion, acknowledges its importance only on the condition that illusion be perfectly counter-balanced by the perception of the objective object. Creativity in potential space is possible only if objective reality is solidly perceived.

In 1915, Freud imagined a stage which would have preceded that of the primitive horde, "the primal human animal passed its existence in a thoroughly rich milieu that satisfies all needs, echoes of which we have retained in the myth of the primeval paradise"

(Freud, 1915c, p. 13). Subsequently, the ice age brought harsh conditions and the struggle for survival, necessitating the formation of the primitive horde. Freud's thoughts on the anxiety experienced during the ice age can be viewed as akin to a Winnicottian hypothesis. Pursuing a lengthy reflection on the question of "whether realistic anxiety or anxiety of longing (overload of libido) is the earlier of the two", he settles upon the first, that is, real anxiety. "Now phylogenetic consideration seems to settle this dispute in favor of realistic anxiety and permits us to assume that a portion of the children bring along the anxiousness of the beginning of the Ice Age" (Freud, 1915c, p. 14). It is obviously tempting to associate this real anxiety of the beginning—cold, darkness, lack of food—with the fear of collapse described by Winnicott. Given the role of the father of the primitive horde, Freud may have first given him this task of protection against the aggressions of nature, but, in *The Future of an Illusion* (1927), this role is clearly given to the mother.

The child of metapsychological synthesis: Instincts and their Vicissitudes

In *Instincts and their Vicissitudes* (1915a), Freud integrates other lines of development with his reflections on narcissism. He is inspired by his discoveries regarding the pregenital stages of the organization of the libido as bringing about particular modes of thought and relationships to objects (anal stage, Freud, 1913b, pp. 311–326; oral stage, Freud, 1915b, pp. 197–200). And he was probably influenced by Ferenczi's account of the origin of the omnipotence of thought. Ferenczi (1913a, p. 51) described with stunning precision the illusion of omnipotence the child may experience when the mother satisfies his needs precisely when they appear. Paradoxically, it is as though, thirty years in advance, Freud had had access to Winnicott's first writings on the illusion of the creation of the object.

In *Instincts and their Vicissitudes*, Freud, without denying the existence of the auto-erotic stage, no longer takes the passage from auto-eroticism to narcissism as a point of reference for the appearance of the Ego. He studies the Ego, referred to for the first time as the Ego-subject, from another point of view, that of the cognitive and experiential dimension, cognitive with respect to the external–internal distinction, and experiential with respect to the localization of sources of pleasure. In a first stage, the rudimentary Ego which now exists at the beginning of psychic life distinguishes pleasure and unpleasure but does not yet distinguish between internal and external. Its first self-organizing task is to situate itself with respect to three major axes of organization:

1. Subject (Ego)–object (external world)
2. Pleasure–unpleasure
3. Active–passive.

In a very schematic way, we may say that the Ego-subject loves "the source of pleasure" and Freud describes three types of "opposition relationship" of loving: loving/being loved (loving oneself), loving/hating and, finally, in opposition to loving or hating, being indifferent. He goes on to describe three stages involved in the transformation of the pleasure-Ego into the reality: the original reality-Ego, the purified pleasure-Ego, the final reality-Ego.

The original reality-Ego in the primal narcissistic state experiences sources of pleasure as coming only from within itself, firstly because of its capacity for auto-erotic satisfaction and then, as Freud explained in a footnote, because of the environment's contributions to satisfying the sexual instincts (which, from the outset, require an object), and the ego instincts. "Indeed, the primal narcissistic state would not be able to follow the development [that is to be described] if it were not for the fact that every individual passes through a period during which he is helpless and has to be looked after and during which his pressing needs are satisfied by an external agency and are thus prevented from becoming greater" (Freud, 1915a, p. 135).

For this rudimentary reality-Ego, centred on itself as sole source of pleasure and well protected from unpleasure by the care of its mother, "the external world is indifferent for purposes of satisfaction" (Freud, 1915a, p. 135). One who has always lived in earthly paradise does not need to envision another type of reality. But this happiness cannot last: all needs cannot be perfectly satisfied and wants bring on an effort to distinguish internal and external through the intermediary of motility. If a disturbing stimulus can be eliminated by "muscular action", it is situated "outside"; if it persists it is perceived as coming from the inside and foreshadows the instinctual urge which must be worked upon. The external world is thus discovered in adversity, and, as such, "at the very beginning, it seems, the external world, objects, and what is hated are identical" (Freud, 1915a, p. 136).

Cognitive development brings rapid awareness that the sources of unpleasure also come from within and that certain pleasures originate in the external world. To reclaim the experienced narcissistic completeness of the beginnings, a new earthly paradise must be constructed through the play of the mechanisms by which the bad is projected outside and the good is introjected within. This is the appearance of the purified pleasure-Ego or of the beginnings of fantasy life in a constantly renewed process of re-creating the original experience of pleasure. The illusion of the constructed narcissistic paradise cannot resist the vicissitudes of life, and the reality principle intervenes, an arduous task, since such a gradual passage towards the recognition of reality is a painful process. The narcissistic omnipotence that the child possesses in the animist phase will be transferred to the protective gods of the religious phase and it is only much later, in the scientific phase, that the reality of the external world, with all its constraints, will be recognized and the final reality-Ego solidly established.

In introducing the notion of the original reality-Ego, Freud establishes the necessity for a basic prerequisite to the appearance of the purified pleasure-Ego and the unfolding of phantasy life. Winnicott, on the basis of his experience with very young children and psychotics, focuses on the exploration of these cognitive and experiential prerequisites. Like Freud, he isolates major organizing axes which enable the exploration of the same phenomena from different angles:

1. Ego, self–object
2. Being–doing (the instinctual)
3. Dependence–independence
4. Creativity–destructiveness (my own synthesis).

He describes three stages in the progress towards the perception of objective reality which follow the same logical times as those put forward in *Instincts and Their Vicissitudes*, but centre on the role played by the object. He describes a time in the beginning comparable to that of the original reality-Ego, a time of absolute dependence where the external existence of the mother is not known, but during which her holding, the primary maternal preoccupation, allows integration as well as a primary identification both to the mother who "is" (beginning of the self) and to the protective environment (beginning of the ego). At this stage, the object is only subjectively real: it is magically created or destroyed. At the period of relative dependence, the object begins to exist outside the area of omnipotent thought, instincts come into play, the feeling of omnipotence is threatened. At this moment, the mother must be "good enough" and not perfect, bringing on anger related to frustration.

> The need for a good environment, which is absolute at first, rapidly becomes relative. The ordinary good mother is good enough. If she is good enough the infant becomes able to allow for her deficiencies by mental activity. This applies to meeting not only instinctual impulses but also all the most primitive types of ego need, even including the need for negative care or an alive neglect. The mental activity of the infant turns a good-enough environment into a perfect environment, that is to say, turns relative failure of adaptation into adaptive success. [Winnicott, 1949, p. 245]

This is the moment of the purified pleasure-Ego described by Freud. Finally, to attain independence and freedom from the danger of fantasized attacks against the object, the final reality-Ego must appear, the depressive position must be elaborated. Fantasy life must be definitively separated from reality. The good mother survives fantasized attacks, and disillusion allows the "use of an object" that corresponds to the establishment of the final reality-Ego.

Beyond the Pleasure Principle:
the child of trauma

In *Beyond the Pleasure Principle*, Freud seeks to explain the phenomenon of the repetition of traumatic experiences that can not be understood in light of the pleasure principle. In this disconcerting text, by putting forward the hypothesis of a self-destructive instinct, the death instinct, he profoundly modifies the systems he had developed. Winnicott never accepted this idea, but from this work, two new ideas essential to building bridges between Freud and Winnicott emerge: the "fort—da" game, which leads to the Winnicottian paradox of potentially constructive destructiveness, and the metaphor of the living vesicle which prefigures the central role of trauma and of holding.

Freud describes his 19-month-old grandson playing with a wooden reel that he throws out of his bed and then makes reappear by pulling on the thread to which it is attached. He understands it as an active attempt to overcome the distress occasioned by the separation from the mother. This is an important advance. In the games of the mythical children described earlier the fulfilment of a sexual desire, of a narcissistic desire, or of the staging of the fantasies camouflaging these desires was always central. Here, through play with a concrete object, that which unfolds on the internal stage is experienced in external reality as a way to find a solution.

In "The observation of infants in a set situation" (1941) Winnicott, in attempting to understand the infant's behaviour with the spatula, developed a profound analysis of the reel game basing himself strictly on Kleinian concepts. He sees in this play an attempt at repairing the fantasized destructive attacks on the mother. In 1954, he returns to it, this time interpreting it on the basis of his own conception of aggressiveness and the depressive position. Aggressiveness is a part of primitive love, it is different from anger and hate. The environment-mother must survive the attacks against the instinctual mother. "The mother is holding the situation and the day proceeds, and the infant realizes that the 'quiet' mother was involved in the full tide of instinctual experience, and has survived. This is repeated day after day, and adds up eventually to the baby's dawning recognition of the difference between what is called fact and fantasy, or outer and inner reality" (Winnicott, 1954, p. 268). He takes up the same thesis in 1963, but there he insists more on the object's own role in survival: "If the object is not destroyed, it is because of its own survival capacity, not because of the baby's protection of the object" (Winnicott, 1963c, p. 76).

From this moment on, Winnicott begins to consider an even more primitive factor involved in the establishment of the reality principle. A letter written in 1963, a note drafted on a train in 1965, and, especially, the new definition of narcissism he presents in describing the pure female and male elements in 1966, reveal his progress towards the notion of the use of an object. In 1968, he states: "In other words, I found myself re-examining the movement to the reality principle from what? I have never been satisfied with the use of the word 'narcissistic'" (Winnicott, 1968–1969, p. 191).

For him, narcissistic illusion, narcissism itself, is linked to the perfect holding of the mother during the period of absolute dependence. The illusion of omnipotence enables both the magical creation of the object and its destruction. In 1968, in "The use of an object" (1968b), the survival of the object and the distinction between fact and fantasy are no longer related to going beyond the depressive position but to going beyond narcissism or the era of omnipotence. It is precisely the object's survival of fantasized destruction, without anger or hate, that enables its use. The paradoxically constructive role of destructiveness, where the object survives, is finally recognized. Finally, in January 1969, in "The use of an object in the context of *Moses and Monotheism*", his last development of the concept of the use of an object, Winnicott seeks to explain, taking into account the mother's behaviour, the origin of destructiveness that Freud had explained through the concept of the death instinct.

Prior to opposing Eros and Thanatos in *Beyond the Pleasure Principle*, Freud had always maintained that aggressiveness was "a universal and indispensable attribute of all instincts—their instinctual [*triebhaft*] and 'pressing' character, what might be described as their capacity for initiating movement", adding "I should prefer for the present to adhere to the usual view, which leaves each instinct its own power of becoming aggressive" (Freud, 1909, p. 141). Winnicott's concept of "primary" aggressiveness closely corresponds to the first Freudian model. The child who eats food he or she enjoys also makes it disappear. The motility linked to impulse can, like fire, either bring about destruction or help conserve life by generating heat. In the end, it is the environment's reactions to this "life force" which will render it constructive or destructive. Concluding his 1969 paper Winnicott summarizes his thought so succinctly that it is worthwhile to cite him completely:

> The fate of this unity of drive cannot be stated without reference to the environment. The drive is potentially "destructive" but whether

it is destructive or not depends on what the object is like; does the object survive, that is, does it retain its character, or does it react? If the former, then there is no destruction, or not much, and there is a next moment when the baby can become and does gradually become aware of a cathected object plus the fantasy of having destroyed, hurt, damaged, or provoked the object. The baby in this extreme of environmental provision goes on in a pattern of developing personal aggressiveness that provides the backcloth of a continuous (unconscious) fantasy of destruction. Here we may use Klein's reparation concept, which links constructive play and work with this (unconscious) fantasy backcloth of destruction or provocation (perhaps the right word has not been found). But destruction of an object that survives, has not reacted or disappeared, leads on to use. The baby at the other extreme that meets a pattern of environmental reaction or retaliation goes forward in quite a different way. This baby finds the reaction from the environment to be the reality of what should be his or her own provocative (or aggressive or destructive) impulse. This kind of baby can never experience or own or be moved by this personal root for aggression or destructive fantasy, and can therefore never convert it into the unconscious fantasy destruction of the libidinised object. It will be seen that I am trying to rewrite one limited part of our theory. This provocative destructive aggressive envious (Klein) urge is not a pleasure–pain phenomenon. It has nothing to do with anger at the inevitable frustrations associated with the reality principle. It precedes this set of phenomena that are true of neurotics but that are not true of psychotics. [Winnicott, 1969, pp. 240–245]

In *Beyond the Pleasure Principle* (1920), Freud returns to the question of trauma he had shelved since 1895. In reworking the problem, he uses the model of the vesicle, the most simplified form of the living organism. To survive in an environment charged with disproportionate energy in relation to itself, this vesicle must be protected by an armour, a protective shield against stimuli. In the mother–child unit described by Winnicott, the role of a protective shield is first played by the anti-intrusion holding of the mother, and then by the environment-mother. Later, this protective role will be fulfilled by the false self.

In *Totem and Taboo* (1913b), Freud attributed this role of protection to the father of the primal horde, who is both threatening and protective. Fourteen years later, in *The Future of an Illusion* (1927), he revisited this question of the first protector. Where in *Totem and Taboo*, he had sought to explain the origins of castration anxiety and the role of the father, he now relates the first helplessness in which the little man finds himself to the necessity to invent gods as protection. He asserts: "In this way the mother, who satisfies the child's hunger, becomes its first love-object and certainly also its first protection against all the undefined dangers which threaten it in the external world—its first protection against anxiety, we may say" (Freud, 1927, p. 24).

Finally, from this model of the most simple form of life, Freud reflects upon the causes of death. Basing himself on the research of the time, he finally attributes death to self-intoxication, a poisoning by the metabolic waste evacuated in an environment unable to make it disappear. For Winnicott, the death instinct, the impulse for self-destruction, is replaced by a deficit of the symbolizing apparatus, by the impossibility of creating a space for play which enables the metabolizing of internal experiences and the elimination of their toxicity in an environment which can receive and transform them.

Conclusion

The five mythical children discussed here serve as an underpinning for the elaboration of the second structural model and in 1923 their different components were reassembled to better render psychical conflictuality. The new theory's power to explain, understand, and interpret, is so great that the mythical children, without disappearing, are relegated to the shade. The ego and the development of the ego become (doubles,) abstract substitutes for the model of the child.

Winnicott, while regularly using the concepts of the structural model, pursues the elaboration of the first theory of instincts, deepening Freudian advances regarding the importance of ego deficits in the genesis of more severe pathologies such as psychosis. The axes of organization that Winnicott proposes, stemming from the distinction between being and doing, bring us back to the same logic that exists between the instinct for self-preservation and the sexual instinct. While Winnicott profoundly transforms the notion of self-preservation, for him the specificity of being human is precisely the capacity to go beyond this way of existing. To be human is not merely to react, survive and adapt, but to live in a creative way before the world. The ego's creative impulse precedes and underlies the sublimation of sexual instincts. Although he rejects the second theory of instincts because of his opposition to the notion of a self-destructive impulse, he comes to describe a creative force that corresponds to the life instinct..

With the discovery of the central role of identification, Freud again modifies his conception of the ego. The axis opposing ego-instincts/sexual instincts is relegated to a second level, and identifications to idealized parents or to their prohibitions are now considered at the centre of the formation of psychical structures—the ideal ego, the ego ideal, the superego—and become central in the elaboration of psychic conflictuality. These three agencies of the psyche have both a topographical and a dynamic meaning: they have great stability, are continually interacting, and can be conscious or unconscious. Winnicott takes for granted the existence of these structures but is interested in another dimension of psychical reality, that of the experiential, of the subjectivation of psychic experience, of the subjective appropriation of the instinctual and of external reality. The self and the false self correspond to subjective experience but also have a quasi-agency status in their topographical and dynamic relation. In his metaphorical language, Winnicott speaks of the false self that protects the true self and of the inviolable sanctuary of the true self. This attempt at structuring does not carve up psychic reality along the same plane, or according to the same logical construction, as the Freudian agencies. It corresponds to a different viewing angle, to a diagonal cut of the Id, the Ego and the Superego.

TRUE SELF.   FALSE SELF.

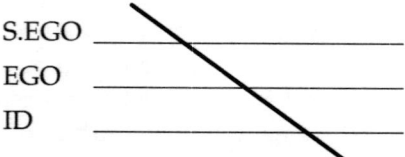

S.EGO _____
EGO   _____
ID   _____

Winnicott writes to his translator: "I think that the user of the term self is on a different platform from the user of the term ego. The first platform has to do with life and living in a direct way; the second, where the word *le moi* is used, the speaker or writer is more detached, less involved, perhaps clearer because of being able to use all that there is of the intellectual approach" (Winnicott, 1971a, p. 47).

In my view, this is a clear illustration of the different approaches of Freud and Winnicott.

Finally, in the Winnicottian topographical theory, the role given to the external object is considered from a different perspective. Freud had described successively the object of sexual instincts, the object of self-preservation, the part-object object, the complete object, the narcissistic object, the lost object of *Mourning and Melancholia*, but he had never addressed, except in the theory of seduction, the active, constructive role of the external object in the organization of ego instincts and sexual instincts. It is precisely this task that Winnicott took on, and one of his greatest contributions has been to shed light on the essential role of the external object in the construction of the internal world. Winnicott was entirely correct in saying that he had both applied Freudian methods to new territories and had remained faithful to Freud throughout his work.

This study of mythical children has attempted to provide an understanding of the complementarity between Freudian and Winnicottian theory, but its approach is quite alien to Winnicott's intellectual processes and its twists and turns could cause an essential dimension of his contribution to be lost. In writing it I have often thought of Winnicott's reflections on scientific truth and poetic truth: "The link between poetic truth and scientific truth is surely in the person, in you and me. The poet in me reaches to a whole truth in a flash, and the scientist in me gropes towards a facet of the truth; as the scientist reaches the immediate objective, a new objective presents itself" (Winnicott, 1965, p. 172).

The poetic words of St. Exupéry, at the end of *Wind, Sand, And Stars* may contribute to understanding another dimension in the comparison between the creative genius of Freud and that of Winnicott:

> I sat down face to face with one couple. Between the man and the woman a child had hollowed himself out a place and fallen asleep. I

saw his face. What an adorable face! A golden fruit had been born of these two peasants and I said to myself: This is a musician's face. This is the child Mozart. This is a life full of beautiful promise. Little princes in legends are not different from this. Protected, sheltered, cultivated, what could not this child become?

When by mutation a new rose is born in a garden, all the gardeners rejoice. They isolate the rose, tend it, foster it. But there is no gardener for men. This little Mozart will be shaped like the rest by the common stamping machine. This little Mozart will love shoddy music in the stench of night dives. This little Mozart is condemned. What torments me to-night is the gardener's point of view. What torments me is not the humps nor the hollows nor the ugliness. It is the sight, a little bit in all these men, of Mozart murdered.

Only the Spirit, if it breathe upon the clay, can create Man. [St Exupéry, 1955, pp. 284–285]

If Freud is the scientist who is passionately searching for the origins of the roses' splendour and the reasons for their wilting, then Winnicott might be the genius who has adopted "the gardener's point of view".

CHAPTER TWO

Early emotional development: Ferenczi to Winnicott

Margret Tonnesmann

Shortly after Freud had published "Formulations on the two principles of psychic functioning" in 1911(a), Sandor Ferenczi wrote a paper in 1913(a), "Stages in the development of the sense of reality", as he felt that Freud had left open how the transition from the pleasure principle to the reality principle during early infancy takes place. The paper is informed by the classical instinct theory of the time, namely the reproductive libidinal instincts and the self-preservative ones, called at that time the "ego-instincts". Ferenczi reasons that development from the pleasure principle to the reality principle is probably due to the replacement of childhood megalomania by the recognition of the power of natural forces and it constitutes the essential content of ego development. He draws attention to the famous footnote in Freud's paper that an organization that is a slave to the pleasure principle and that can neglect the reality of the external world is a fiction, but one that is almost realized provided one includes with it the care received from the mother. Ferenczi then points out that this is realized in the embryo's existence in the womb where there is indeed total environmental supply and with it absolute omnipotence. There is no wish/impulse yet. When, during the post-uterine existence, this stage is—as Ferenczi put it—rudely interrupted, it is the loving and empathic nursing care that gratifies the first wish/impulse of the infant. In magic hallucinatory omnipotence the infant can imagine satisfaction in positive and negative hallucinations. As the infant's psychic organization grows, what had been simple discharge phenomena of unpleasant affects now obtain a new function and can be used to give signals, so that hallucinatory ideational identity can be followed by satisfying perceptual identity. The infant can maintain its omnipotence with the help of magic gestures, which, in time, become more and more complex, but also more specialized. They all call for prompt satisfaction, which is given by mother's loving attention and appropriate nursing care. But the infant experiences them as part of the self and he is not aware of mother's administrations to satisfy his needs.

Ferenczi conceived of this earliest development as the introjective omnipotent stages which in time give way to the beginnings of the projective reality stages of the ego. The infant now experiences, often painfully, that the outside world does not always obey his magic gestures, and instant gratification of his wishes and wants may be absent or delayed. In a further advance of adaptation, the Ego starts to distinguish between subjective psychical contents, that is to say, feelings, and the objective content of sensations. The outside world, however, is at first endowed with life by the infant during the animistic period of development. He seeks in the reality-objects his own body organs and activities, which is the beginning of symbol-formation. He also learns to represent the outside world symbolically by means of his own body. Ferenczi is aware here of the importance of the environmental provision, when he states that it is because of the understanding, loving care the infant receives from his mother that he need not give up the illusion of omnipotence yet.

In time the baby starts to make use of speech-symbolism, starting with the imitation of sounds and noises. It discovers that this allows for a much simpler and more varied representation of objects in the outside world than was possible with gesture-language. In further development, conscious thinking makes speech-symbolism possible by association with thought processes that are in themselves unconscious, lending them perceptual qualities. It is the development of conscious thought that advances the ego's adjustment to reality, as Freud had already said, but it is the continuation of mother's care that, by guessing the child's thoughts, allows him a period when he can experience his own thoughts and words as having magic power. Referring to Freud, Ferenczi agreed that it is only with the child's psychical detachment from his parents that the feelings of omnipotence give way to full appreciation of the force of circumstances.

What seems remarkable about this 1913 paper is that it represents a highly intuitive and detailed study of ego development in infancy and it also recognizes the importance of mother's adaptations to her infant's needs for the undisturbed continuation of his maturational omnipotence. But it is a paper of classical orientation and it basically views development as a series of internal adaptations. It conceives of the infant in terms of a one-body psychology, to use Rickman's classification of a one-body, two-body, three-body and multi-body psychology.

What may also be of interest is that, in this paper, Ferenczi talks tentatively of the idea that in psychoneurotic pathology not only is there regression to fixation points of libidinal development, but in primary repression, a developmentally corresponding part of mental functioning is also arrested and does not take part in further development with the rest of the ego. He reasons that the mechanisms of neurotic symptoms are determined by regression to this early arrested ego-part. Hysteria, for example, is characterized on the one hand by regression to early libidinal fixations, but on the other, also by regression to the corresponding arrested fixations of the ego, that is, to the stage of magic gestures that characterizes conversion. Also, in obsessional neurosis, there is regression to an arrested ego-part at the stage of magic omnipotent thought.

In the introduction to her first book, *Psycho-Analysis of Children* (1937), Melanie Klein expressed her indebtedness to her two teachers, Sandor Ferenczi and Karl Abraham. She explicitly states that, apart from his strong and immediate feelings for the unconscious and symbolism, Ferenczi impressed her by his unusual empathy for the psyche of the small child. She also says that she owes to him the foundation for her personal development as a psychoanalyst. She characterized Abraham as her mentor and deeply appreciated his highest expectations of the human and scientific achievements of his colleagues; this, she said, had inspired her. When she came to England in 1926 she had had analysis with Ferenczi, whose capacity for emotional understanding and relating to children she had admired, and with Abraham, whose late work concerned the fate of the libidinal object in development and pathology. As she herself acknowledged, both analysts were important for the development of her own theories of child development.

Her ideas on early object relations stimulated discussion in the British Society, where there had already been great interest in early development of affects by analysts like Ernest Jones, Edward Glover and others. In her classical paper on affects in 1937 Marjory Brierley gave affect-cathexis from the beginning high priority and said that, at the beginning, the affect is the object for the infant. It is the cathexis of the object, rather than the emotional charge of the ideational representation of the impulse, that is central to all the various object-relations theories.

Melanie Klein developed her theories of early object-relations while remaining committed to instinct theory. Her concepts assume instinctual conflicts with objects manifested in unconscious phantasies, and activating the primitive defence-mechanisms of an operative primitive ego from birth. Hence, her theories of object relations are also of a one-body psychology. Supported by the loving care of the nursing mother, the developmental processes unfold according to the infant's constitutional forces which have built the structure of the child's internal object world.

It was different for those British analysts of an object-relations theoretical orientation, Balint, Fairbairn and Winnicott, but also many others, who conceived of object relations not primarily as the cathexis of the object of the instinctual impulse, but as an intersubjective emotional process, operative from the earliest dependence of the infant on the nursing mother. It is this that contributes the importance of the facilitating environment for the infant's maturational processes. This is then, a two-body psychology. Fairbairn stated that the ego is from the start not pleasure-seeking but object-seeking and Balint was at pains to insist that there is no primary narcissism, but secondary narcissism from the beginning, as the narcissistic solution to early object-relating.

Donald Winnicott conceived of earliest development as a mother–infant unity. He coined the phrase, "I cannot conceive of an infant, only of a nursing couple". His main concern was the study of ego-relatedness, that is, object-relating apart from Id considerations. Contrary to Fairbairn's view, he did not give up instinct theory altogether, but stressed that instinctual impulses are an important back-up for ego-relatedness.

Winnicott felt that psychoanalysis had concentrated its attention on psychic reality and shared reality, but neglected the intermediate area of experience, which is neither intra-psychic nor shared reality but at the border of both, and both contribute to it. This third area is a potential space and in Winnicott's conceptualization of infant development, it is the experiential, emotional quality of the infant–mother unity that is at the centre of his considerations. He conceived of an infant at the very beginning in absolute or double dependence on the nursing mother. The infant is dependent but has no awareness of it yet. The ordinary devoted mother relates to the infant with what he called maternal preoccupation, which is given to her in health, prepared during the last stages of pregnancy, and lasts for a couple of months. At the beginning she holds the infant's ego, as Winnicott said, so is aware of her infant's needs. At first the infant has only motor-sensory experiences and is totally merged with mother in a state of anxiety-free un-integration, a kind of continuation of the intra-uterine existence where physiology and psychology are not yet differentiated and the environmental provision assures aliveness of tissue. Ferenczi describes the nursing care of the post-uterine infant in similar terms, but, for him, it is the mother's loving administrations of keeping her infant warm and protected from noise and light that approximate the infant's wish to go back into the wishless intra-uterine state where everything was provided for. Winnicott maintained that the ordinary devoted mother meets the infant's needs by empathically understanding what the infant is feeling. She makes sure that his experience of continuity, of going-on-being, is not interrupted. Winnicott demarcates from it the mother–infant relationship built on satisfaction of instinctual impulses.

The mother also facilitates the infant's experientially creating the object, as Winnicott called it. The infant has a wish, a want for the breast and at this moment the mother presents the breast to the infant. The infant omnipotently experiences that he has created an object, the breast, just when it was wanted. The hallucination is here a creative gesture. This is akin to Ferenczi's stage of hallucinatory magic omnipotence when perceptual identify follows the ideational one, but, for Winnicott, it is the experience that leaves memory traces of a special kind.

If, however, the mother is insensitive to the infant's needs and presents, let us say, the nipple, in an unsatisfactory way, the infant's feelings of continuity-of-being are impinged upon and, whereas, in good enough mothering, the infant can gather such occasional failures under his omnipotence, frequent crises of not good enough mothering lead to early dissociation. The self withdraws from communication and instead a compliant, false self develops, accompanied by premature mind activity. Spontaneous affect signals disappear and instead the infant only reacts compliantly, and so defensively, to stimuli. Winnicott assumes that this very early split protects the true self from further impingements, but it also prevents its further growth and it can lead to severe pathology of childhood psychosis and autism. For Ferenczi it is regression to arrested parts at the stage of magic hallucinatory wish-fulfilment, that constitutes the mechanism of psychotic symptoms.

According to the one-body psychology approach of Ferenczi's, ego-development in early infancy is due to the adaptation to increasing frustration of the infant's omnipotent wishes and wants. In the course of development the infant experiences that not all its urges find instant magic satisfaction, and it slowly dawns on him that there are hostile forces in the outside world, for example, when an object he stretches his arms out for does not come to him. It is from the experience of this painful discordance that the ego learns to differentiate between the outer world and the psychic feeling world. In other words, the infant perceives the separateness of objects through frustration of his omnipotent wishes.

Winnicott's approach is that of a two-body psychology. He conceptualizes this developmental step differently: when ego relatedness has become possible, there develops a space between mother and infant. It is the area of illusion, in which the infant's subjective relating is imaginatively and experientially enriched. He refers to the observation that, early on, when infants are vigorously sucking the breast, they may concomitantly stroke their lips with a finger or caress the breast with their hand. Libidinal and aggressive impulses are still un-integrated and the infant may experience them as coming from outside. For the infant, he says, the impulse is just like a clap of thunder. In a primitive love-impulse the infant may wish to destroy his subjective object joyfully and, Winnicott says, give it cavalier treatment, but there is no malice in this: "I love you so I eat you". Here, the good-enough mother will understand the importance of her survival of the attack. It is one of the most important developmental steps, as the infant's discovery of the survival of the destroyed object releases it from his omnipotent control. The infant can now relate to a separate object. In Winnicott's conceptualization, it is not the absence of gratification that introduces the infant to shared reality and with it, a separate object world; it is the survival of the object he has destroyed in subjective intention that matters. It now can be trusted and used. In health the infant has now reached unit status with boundaries, and ego-relating is enhanced by the triad of introjection, projection and identification. Aggressive and libidinal impulses get fused and in time, the self will take responsibility for them. It is only then that we can speak of a hateful destructive impulse and also of developing concern for the separate object and its intra-psychic imago.

It seems to me that it is here, in the different assumptions about the infant's learning of and adapting to shared reality, that the contrast between Ferenczi's one-body psychology and Winnicott's two-body psychology is striking. In 1926, in a second paper informed by Freud's final instinct theory, Ferenczi further discussed development towards the reality principle. He stressed that, as long as the infant is in the stage of introjective omnipotent development, he has no feelings for the object, neither good nor bad ones. As long as the object is always there when needed, it is experienced as part of the ego. But, when the object remains absent when needed, for example, when the infant feels hungry but there is no breast yet, we can observe that the infant reacts with uncoordinated movements and screaming, comparable with an adult's expression of rage. Ferenczi reasons that a defusion of instincts takes place here and the destructive part takes precedence. The absent object is now hated. When, however, the object re-appears and the infant finds it again, the libidinal part takes over and the re-found object can now be loved. This is in line with Freud's statement that all object-finding is a re-finding of it. It is from the first experience of the absence of the object that is needed—or, as Ferenczi said in 1913, when the infant discovers that not everything obeys his will—that the infant is introduced to the notion of reality-objects that are ambivalently hated when absent but loved when re-found.

Winnicott's assumptions are different as he did not accept the concept of the death-instinct. He traced the roots of aggression to prenatal life and saw, in the muscular movements that meet opposition, the earliest manifestations of pleasurable aggression. At the beginning these movements are physiological me, not-me experiences. The aggressive impulse is purposeful but, in subjective omnipotence, the infant does not know about it; he is pre-ruth rather than ruthless, as Winnicott said. Only after the object has been released from the infant's omnipotent control can he experience hate towards the now separate object.

As I have already said, in further development Ferenczi assumes an animistic phase when the infant endows objects of the outer world with life and seeks to find again in his objects, his own body organs and their pleasurable activities. It is the stage of the beginnings of symbol-formation, enriched by imitation, imagination, and experimentation. In time, the child develops speech, and conscious thinking makes speech-symbolism possible by becoming associated with unconscious thought-processes.

Winnicott emphasized that, in further emotional development, it is the child's dependence on the mother, who is now experienced as a separate object and, in health, a trustworthy one, that is important. The mother continues to provide understanding ego-cover, appropriate to the maturational age of her child. She will now start to disillusion the infant, let it wait for a bit, etc. Whereas impingement during earliest development leads to catastrophic pathology, it now assumes positive value as it stimulates the infant's capacity to communicate. Instead of elaborating the animistic stage of development, as Ferenczi had done, Winnicott's interest was in exploring further emotional development in the third area of experience. His concepts of the transitional object and transitional phenomena are central to an understanding of the vital position he gives to ego-relatedness and the development of the individual's interactional emotional relating. The first object of which the child takes possession and which is neither a projection of an internal object nor a shared reality-object, though both contribute to it, remains in the experiental space. It has to have features of both the self and the mother and it has to have all the characteristics of surviving when used. It should be indestructible and remain the same, however maltreated it is at times by the baby's vigorous love and hate. Winnicott accepts that the transitional object is at the root of symbol development and represents the infant–mother unity, but he stressed that, for him, it is the use the infant makes of his transitional object that is important. It covers the whole range of the emotional experiences of the self. When, with further development, the transitional object is forgotten, as the baby's interests widen into the area of transitional phenomena, the latter refer to the child's self-absorbed playing and later to cultural experiences, in the widest sense of the term. They cover everything of which we say, it is meaningful to us. The core self, or true self as Winnicott called it, to contrast it with his concept of the false self, remains, in his assumption, an isolate, and is incommunicable. But it actualizes itself in the transitional space that he called the third area of experience. Winnicott maintained that the child's playing is a capacity that remains active in all healthy-enough human beings throughout life. Playing is doing, he said, and he differentiated it sharply from narcissistic, libidinal daydreaming. He also drew attention to the fact that, when id excitement reaches a certain threshold, it interrupts the child's playing. Playing was, for him, not just mastery of trauma, nor was it only sublimation of instinctual impulses. What matters in playing is the self's actualization and the creativity of ego-relatedness. It is from these assumptions that he said all meaningful relationships between human beings, and also the psychoanalytic therapy process take place, in a space to which both partners contribute and where two areas of playing overlap. In adult analysis, he sees playing manifest itself in the choice of words, in the intonation of voice, and in the sense of humour.

I have tried to compare and to contrast two psychoanalytic theories of infant development. Ferenczi's paper of 1913 must be the first, or one of the first papers on Baby Observation. The infant's development is viewed in terms of the classical theory of the time, namely, the ego's adaptation to the demands of shared reality, with the aim of finding satisfaction for the tension states that are caused by the growing infant's ever increasing wishes and wants. Ferenczi views the infant in terms of a one-body psychology, but he also describes a mother's nursing care at different stages, so that the infant can live with appropriate feelings of omnipotence and the formation of pathogenic fixations and arrests can be minimized.

Winnicott's object-relations theory of infant development is a two-body psychology. He views development as evolving from the infant–mother unity, with its interactional emotional dependence. The unfolding of emotional experiences in ego-relatedness and the actualization of self in creative pursuits are, for him, the base of healthy development. Pathology may arise when owing, to extensive failures of the nursing mother, the infant's continuity-of-being feelings are repeatedly impinged upon. An endopsychic defensive adaptation to shared reality develops in a false-self organization with premature mind activity.

During the 1920s, Ferenczi treated some severely disturbed patients and difficulties arose when these patients experienced his classical benevolent, neutral analytic stance as being cold, harsh or aloof towards them. To bring the analytic process forward, he relaxed his attitude and encouraged the patients' tendencies to regress during the sessions. They then re-enacted, in a trance-like state, childhood memories and Ferenczi responded by trying to address in them the child they had become at such moments. When, after a while, he brought such episodes to a close and addressed the adult patient again, the patients reacted with vehement anger. Ferenczi became aware that the patients had first regressed to a pre-trauma stage but, with his change of approach, had re-experienced a childhood trauma that they could now recall in memory. This led him to investigate the exogenous factors in infant and child development, in particular, those traumatic events in the infant–mother and child–mother relationships that were of pathogenic significance. His theoretical orientation had now shifted from a one-body psychology to a two-body one. He felt that it was rather naive of him to re-discover what he had, after all, known, but neglected for twenty-five years. At the International Congress in 1929, in Oxford, he said that, however half-worked out his theoretical statements were, he was convinced that a proper evaluation of the long neglected traumato-genesis was necessary for our practical technique and the theory of our science.

It is with the evaluation of pathogenic early traumata that Ferenczi's and Winnicott's concepts, to some extent, converge, as both held the same basic assumptions, namely that the mother–infant and mother–child interactions are of vital importance for the emotional and mental health of the individual. Both authors assume that privation and de-privation, to use Winnicott's terminology, lead to narcissistic splits of the self and only by re-experiencing such early traumata during analysis can these splits be healed.

When traumata have occurred before the infant has reached unit status, in Winnicott's formulation or, in Ferenczi's words, before the infant has reached the stage of development when thought has completely developed, they are only registered in physical memories. Winnicott called them "frozen" memories and stressed that they often accurately resemble the original trauma. Ferenczi stated that such memories can only be repeated in transitory hysterical symptoms that signify regression to the stage of magic gestures. In the analytic situation they have communicative emotional value in the analyst–patient relationship. Winnicott stressed that such severely regressed patients need management rather than interpretation and the analyst has to provide "holding" for the vulnerable, dependent patient. Ferenczi also said that such patients, who often present with a loss of desire for life, feelings of having been abandoned and who also show signs of having turned the aggression against the self, need a period of indulgence preparatory to later analysis.

Ferenczi's main interest, however, was with those infantile traumata that the patients could recall in memory. He conceived of the traumatogenic factor as the mother's, or, in cases of the child's sexual or violent abuse, the adult's failure to respond to the child's innocent, guilt-free, tender feelings and phantasies of passive love. Instead, the mother reacts with feelings of love and hate that belong to the adult's passionate emotions and they are often consciously denied. The child now feels not understood, abandoned, not confirmed in the reality of his own emotional state and he becomes confused and frightened. He instantly identifies with the aggressor, leading to a split in the self and endopsychic manifestations that are similar to those described by Winnicott as false-living in cases of false-self development. Time does not permit me to discuss Ferenczi's attempts to find a technique that would not only repeat the trauma, but also allow the patient to experience, in the analytic relationship, the analyst as a new object, who responds with complete frankness about his feelings when the patient experiences him in the transference as the aggressor. They were early attempts to accommodate counter-transference for the benefit of the patient.

Winnicott's conceptualization is different. He conceived of false-self disorders as defences to protect the true or core self from traumatic environmental intrusions. Another category of response to traumata is the antisocial tendency of a child that feels it has the right to take back what it once had, but was taken away from him. For example, mother's love when another sibling is born and, sometimes, owing to external circumstances, she had to withdraw some of her attention. Stealing and lying are characteristic features of the antisocial tendency and, when not given attention, can result in massive character disorders with secondary gains. Winnicott was sceptical about the value of psychoanalytic treatment in such cases.

Sandor Ferenczi died at the age of sixty and with it his research into the traumatogenic origin of self disorders and his search for a technique that could utilize counter-transference in the best interest of the patients came to a premature end. On several occasions in his last papers, he makes a plea for a more thorough analysis of practising psychoanalysts and he expressed concern that otherwise, a situation could arise when patients had become better analyzed than their analysts. Fifteen years later, Winnicott can take training analysis for granted when he requires that the analyst has to understand his own guilt about his primitive unconscious destructive impulses when treating patients who suffer from narcissistic depressions and who need the analyst to survive or, when treating psychotic patients, must know that the analyst has to be able to experience and to contain his undisplaced simultaneous love and hate in the counter-transference.

Ferenczi was always somewhat ahead of his time. That was already so when, in 1913, he wrote his fine paper on baby observation, focusing on early ego development in terms of the various stages that lead finally to the baby's adaptation to reality. As I have already said, he stated there that primal repression is accompanied by a corresponding arrest of parts of the ego. In Fairbairn's two-body object relations theory, object-ego relationships are split, repressed and constitute psychic structure. In his late papers Ferenczi discussed theory and technique of self-disorders resulting from infantile pathogenic traumata. This was also ahead of his time, as the understanding of the communicative value of emotions in an intersubjective transference–counter-transference relationship was neither comprehended nor practised in 1933. If he could have survived for another fifteen years or so, would he have developed his traumatogenic theory in similar directions to those of Daunt or Winnicott or even Fairbairn? Would he have come to conclusions similar to Paula Heimann's in 1949 or Winnicott's in 1947, or Pearl King's in 1978, concerning the handling of the counter-transference in psychoanalytic therapy?

I have tried to trace, in Ferenczi's contributions to psychoanalysis, the development from a one-body to a two-body psychology that foreshadowed those object-relations theories that Donald Winnicott and other British psychoanalysts have developed and that are practised, in particular, by analysts of the Independent Group of psychoanalysts in Great Britain.

CHAPTER THREE

Infant observation: what **do** you see?*

Abe Brafman

Infant Observation only started life as an academic discipline in the late 1950s when Esther Bick introduced it to child psychotherapists in training at the Tavistock Clinic (Bick, 1964). It has now become part of the training in a large range of disciplines and is the subject of an international journal, *Infant Observation*, and many books. After a brief historical overview, I propose to discuss the nature, goals and rationale of Infant Observation under three headings: Curricular discipline, Research, and as a test of a student's capacity to learn from experience.

History

The last century saw a growing interest in the emotional and psychological development of the child. One line of work focused on examining the behaviour and establishing the cognitive

---

*After an earlier paper on this subject (Brafman, 1988) I was asked to write on my present views on the observation of babies. To preserve clarity, some points are repeated here.

capabilities of the growing infant, while longitudinal studies aimed at delineating continuities and discontinuities in the progress from infancy to adulthood. Although these studies have produced fascinating findings, few, if any of them are automatically applicable to all subjects. This is to be expected from statistically based investigations. We continue to believe that "the child is father to the man", but time and again when trying to determine the characteristics of a particular individual, we face the old arguments over the relative importance of natural endowment and the environment and lived experience. If the focus is on the adult, it is not difficult to postulate which features of his childhood might be relevant in explaining any of our findings, but the reverse process is seldom successful. There are now studies showing how people diagnosed as autistic in childhood develop into adulthood, and these findings have helped in recognizing early presentations of psychological pathology that persist into later life. But when we focus on a "normal" child, it is virtually impossible to predict development, since environmental influences appear to trigger off continuous adaptational changes in that individual.

In the psychoanalytical world, Spitz (1950) alerted us to the consequences of leaving babies without significant human contact and argued that infants needed human/maternal nurturing if they were to develop normally. Bowlby (1969) and Robertson documented the consequences of separating children from their parents, and they focused on the dramatic, visible signs of their distress. Winnicott's description of the "spatula game" (1941) was based on his observations of babies' behaviour, much along the lines of Freud's description of his grandson's "fort-da" game (1920). Though these authors postulated links between observable behaviour and underlying affects, they concentrated on the children's visible reactions to how adults treated them.

There is a dramatic, qualitative change when observations of behaviour lead to the formulation of what unconscious fantasies, affects, and impulses are the cause or the response to that baby's experience of the world he inhabits. Are these theoretical postulates based on that particular baby, or are they the result of psychoanalytic work with older children and adults? The former involves finding ways of checking the validity of our inferences, the latter presents the insoluble problem of being, by definition, self-validating.

Already in 1905, Freud had written:

> Psychoanalytic investigation, reaching back into childhood from a later time, and contemporary observation of children combine to indicate to us still other regularly active sources of sexual excitation. The direct observation of children has the disadvantage of working upon data which are easily misunderstandable; psychoanalysis is made difficult by the fact that it can only reach its data, as well as its conclusions, after long détours. But by cooperation the two methods can attain a satisfactory degree of certainty in their findings. [p. 201]

Analysts began to work with children in the 1920s. Hug-Helmut, Anna Freud and Melanie Klein began to analyze children, and, in 1926, Anna Freud together with Dorothy Burlingham, Eva Rosenfeld, Peter Blos Senior and Erik Erikson opened a school for children aged between 7 and 13 in Vienna (Tyson, 1996, p. 394). But it was only when Anna Freud created the Hampstead Nurseries in London, that the concept of "observation", *sensu strictu*, of young children, came into existence.

Besides seeing children in analytic treatment, analysts wanted to observe ever younger children to find validation for the psychoanalytic theories of human emotional development that had originated from work with adults and older children. In the forties, Mrs Bick (1964) introduced "infant observation" as a discipline in the child psychotherapy training at the Tavistock Clinic, but it was only in 1960 that this was included in the training curriculum of the British Psychoanalytical Society. Since the seventies, there has been an increasing number of trainings that have adopted this discipline all over the world, though there is a recognizable difference in the theoretical and technical frameworks within which this is practised at each training centre.

Curricular discipline

The inclusion of "infant observation" in the training curriculum follows from the belief that it represents a valuable introduction to the work with children and adult patients in analysis or psychotherapy. A number of arguments are put forward to justify this claim:

1. The student is exposed to intimate and delicate situations that quite often become charged with considerable emotional tension: this can arouse feelings and impulses in the student with which he or she may not be very familiar.

   He or she may then experience anxiety and discomfort, and often quite strong impulses to become an active participant in the baby–mother interaction. This is an early opportunity for the student to learn how to recognize his or her urges, but contain them for appropriate scrutiny. This will help to learn more about him or her self, at the same time as obtaining a close view of the struggles experienced by someone holding full responsibility for a helpless dependent person. Because the couple in this case is an infant and its mother, the student can gain first-hand knowledge of what is involved in these fundamental developmental stages of human beings.
2. Psychoanalytic theories postulate the origins of adult pathology in the early months and years of life, and the student can observe the actual interactions that might constitute evidence of the inborn endowment of the baby, as well as the reactions to the stimuli from the environment. At the same time, the student can learn the impact that bearing and nursing an infant has on a woman, and the changes imposed on the life of the marital couple.
3. The changes occurring from week to week help the student to realize how subtle, but significant, are the effects on the infant of physical and cognitive maturation, and of interaction with the mother. Perhaps one of the most valuable lessons to be learnt from this exercise is the power of the mutual influences that baby and mother exert on each other. As weeks and months flow by, the observations will demonstrate how each baby and each parent have their own highly personal characteristics which, in the course of time, create their own typical pattern of interaction. Because each student has his or her own private view of what is right and wrong, good and bad, in infant care, comments describing observations as functional or dysfunctional, healthy or pathological, will frequently appear in observers' reports. Subsequent discussion of these comments will help the student to recognize whether they are fair assessments of the observed baby–mother or whether they stem from personal views and experiences.

4. If students are encouraged to formulate predictions of how baby and mother will evolve, they can soon discover that, in the vast majority of cases, the potential for normal development is far more real and powerful than their anxieties and preconceptions would ever have believed possible. In terms of future clinical work, the student would find here a powerful example of the importance of checking each impression over a period of time before assuming it constitutes a permanent trait.
5. The most frequent argument put forward to justify the observation of infants is that students have the opportunity of watching *in statu nascendi* the phenomena that shape their future adult, child and adolescent patients.

In practice, it is difficult to establish the real value of each of the above arguments. There is no doubt that the observations produce a considerable emotional impact on the student and this allows teachers to help him or her to recognize their areas of emotional vulnerability, as well as the importance of keeping their own anxieties in check, without interfering unduly in the interactions they observe. When the student is able to compare his or her preconceptions with the actual unfolding of the infant–mother development, he or she can also gradually gain insight into how personal life experiences influence his or her perception of the world.

However, I have never been convinced that infant observation gives students any additional insight regarding their view of their patients. In spite of the fact that this discipline is undertaken right at the beginning of the training, students finish their observations using the same theoretical spectacles with which they started their visits to the family. This may be due to the fact that most, if not all, our students have been through complex previous trainings. Perhaps more important is the fact that students have already had one or more years of personal analysis before the start of the observations; this also influences their perceptions and formulations.

Most students purport to have enjoyed their infant observation and to have learned from it, which may well be sufficient reason to keep this discipline as part of the training curriculum. I find it sad, nevertheless, that it is only a rare student who will react to the observations by discovering a new interest in children or even in the complexities of early human development. Somehow, most students see infant observation as one of the steps they need to undertake before reaching their goal of becoming psychoanalysts or psychotherapists—of adults.

To my mind, the main advantage of Infant Observation as a curricular discipline lies in the unique opportunity it gives us of teaching students how many different hypotheses can be raised to explain every single particular aspect of the infant's behaviour and interaction with the mother. Intellectually, every student finds this a valuable discovery, but it is not often that these alternative explanations will lead them to question the theoretical framework of their personal analysis.

Research

I quoted Freud's caveat concerning speculations about the Infant's unconscious thoughts and feelings. Anna Freud (1969) also warned against "turning understanding and any degree of intuition into a belief that ultimate information has been obtained about the unconscious, underlying meaning of these behaviours". Melanie Klein (1952) wrote that observations of "an infant's behaviour during the first year of life" should substantiate (*sic*) the concepts derived from psychoanalytic work with young children and with adults whose analysis was carried to "deep layers of the mind". But she stressed the limitations of such evidence "for, as we know, unconscious processes are only partly revealed in behaviour, whether of infants or adults". In spite of these words, she goes on to make a comment that has set a pattern for much future work in infant observation: "if we are to understand the young infant, though, we need not only greater knowledge but also a full sympathy with him, based on our unconscious being in close touch with his unconscious". Presumably based on this imponderable "close touch" with the unconscious of the infant, Klein writes: "The newborn infant suffers from persecutory anxiety aroused by the process of birth and by the loss of the intra-uterine situation. The initial attitude towards food ranges from an apparent absence of greed to great avidity" (Klein, 1952, p. 238). These are interpretations that have become characteristic of Kleinian based infant observations but similar positions can be found in other authors. Seligman describes this very accurately:

> We have the aggressively fantasizing baby of Melanie Klein and her followers (Isaacs, 1948); (Klein, 1952), the merging infant of Margaret Mahler (Mahler, Pine, Bergman, 1975), the need- and pleasure-driven baby of Anna Freud and her colleagues (A. Freud, 1965), and the active object-seeking baby of Kohut and his followers (Kohut, 1977); (Tolpin, 1980), to name but a few. [Seligman, 1993]

There is widespread agreement that our theoretical framework influences our observations of babies, for example, "the interest and orientation of the observer determines not only the selection of the data, but also their interpretation" (Kestenberg, 1977, p. 395). It might be interesting to quote the arguments put forward by Richard Gregory, Emeritus Professor of Psychology at Bristol University (1998). Gregory asks a strange question: does the brain receive or make sensations? It turns out that "some 80% of fibres to the lateral geniculate nucleus relay station come downwards from the cortex and only about 20% from the retinas". He gives the amusing example of listening to a tape recording of an audience clapping: "in the kitchen it sounds like bacon frying, in the garden on a dull day it sounds like rain". If you look at a frontal image of a rubber mask depicting a face, you would take it for granted that this was a whole head, until, once it was turned sideways, you might find the mask was hollow. Gregory writes: "Though seeing and hearing and touch seem simple and direct, they are not. They are fallible inferences based on knowledge and assumptions which may not be appropriate to the situation" and "perceptions are predictive hypotheses, based on knowledge stored from the past". Again: "From patterns of stimulation at the eyes and ears and the other organs of senses, including touch, we project sensations of consciousness into the external world". So, what you SEE NOW is entirely dependent on the past experiences which your memory brings to the fore to make sense of the current patterns of stimulation.

In the psychoanalytic world, Green argues passionately that our understanding of the unconscious is derived from our analytic work with patients. "Bion's capacity for reverie of the mother, essential in his thinking ... was born from the setting, and is not applicable to infant observation ... No infant researcher could have discovered the concepts of projective identification or reparation, which were drawn from the couch" (2000). And the same position is found in Wolff: "Psychoanalytically informed infant observations may be the source for new theories of social–emotional development, but they are essentially irrelevant for psychoanalysis as a psychology of meanings, unconscious ideas and hidden motives" (1966, p. 369).

But there are analysts who hold a different view and a growing number of them are devoting their efforts to early infantile development. The International Psychoanalytical Association has now established a "Research" department. Perhaps this is an unavoidable development, as it follows the trend among biologists and psychologists to utilize statistical studies as the source of credibility and respectability for theories, otherwise not considered properly scientific. This is the re-appearance of the old debate about the scientific status of psychoanalysis. Personally, whether it is Klein's assertion that an observer's interpretation is valid as long as his unconscious is "in close touch with (the infant's) unconscious" or laboratory researchers claiming validity for their findings because of numerical "evidence", I believe these are self-fulfilling claims that add little to psychoanalytic theories.

These are important issues that will involve many analysts in work and argument for many years to come, but we should separate out analytic research in laboratory conditions from the discipline of "infant observation" as part of the analytic training. Each student will only have one infant and family to observe, and this, by definition, gives him no chance to compare his perceptions with others made in a different family setting. Nor will the same infant and family be observed by another student for comparisons to be made of their views. If we can accept that the student is learning to develop observational and conceptualizing skills, we are on safe ground, but to transpose a student's findings to the level of "research" is a vitiated step.

Testing the student's potential for learning

A working class family was being observed by a student who happened to be quite well-off. When the baby was some five months old, the student reported making a visit to which she took her own six-year-old son. The student reported the mother's comments about the beautiful clothes the little boy was wearing and her acknowledgement of the sophistication of his manners and speech. The other students in the supervision group were surprised and embarrassed. A difficult discussion followed. The group felt the observer had been insensitive to the mother's feelings about herself and about the observer's private life. But the observer argued this was not true and she could not agree that the presence of her son would have influenced the mother's feelings and behaviour in any way. Another student reported being offered a cup of tea at each visit, which he consistently declined to accept. As this was discussed, it emerged that he came from a culture where it is considered rude to accept any food or drink when first offered; only when offered a second or third time can this be accepted. Once the group commented on the possible feelings the mother might have about the observer's refusal, he recognized it was up to him to put aside his personal customs and adapt to the mother's cultural preconceptions.

These are rather crude examples of situations where a student's behaviour has to be assessed in relation to his or her awareness of the needs of someone they meet in a clinical situation and their capacity to scrutinize their own behaviour. Many analysts and therapists have now adopted a posture where a student's behaviour is automatically seen as a counter-transference response to the patient or, in the context of infant observation, to the infant or parent being observed. This is a serious mistake in a teaching context, since it can deprive the student of valuable learning experiences.

It is extremely important to differentiate the extent to which a student's particular behaviour stems from their own personal experiences or is only a temporary, context-limited response to stimuli with which they have to deal. It is only by establishing the origin of a specific response that we can decide about that student's capacity to see himself as the object of observation and scrutiny. It is obvious that no two students will deal with the same baby–mother in the same way, and it is prudent to accept that all students will "make mistakes" at some point; this is one of the reasons infant observation does not lend itself to being an instrument of research. But most "mistakes" have no significant consequences and only become relevant as part of the training process.

Most psychoanalytic and psychotherapeutic trainings assess the abilities and progress of students on the basis of reports from lecturers and supervisors of training cases. Infant observation constitutes an equal (and arguably better) field to observe a student's capacity to relate to others in a clinical situation, to deal with comments from colleagues and teachers, look at him or her self in a critical manner and to be able to change their views and behaviour, that is, to learn from experience.

Summing up

It will have become clear that I value infant observation as an introduction to the formal training in analysis or therapy, but not as an instrument of research. Theories of psychodynamic development will not change through observation findings, since by definition those findings already result from theories derived from work with patients in a clinical setting. But the observations conducted over the period of some twelve or more months give the student a precious opportunity to discover how today's anxiety gives way to tomorrow's new developmental achievement. This is not just "the mother's anxiety", but the student's occasional assumption that he or she has identified a pathological trait and the subsequent slow unfolding of further developments that gradually bring confirmation or correction to these views. In other words, this is an exercise where the student can prepare himself for later work with patients, where there is little room for dogma, and where careful awareness of diverse possible interpretations brings continuous learning.

I find it regrettable that so many infant observation courses are used to convince students of the validity of specific theories. Precisely because these seminars take place at the beginning of the training, students find it particularly comforting to discover neat and precise explanations for their baffling findings. If, instead of being helped to discover which theory will best fit individual perceptions, the student is simply expected to accept the theory adopted by his or her teachers, this comes to constitute an overt or covert process of indoctrination. I believe that the observation of infants allows little room for certainties and definitely minimal scope for predictions of future development. Only the careful noting of each piece of infant behaviour and its corresponding connection with parental input will enable the formulation of hypotheses that subsequent observations will confirm or correct. It is this rich field of diverging possibilities that gives the seminar leader the opportunity to show students that there are many different ways of interpreting each datum: only this approach will help students to discover their own explanation for their findings.

I have always hoped that observing a baby would make a student discover the beauty and the excitement of observing a growing, developing human being. Virtually every single adult will know of what happens as babies grow into childhood and adolescence, but, surprisingly, few adults have actually accompanied closely the pleasures and pains of bringing up an infant/child. It is easy, perhaps facile, to postulate that repressed traumatic memories of early life lead some people to shy away from babies and young children. Whatever the reason, all trainees can put forward endless theories of early development, but only a few actually welcome the opportunity of coming close to a baby. In practice, those who feel comfortable with children and actually want to work closely with them move towards trainings specializing in work with children, while those who come to analytic or psychotherapeutic trainings are mostly interested in seeing adult patients. They clearly feel more comfortable dealing with the "conceptual infant" (Stern, 1985) than with real babies. Infant Observation, sadly, becomes no more than one of the disciplines leading to their desired qualification.

CHAPTER FOUR

Defects of inscription in language: Anne and Anna

Catherine Mathelin

That morning, as soon as I entered the neonatal intensive care service where I work as an analyst, I knew that emergency was in the air. We are very familiar with this particularly oppressive atmosphere: it is imbued with high tension, and, at the same time, with great calmness. Never a feeling of panic, no haste. The more precious the minutes, the more the team seems to be immersed in timelessness. Two little girls had been born an hour apart, their first names, Anne and Anna, almost identical, as the circumstances of their births had been.

Anne, born at twenty-six and a half weeks, weighed eight hundred and fifty grams, Anna eight hundred and twenty grams at twenty-seven weeks. While the medical staff bent over the incubators, placed catheters, intubated, ventilated, the two mums waited in their rooms in the maternity ward for the doctors to deliver their verdict.

Lila, Anne's mother, had come to the maternity ward at risk of giving birth prematurely, three days before the child arrived. The obstetricians had done all they could to postpone the onset of labor, but their various attempts had failed, and Anne had been delivered vaginally after an unproblematical labor. The very same evening,

Lila, though she was walking unsteadily, had nevertheless come to see her daughter. Standing beside the incubator, very affected by the imposing machinery, the many electrical wires, the sounds of the monitor, and the puffing of the oxygen, she listened to the nurse's explanations, refused to touch her baby, and said, weeping, "She's too little! She's not going to make it!"

She didn't come to see her daughter the next day and appeared on the service only late the day after that, at the time of her appointment with me. I ushered her into my office. She began the interview by saying that she didn't dare ask me for news of Anne. Was she dead? Wouldn't it be better for her to die in any case? And then, even if she didn't die, no doubt there would be after effects of this intensive care. She thought constantly about her daughter's death: "The sooner the better; I can't let myself get attached to her".

Obviously, when she had spoken like this on the unit, she had been made to keep quiet. Since I let her talk about Anne's death, she continued, "It would be easier for everyone, and yet this child I was carrying was my only happiness, my only hope. She was what kept me alive".

Lila had been in France for two years. Of Algerian origin, she lived with her sister and brother-in-law, having fled a family she considered too strict. Soon after her arrival in France, she had fallen madly in love with a handsome, rich, intelligent man. Her Prince Charming announced he was married and a father on the day when, filled with pride, she told him she was pregnant. Her fairy tale then turned into a nightmare. He asked her to resign herself to an abortion, and she categorically refused. He therefore decided to end the relationship, and Lila set about looking for work to help her sister out financially. "It was hard", she said, "but my baby and I were going to cope with it together. I wanted to fight for her".

I pointed out that today her little daughter was fighting against death, no doubt thanks to the strength Lila had given her from the time when she was in her belly. Lila seemed to emerge from her torpor and said, "I'd like to go to see her, but the doctors seem so pessimistic that I don't have the nerve to tell her to keep on fighting". I asked, "What would you tell her?"

"I'd tell her not to give up, that she's strong and will pull through".

"What's keeping you from doing that?"

"I have the impression that I don't belong there, that just the specialists do, that they're the ones who know, not me".

I told Lila that only she knew where she belonged now and what she had to say to her daughter. No matter what the doctors said, she could give herself permission to listen to her child with an ear that was different from theirs, and to speak to her with a different voice. Nothing forced her to think the way they did. When she left my office, Lila went directly to the neonatal ICU (Intensive care Unit). When I entered the airlock in turn, two hours later, I saw her seated beside her baby. I simply opened the door of the incubator part way and told her, "Like this she'll be able to hear you", and then left them alone, busy with their conversation. That evening, up to the time the service closed, and on all following days, Lila talked to Anne without stopping.

Some time after that, the baby weighed only seven hundred and eighty grams. Lila, for her part, began to give the medical staff a hard time. She often asked to see me, but on some days the supervisor called me in more for the team than for her, when they were fed up with her shouting, her tears, and her aggression. Clearly, what was most distressing to them was when this aggression was directed at her daughter: "It's as though she wanted her dead—does this mother really love her?"

Lila questioned the team incessantly, and at the same time Anne seemed less present, as though she had withdrawn into her pain, no longer seeking our presence or reacting to our attempts to get a response from her. The medical staff, observing her remoteness, blamed her mother. For a neonatal ICU, the only way to love a baby is to want it to live at any cost. When the parents don't go along with this, when anxiety makes them doubt, when they anticipate a mourning that they think is probable, doctors and nurses are tempted to experience them as "bad". The child seems to be the "receptor" of these different tensions between parents and staff, and we have often observed that this can have a marked effect on its state of health. Only if guilt and hate, not just love, can be expressed and acknowledged can mutual trust be restored.

Through talking with Lila and working with the nurses, through watching for the smallest sign of suffering in Anne and the most fragile attempt at communication, and emphasizing that it was possible to respond to her in turn, the dialogue among Lila, Anne, and the team got underway again. In a sense Lila was taken into care at the same time as her baby. "This mother is hooked on us", one of the medical staff said to me one day, "the way her baby is to our IV's (intravenous drips)". For her part, Anne kept getting better. She commanded everyone's interest and respect.

However, when the doctors decided to take her off the ventilator on her fiftieth day of life, problems arose and slowdowns in heart rate appeared. When Anne fell into a slumber that was too deep, the monitor began to shriek until only a straight line was traced on the screen. She very quickly understood that she was risking her life by sleeping, and clutching our fingers for hours on end, she fought against sleep. The mere fact of being near her and talking to her, without any resuscitation techniques, made her heart rate increase again and re-established her CPO_2 (oxygenation evaluated by a skin sensor). Anna mobilized things in such a way that someone stayed by her side all the time. "It's odd", an intern said to me one day. "You'd think she replaced the oxygen with the words she's asking us to say to her".

It seems that talking to Anne made it possible for her to lose an essential part of herself. This machine, which raised her thorax in a regular rhythm, blocked her head, and, by keeping her alive, had up to now been a part of her body. When it was taken away, she was deprived of sensations that had enabled her to construct herself. She must have felt panic when the machine was removed. When we explained to her that she may have been suffering from the hole in her mouth area, and that she was certainly afraid, we were able to believe that an initial element of loss was being constituted for her. The hole could now exist in another way: our words constituted it without "plugging" it. The rhythm of the sound of our voices didn't have the regularity of the rhythm of the machine, but for Anne it carried her desire for life.

During this period, the mother once again lost her footing. "She can't go on; let her die; she doesn't want to live; it's better if she dies", but as she was about to leave, she would whisper into Anne's ear, "Hang in there tonight. I'll be here tomorrow". New sessions with the mother and the diminution of the brachycardias restored calm in the team and in Lila, who said to a supervisor one day, "My daughter and I owe our lives to you". At Lila's request, Anne's father came on the service. Afterwards he came back regularly to talk to her. He reported that she had given him the strength to stop trying to escape, the strength to take responsibility for what he called his mistakes in life. The story could be spoken. Several weeks later, the father asked to recognize Anne legally.

When Anne left the service at the age of one hundred and forty days, she was accompanied by her mother and her father. Regular followup visits were normal. She always seemed happy to come back, and she smiled at the nurses, whom she recognized each time. Today, four years later, Anne is a merry little girl, in perfect health. A note in her chart indicates that she cried for the first time during her last checkup. She didn't recognize anyone anymore and refused to be held in the arms of the white-uniformed nurses. She had truly left us, forgotten us. She was now fully oriented toward her parents, and we could consider our work with her completed.

At the same time, Anna was growing bigger on the service. Born at twenty-seven weeks and weighing eight hundred and twenty grams, she developed in about the same way as Anne and did not pose any special problems. Her lowest weight was recorded at seven hundred and sixty grams, and, like Anne, she was intubated, ventilated, and put on IV drips. Although they followed approximately the same course, their histories were very different.

Anna's mother, Lise, had come as an emergency case to the maternity unit following a major hemorrhage. Birth had already begun, and there was no question of trying anything to stop it. Anna was born vaginally after an uneventful labor lasting one and a half hours. Her mother came to our front desk the next day, asking to see the doctor responsible for the hospitalization. After speaking with him, she had gone in to see her daughter, but the doctor and the nurses were all astonished to see how little this mum reacted. She had compliantly touched the baby when this was suggested and very politely thanked the doctor for all his trouble, without asking a single question about her daughter.

The first meeting with me was strange, leaving me very anxious for Anna. After I had explained the work of the unit to Lise and spoken at length about her baby, she remained silent, as though all this had nothing to do with her. Sitting there resigned, she seemed calm and said she had no questions for me. When I asked her whether she was anxious, she replied, "We'll have to see. She's not too strong, so there's no way of knowing what will happen". Then she got up and left my office as she had done the previous day with the doctor, without asking me anything and forgetting the Polaroid photo of Anna that I had just given her.

One of the customs we have established on the service is to give each mum a photo of her baby to take with her to her room in the maternity ward. Similarly, we invite the parents to bring the baby a personal object, a toy, or an item of clothing that we leave next to the child's incubator or bed. The mothers say they are very attached to this entry ritual, as to the other ritual that consists in suggesting, when they first visit the baby, to explain to it that it hasn't been abandoned, that she is entrusting it to the nurses, whom she names, to be cared for.

Anna's mother had refused to speak in these terms to the child: "There's no point in talking, since she doesn't understand us. It's better to say nothing". With that she left, all sweet and smiling, leaving the nurses at a loss.

During another session with her, I questioned her again: "It's funny, but you talk about this child as though she weren't yours". "Yes", she replied, "it's true that I haven't been able to bring myself to do that. I've just left the maternity ward. I have a lot of work at home, and besides, I think I'm not going to be able to come anymore. Are you going to think that's bad?" When I told her that we weren't in a position to make any judgments about her behavior but were only trying to help the two of them understand and know each other better, Lise reported the following: she had been married for four years and already had two daughters, one three years old and one nine months. She was still breastfeeding the little one and didn't think it was possible to become pregnant before the child was weaned. It was on the occasion of an ultrasound ordered by her internist, to whom she had come complaining that she couldn't get her stomach flat again, that she learned that she was four months pregnant with a little girl. She then decided, with her husband's agreement, to hand herself over to a back-street abortionist. It was the panic of the hemorrhage triggered by this procedure that had brought her to the hospital, where she didn't think she would give birth to a living child. In talking about this birth, Lise mentioned another, her own. Her mother had been fifteen at her birth, and Lise said she was convinced that she, too, was born following a failed late abortion. She didn't know who her father was, and her mother, now no longer there, had taken her secret to the grave. But Lise was sure that she had been the product of incest: everything in her mother's behavior, she said, led her to believe that.

In the following weeks Anna had some problems with feeding. Lise came to see her but never stayed more than ten minutes. She never said, the way Lila did, that she would wish for her daughter's death. She was self-effacing and spoke to no one. I noticed that at this time it was also becoming harder and harder to talk to Anna. When I went over to her, it made me anxious to observe that she responded very little to my presence. Still on the ventilator, she spent hours looking fixedly at a point to the left—perhaps a reflection on the ventilator hook-up? It was increasingly difficult to attract her attention.

We are always very anxious when, after a few days, children on ventilators begin to fix on a precise point on a piece of apparatus, to which they seem to cling like shipwrecked people to a life preserver. These children in a state of abeyance and a state of suffering were no doubt trying to rally, to take hold of themselves, by clinging to an external point, perhaps to fight against the fragmentation brought on by pain and panic. The type of work we can do with them at those times is reminiscent of the treatment of autistic children. What is missing in the drive mechanism here? These newborns teach us how this mechanism, precisely if it is only a mechanism, that is, attached to a machine, can be prevented from establishing itself. Long hours spent next to such children, talking to them again and again about their history, the care they are undergoing, and their parents, sometimes enables them to come back toward the world. Words and still more words, a "music of words" written by a "voice pen" that would make it possible for them to construct themselves and would give them the content they lack.

But what do they understand of these words? Do they grasp their meaning? Or rather the intention and the affect?

We come out of these sessions exhausted, drained, in a state close to the one in which we find ourselves at the end of certain sessions with autistic children. What part of ourselves do they take with them? It is only once contact has been established and the baby is back among us that we try to decode each of its signals as attempts at communication. The main part of our work from then on will be to enable the parents, especially the mothers, to give themselves permission to recognize by themselves the child's appeals for help and to respond in their own way.

It isn't easy for a mother to reclaim her child after a stay on the neonatal unit. It may take a lot of time before it becomes "hers". For the drama of these mothers of premature children is also being premature mothers and thus, unlike those who give birth normally, being unable to suffer that illness that Winnicott calls "primary maternal preoccupation" and that enables them to imagine their child. In this case, they ascribe a psychic apparatus to the baby, who is already presumed to be a subject. It escapes the mother and can then be hers only on condition that she can recognize it as separate from herself and can find herself lacking. In contrast, mothers next to incubators most often suffer from an inability to conceptualize their baby. Whom does he or she resemble? What does he or she feel? Who is he or she? In this situation, in which it is impossible to say, the mothers become paralyzed, trapped between the doctor who knows better than they do, the mourning of the end of their pregnancy, and the real risks of the child's death.

The relation between mother and child will not find its course easily, even if the team, full of good will, do their best to put the babies in the mum's arms. This separation that comes as an additional separation in the brutal and often mute hospitalization of the newborn seems to cancel out the cut by redoubling it, thereby preventing it from truly operating, that is, preventing it from becoming symbolized. There is no baby-blues day on a neonatology service.

The most precious aspect of the hospitalization period will be to facilitate the cut, the loss, the third entity. Calling medical omnipotence into question, we will in time be confronted as a team by the work of mourning, and it is also in the work of loss and separation that we will have to support the parents, so that each one can refind himself or herself in the position of subject.

Nothing of this work could be done with Lise. Around the fiftieth day of Anna's life, the doctors thought that, as with Anne, she was able to breathe on her own. At this time the mother was coming only once a week, and so it was in her absence that we stopped the machine. But Anna was unable to breathe on her own, and each time everything had to be connected up again. One morning when I arrived on the service, I was told that Anna was finally weaned!

A solution had been found: she could do without oxygen as long as the sound of the machine was allowed to continue at her side. Anna clung to the sound of this machine, just as, at the same time, Anne was clinging to our presence, our speech, and the words uttered by her mother. But this was quite another music; a mechanical music that could not presuppose a subject in Anna. If the machine became the sole possibility of identification for her, as we often see in autistic children, nothing could convey desire. Did this impossible desire reflect the mother's refusal to want this child? Or rather, and more likely, as we saw it, did it reflect the mother's childhood, in which the impossibility of inscribing a history had left desire and filiation in a state of breakdown, preventing the trauma of birth from being inscribed?

I suggested that the team get together to talk about this miracle solution brought about by the machine. After this meeting, the team, highly motivated, mobilized a little more around Anna, but failed once again in the work with the mother. "We don't hesitate to take her, because she never says anything if we suddenly have work to do and have to put her back to bed", said the nurses' aides. The head doctor disapproved of these signs of "special treatment" and asked that no distinction be made between Anna and the others. But it was no use. "Anna is always alone", the nurses' aides said. "She needs company".

When I tried to explain to the team that this company would be her undoing, that the bond with her family must not be cancelled out by our zeal, I wasn't listened to. Anna was too strongly invested and her mother too forgotten for our orders and warnings to alter the team's transference to this baby. Before Anna left, we anxiously notified the Mother and Infant Protective Service to arrange for a paediatric nurse to make home visits.

Anna was one hundred and twenty days old when she went home. Only her mum came to call for her. We have a traditional exit ritual. The nurses each take the time to come to say goodbye to the baby, other photos are taken, the doctor sees the parents one last time. All these symbolic reference points enable the child and its family not to wipe out the memory of this transition but to build on it and integrate it into the child's history. But here again the mother refused: she had no time, and it wasn't possible any more than the entry ritual had been. Lise was too busy; her two daughters were waiting for her. An intern pointed out to me, a bit before they left, that Lise never said "my three daughters" but always "my two daughters". And indeed, what was the place of this third child?

As was the case with Anne, the exit report noted that Anna was in perfect health, with no apparent after-effects from intensive care. Normal CT scan and EEG; blood and digestive evaluations normal, as was the respiratory evaluation; perfect hearing and vision tests. The clinical examination was satisfactory: Anna was an energetic and vigorous little girl. As with Anne, the neonatology unit could be proud of a job well done.

Ten days later, the local Emergency Medical Service returned to the hospital, bringing the body of Anna, who had died suddenly during the night. The autopsy confirmed that this was surely a death without apparent cause.

What I hear, I can't write

On sideboards in the empty living-room: no ptyx,
Abolished trinket of the resonant absurd,
(For the master has gone to draw tears from the Styx
With this sole object of which Nothingness is proud.). [Stéphane Mallarmé]

"What I hear", Marion said, "I can't write". At age eight, Marion was in the second year of primary school and an academic failure. One after the other, her teachers had come up against the same problem. She was very brilliant in oral communication, caught on quickly, and knew her lessons perfectly, but since beginning elementary school she had been unable to write.

Born under X and adopted at the age of three months, Marion, according to her mother, had had an unproblematical childhood. Everything had gone normally until the time when she had been asked to write. Already in the middle stream the teacher had noted her disinclination to make marks on paper. Nothing was drawn on the sheet, no trace left there.

Marion's birth parents were of Mali origin. Her adoptive mother remembered being astonished when, at age three, Marion had begun to sing Mali lullabies. A friend, herself raised in Africa, had recognized them. And then the songs fell silent, at about the time when Marion's adoptive father died. She had just turned four. An unproblematical childhood.

"As soon as I write", Marion said, "I don't know how to remember anymore. That's why I don't write".

Clinical experience teaches us that many adopted children have trouble learning how to write. What is it in their history that can't be written? No trace on the white paper, nothing, and yet traces existed for Marion, insistent oral traces that had returned when she sang the lullabies.

Even if it is not written, the oral trace is inscribed, and psychoanalytic practice proves this to us every day. Traces of words that mark the body of hysterics, metaphors that lead obsessionals astray. Representations of things, representations of words, mnemonic traces are at the very heart of Freudian metapsychology.

Traces are found in language, depositing elements there, elements that, little by little, constitute it, transform it, as Georges Arthur Goldschmidt emphasizes when he works on the relations between the invention of psychoanalysis, the rise of Nazism, and the German language.

Marion recognized oral traces, but her hand would not let her inscribe a written trace on paper.

The trace left by the hand involves the gaze. At the beginning of life the baby "sees" with its hands. When the child is old enough to write, its hand, writing letters, will make traces visible. "Writing remains", it is said. What remainder did Marion not trust? What was the misfortune of which she did not want a trace to remain?

For the child, the trace can be experienced as improper. The age at which he learns to write corresponds to the age at which he learns to control himself; to speak or not speak according to the occasion; to talk in a certain way to some people, in another way to others. The age at which he is taught what is done and what is not done. You have to write between the lines; the letters have to be a certain size; you have to control the way your hand moves. The paper must remain clean. The fear of an ink blot or erasure mark is always there.

This phase of life harkens back to the difficulties or successes of the time of anal castration: "He doesn't do anything—that is, doesn't 'make' anything—in school".

As Freud says, the symptom is overdetermined. If anorexia reflects the inhibition of the oral drive, if the anorexic eats "the nothing", the academically failing child puts all his energy into doing or making "nothing", or knowing "nothing".

Some children will stumble over the injunction "do" or "make", others over "learn", still others over "shine and make me shine". To succeed is to assume a phallic position, which sometimes complicates the hand the child is dealt. Where inhibition is concerned, the anxiety is even greater to the extent that it is identified with *objet a*, the drive of the Other. The demand of this Other has a direct influence on the child's body, triggering annihilation fears in him. He cancels out his desire and plays dead in order to survive. Anxiety signals danger, and protective inhibition is immediately established.

"All desire to know", Annie Cordié explains, "as well as the prohibition relating to it, originates in the fundamental drives. At its root, we find all the *objets a*: oral, anal, and scopic, as well as the voice".

The child's development will depend on the "metamorphoses" of these objects, their progressive erasure of the real, their "sublimation". *Objet a* will be included in language through fantasy, while the drive will remain closest to the jouissance of the body.

When the knotting of the symbolic, the real, and the imaginary takes place, with a predominance in each register—the real for the drive, the imaginary for fantasy, and the symbolic for desire—therapy will make it clear which of the *objets a* is at the origin of a child's particular inhibition. But can the mishaps in learning to write be deciphered in this dynamic? Can we equate the desire to know and its corollary, academic inhibition, with the failure in learning to write?

Certain children who can't write, and who are therefore in a lot of trouble at school, do not hold back from learning. They are not in a state of inhibition. They learn, and sometimes even greatly enjoy doing so, but they can reproduce their knowledge only in the oral mode. Can we then speak of inhibition? Knowledge is surely different when it bears exclusively on the question: How is it written? Does it leave traces?

"It's odd", Marion's mother said. "She learns the text and can say it aloud, but she can't write it". This mum was an actress, and her repertory was in the classic theatre. She said of her profession, "It's hard to efface yourself behind the text all the time. An actor doesn't speak. What I mean is, he's not the one who is speaking. He says what's written. I lend my body and my voice, but it's the text that does the speaking".

And she also complained about her difficulty in speaking with her daughter: "You understand", she said, "when I talk with Marion no one writes dialogues for me, so what am I supposed to say to her?" Nor had she been able to talk to Marion about her father's death. On the contrary, she recited to the child the phrases that the social-service agency had written for her: "I'm very grateful to your birth mother. Thanks to her entrusting you to me, I was lucky enough to have a little girl like you".

The actor lets someone else speak with his voice. Since her father's death, Marion had been failing in school. In the face of these problems, she gave up; nothing spoke to her anymore. Freud described the desire to learn or understand, the wish to know, as a drive, the epistemophilic drive, connected with the life instinct. In the *"Three Essays on the Theory of Sexuality"*, he explains how the child awakens its intelligence by becoming interested in sexual problems. But sexual curiosity also refers to the question of origins. An adopted child, more than others, will try to find an answer. He will investigate desire and jouissance. What does this mother want from me? She didn't bring me into the world, so why did she choose me? What is going on in the primal scene?

We only have to listen to a child, adopted or not, to hear that the object of the epistemophilic drive has to do with origins. "Who made me?" The question of origins, of sex, of death, affects children at the bodily level. They know without knowing, with a knowledge, as Lacan says, "that does not include the least cognizance, in that it is inscribed in a discourse of which, like the messenger slave in the custom of antiquity, the subject who wears under his hair its codicil that condemns him to death knows neither the meaning, nor the text, nor in what language it is written, nor even that it was tattooed on his shaved hide while he was sleeping".

What the adopted child knows of his origins can't easily be written in a school notebook. The trace becomes threatening then.

Medhi, age five, had been adopted at three months. Born under X, he had waited in the hospital's nursery ward during the obligatory delay in meeting his new parents. Today he is in the upper stream in pre-school and has been labelled by the school "a danger to himself and others". When his parents come for a consultation, he has to be dismissed from the premises, which is a sign of his inability both to take an interest in any activity and to comply with instructions. Furthermore, he finds it impossible to copy letters of the alphabet and refuses to learn to write his first name or to make any drawing that isn't dirtied or torn up. What worries his teacher even more is his tendency to escape. Not only can he not stay still in front of a notebook, but he leaves the classroom, on the lookout for a half-open door to run out of as fast as he can. He gets away and leaves the school grounds. Most often he is brought back by the police, hours later, having been found a mile or so from the school. He runs away both there and at home. He's a fugitive. When I ask him where he's going, he answers, "To look for the lady", and when I ask for details, he says, "I'm running so that she can catch me".

The parents explain that this running away dates from his entrance into the upper stream and began during an autumn vacation in Brittany. He had run toward the sea. They found him still standing there, paralyzed, on the beach, saying that he was afraid of the mark, the trace his feet left on the sand. It was this trace that had stopped him. During that vacation the parents had decided to begin teaching him to write.

Several sessions later, when he was talking to me about school, Medhi said to me, "The teacher wants me to write words, but I don't want to. Words are dirty. Lies make them dirty". What lies had been told to Medhi? He was destroying himself so as to be found at last and, at the same time, so as never to be found. But what traces were setting a limit to his running?

His adoptive parents, very concerned to do the right thing, had spoken of the adoption in the same terms as those used by the personnel in the nursery ward: "What luck that your birth mother wanted you to have a happy life and gave you up for adoption. She left a letter to say that she loved you and that her thoughts would always follow you".

Medhi's mother had left a written trace that, despite what nursery staffs think, was perhaps not the kind to reassure him. Isn't there good reason to become delusional when you know that you're always being followed?

When he was old enough to write his name, this remarkably

sensitive and intelligent little boy went crazy and began to run away, both to escape and to be caught. He was terrorized by the written trace of a name that he could not manage to make his own, and by a different kind of "letter" that he could not escape and that, as it were, followed in his tracks, his trace. Medhi's father, himself in great distress, found it impossible because of his personal history to transmit to Medhi a true family name.

How to make a father one's own? To disrupt the relation of the mother, the capital-O Other, to the child as her *objet a*, will the signifier X, the mark of the unknown, do the job? Will the name given at a later time be enough? How to make it possible for a place to be cleared and for the *infans*, the one who cannot speak, to become a subject in his own right? This place in which the name of the father comes to be inscribed is in fact just the signifier of the mother's lack. Does this lack have a different status for adoptive mothers? In being redoubled, doesn't it cancel itself out? Don't these mothers remain "too full"? Yet it is on the basis of the lack that the child will be able to escape the jouissance of the Other, able to inhabit language and not to speak in the place of an other.

If an "elsewhere" does not appear to capture the mother's desire, psychosis will plunge the child into a devastating imaginary made up of violence and aggression. Transitivism will remain in the foreground, and the child will know neither who he is nor from what position he is speaking. Even if not all of them are psychotic, don't adopted children all have to come to terms with the Name-of-the-Father and the question of the symbolic a little differently from the way other children do?

Fleur was six years old. Adopted at nineteen months in Rumania, she had arrived in France in a state of autistic withdrawal that alarmed the pediatricians. With patience and understanding her parents had brought her back to life.

She became a lively and intelligent little girl who got good grades in school, except in writing. Finding it impossible to write in the first year of school quickly makes a child a pupil in trouble, and the anxious parents came for a consultation in order to complain.

As Jean Berges and Gabriel Balbo remind us, parents usually come to demand justice against a child who is monopolizing their jouissance. They are not complaining; they're lodging a complaint. They have the feeling that the child wants to impose her will, deprive them of the pleasure of shining thanks to them. This is certainly the case for many children who try to control the jouissance of the Other, at the price of symptoms that are sometimes very disabling.

Fleur's symptom was school. After having made her parents her saviors who rescued her, as the doctors had told them, she was now making them parents of a child who was an academic failure, called in regularly by the teacher. They questioned themselves and blamed themselves. This brutal disillusionment made them suffer: "What's happening with Fleur?" they asked. "What did we do to make this perfect little girl such a problem today?"

During this time Fleur displayed an attitude of offhand tyranny. "I don't feel like writing, so I won't. I'm the one who decides, even if Mum cries", she said. But if you listened a little harder, you could hear her fear of failing or of making a mess, her fear of being inadequate. Because it was impossible to show her parents her distress, she had to remain all-powerful, and she was perfect at it. For that purpose it was better to avoid the hazards of being an apprentice. She could not fail, for fear of showing her parents a disappointing image of themselves.

It took a long time for Fleur to be able to talk, in the sessions, about the loneliness and fear she had experienced as a baby. Her parents spoke of this adoption as a fairy tale: "We chose each other right away and loved each other". A beautiful story, indeed, that did not leave Fleur with the possibility of bearing the traces of her past. Today she was a prisoner of that forbidden representation. It was only after she enacted, session after session, the adventures of a little girl dead of cold and fear, abandoned on a desert island, that she could find the inclination to write and, at the same time, an identity.

At the beginning of the sessions she had asked me, "Do you have the same name as me?" I reminded her of my name, and she insisted, "You're my mother, so you have to have the same name. Mum said so. Can your name be written?" I asked, "What about your name: can it be written?" "No", she answered. "I lost the letters. Mum said I chose her, so I can choose another mother if I want. I choose you. I don't care what name they write on my notebook".

It is surely this freedom that prevented Fleur from writing, in the same way that it paralyzed Anne, a woman of thirty-four who was referred to me by the neurology service of a Parisian hospital.

This young woman had lost the ability to write. It had become impossible for her to form letters. Her hand no longer obeyed her thought, the words did not form or take shape anymore. The most sophisticated medical examinations had revealed nothing. and, out of desperation, the doctors had advised her to consult me.

Several weeks earlier, when nothing in her life indicated a problem, she had learned that her three-year-old son was afflicted with a weak X chromosome. Difficulties in preschool, a major delay in language development, and psychomotor problems had led the school to have the parents see a neurologist.

"This discovery of the weak X", Anna reported, "brought all my own weakness back to me like a blow. I was born under X, and now it's this X that comes back with the force of a boomerang. And there's nothing I can do about it; it's a disk that my computer can't read. No writing appears on my screen".

Adopted at the age of three months, Anne always knew the truth, but she described the great effort she had made not to know anything about her history. All these years she had kept the circumstances of her birth outside her field of representation. As she told me, "X is the symbol of the unknown. It's outside of language for me. I can't even think it. It can't be named. I can't talk about it. Ever since I heard the diagnosis, I can't write anymore".

Several days later, Anne tried to drown her son in the bathtub. The father, and then the emergency medical service, were barely able to save the child's life.

Anne was terrified when she came to the next session. "I should be hospitalized; I'm dangerous; I know I'll do it again". She was overcome by the idea of murder with a blade. Knives, scissors, and all sharp objects frightened her. She was convinced that she would take one in order to kill, convinced that she was a criminal who was dangerous not only to her son, but also to her husband and to me: "The glass ashtray on your desk frightens me. I feel like throwing myself on you and mortally injuring you. I have nothing more to lose. Not being able to write makes me crazy, maybe more than my son's illness".

She had indeed written. A professor of linguistics at the university, she had done her dissertation on Mallarmé. Killing her son, she said, would be the only way she could eliminate any trace of X, the only way to make sure that there would be no remnant of the history of her birth: "I'd be free of it. There would be no more evidence that all of that had happened, and I could do as I did before, live by setting aside that phase of my life, leaving it outside of everything".

One night she dreamed of her son's body barred with the letter X. Next to him a word could be read: PTYX. Her association was: "It's the little X [petit X], as if this had become his family name". Under this word she also saw Mallarmé's name written. Upon awakening, she recognized the "ptyx". This was a word in one of Mallarmé's sonnets, "Sonnet in X". She had forgotten all about it, although she knew it perfectly and found it very beautiful. She recalled each of the lines during the session, and said, "Isn't the Ptyx the river of hell?"

The next day she was once again able to sign her name "robotically", but writing had not yet returned. "I didn't think that any X could be written", she said, "and I had forgotten this sonnet".

Here is Mallarmé's "Sonnet in X":

> Its pure nails dedicating very high their onyx,
>   Torch-bearing Anxiety, this midnight, sustains
> Many an evening dream burned by the Phoenix That no funerary
>   amphora retains.
> On sideboards in the empty living-room: no ptyx, Abolished trinket
>   of the resonant absurd (For the master has gone to draw tears
>   from the Styx With this sole object of which Nothingness
>   is proud.)
> But near the vacant window in the north, a gold death-agony,
>   perhaps in keeping with the scene Of unicorns rushing from the
>   fire against a nix.
> She, deceased and naked in the mirror, though In the frame's
>   enclosed oblivion is fixed, As soon as it appears, the septet's
>   sparkling glow.

Anne too was poorly defended (*mal armée*). She had undoubtedly been able to identify herself in the mirror, by way of the signifier, with this lacking man. A temporary substitute, crutches that had been precious in her adolescence. A man serving the paternal function could give her something of the castration that might perhaps enable her to acknowledge herself as a woman. If a man who is called *mal armé* can write such a beautiful poem, then she too could make something of the "X".

"When I began to read Mallarmé", she said, "what surprised me is that I found only meaning where other people were feeling lost".

Anne's weakness also consisted in an impossibility that she recognized in herself and feared: when she wanted to listen to someone talking, she could not grasp the meaning of the words. It was as though she had become disconnected from language, with no anchoring point. She put it very clearly: "I'm like a mountain climber who's falling. Someone says something, and I feel myself dropping down, without anything to hold onto. I fall into a hole of desire. There's nothing symbolic to catch me. It's horrible when the only signifier left is in a panic. Everything refers to something else. There's no signified to keep me on the road, and human beings become absent to me".

Recalling the work of Louis Ferdinand Céline during one session, she said to me, "When I disconnect, people become blurred. They pass by like ghosts, as Céline says. If I understand them, I'm scared that they'll stick to me, that they won't be able to go away from me, that they'll become doubles. Céline said about those kinds of people that they "turned into a puppet-show". My mother passed by like a ghost for my whole childhood. Maybe that's more reassuring than if she'd turned into a puppet!"

Anne had lived with her adoptive parents, or rather alongside them, in absolute distrust. She knew that she hadn't come from her mother's belly, but no one ever discussed this with her. She had heard it spoken of and hadn't wondered about it any further. Even in adolescence the idea of looking up her origins had never crossed her mind. "Those parents", she said, "were nothing to me". The others had never existed. "It was terrible and wonderful at the same time, because it gave me freedom without limits". And she reported the feeling that she reinvented her life anew each day. She had never wanted to know anything about her background, or even about the family history of her adoptive parents: "Knowing something about my family wasn't a concern of mine. In any case these were givens that weren't legible for me". And she still did not want to know anything about this, to the point of thinking of getting rid of her son.

This revelation, the surplus of the real that came back to her in the form of X, prevented her from writing.

Nothing had happened. She had lost nothing. In giving birth to herself each day, she maintained the delusion of her omnipotence. A week after the dream of the sonnet, she awoke doubled over with pain. "I had never felt anything like this", she said. "It was like a wound from an entirely new kind of violence that kept me from breathing. I didn't understand what was happening to me. I needed something to calm my anxiety, but I didn't know what. Smells overwhelmed me. I was aware of all of them, as though up until then none had ever really gotten to me. My sense of touch had also changed. I felt under my fingers the smoothness of a cloth, the velvet of peach skin; the moistness of the peaches knocked me over. I'd never known anything like that before. I suddenly felt like going out into the street. It was hard for me to walk. Suddenly I heard a woman's voice coming from a store nearby. A strong, clear, and merry voice, and it was then that I understood my suffering. I wanted my mother's body. I also understood that I could never find that body again, even if I found my mother. It was her body at the moment of my birth that I needed, and I had lost that body forever. The violence of that cut was what I felt". Cutting objects were what she was afraid of using as murder weapons.

Some time after the sonnet dream, after finding the trace of the lack, and after realizing that her mother's body was lost forever, Anne once again found it possible to write. "I'm sure", she said, "that I was afraid of having killed my mother. Maybe that's why I was terrified of the idea that I might be a criminal. It's so much less painful than thinking that she could abandon me".

Another Anne, Anne Ernaux, the author of a book *La Honte (Shame)*, said the following in an article in *Le Monde* on March 31, 2000: "When I write, I have to find the right words, those that are in accord with what I have seen and felt. It is a frightened vision of the real". In her book, she speaks of her background, rejecting her past, her identity. She earned an advanced degree although her parents owned a café, and she speaks of her shame and the great difficulty she had in school when she had to pass from speech to writing, the contempt she felt toward her parents who did not know how to write, and her guilt at having betrayed them: writing the right word is a frightened vision of the real.

It is the encounter with this real, the shock of coming up against it, that Anne described when she spoke of the return of the X. Aren't Medhi's footprints on the beach of the same order? That excessive freedom, that jouissance that has no limit set to it and is not channeled, can only lead to the banks of the Styx. This river of hell conferred invulnerability. Achilles bore the mark of his immersion, since his mother, renouncing his omnipotence, had held him by the heel. By what father had she been marked, so as to save her child's life by leaving him this trace that made him a mortal and humanized him? The incomplete operation of the Name-of-the-Father is surely what points to the problem in the cases I have discussed. A defect in the fabric of the symbolic, impeding the construction of the subject. In order to write, didn't Medhi, Fleur, and Marion, lacking a father, all face a task like Anne's, the task of decoding that other language, the one that too great a jouissance had kept them from reaching before?

Response: Angela Joyce

WHAT I HEAR I CAN'T WRITE

Themes
1. How the child's history is represented in the parents' minds—both the adoptive and birth parents and its impact upon the representation in the child's mind. The role of the parents' mentalization of the child's history for the representation in the child's mind. Suzanne's dream of the assassin who murdered the primal scene.
2. The desire of the other—being an object rather than being the subject of one's own desire. This is annihilation of the self. How is this connected to the need for the infant to be brought to life through being claimed by the object i.e. by being the object of the other's desire.
3. The primal scene of the adopted child is complicated—the impact of loss on the representation.
4. The place of the father—being born under X.
5. Being born into the *jouissance* of the parents, or rather adopted into the adoptive parents' *jouissance*, but also having to contend with the hatred and murderousness of the birth parents?

6. Concreteness of the thing representation; if it has not been mentalized, perhaps it remains so, and cannot be symbolized. The absence of any shared symbolized representation of the prehistory i.e. that which does not include the adoptive parents. The presence of the unmentalized, unsymbolized history has no existence in her mind, is then experienced as a bizarre object.
7. The encounter with the Real, the raw unprocessed data of experience.
8. "The incomplete operation of the name of the father—a defect in the fabric of the symbolic, impeding the construction of the subject".

Themes that come up throughout the papers
1. The nature of the real external object and its role in implementing the life drive of the baby. The balance of love and hate and its impact.
2. The role of history, both of the inter-generational kind and individual history as it is lived.
3. The role of speech and language in the creating of the link between object and infant. Representation in the infant's mind—how is it created and what is the role of the various imputs from the object?
4. The role of the clinician—both the analyst and the staff of the ICU. Institutional processes and how they are affected and affect the patient.
5. The machine in the infant's life.
6. The role of the "law of the father".
7. The way the parents claim the infant—and when. How to symbolize and represent an absence.

CHAPTER FIVE

Creating transitions in the lives of children suffering from "multiple traumatic loss"*

Monica Lanyado

A number of years ago a three-year-old boy was referred to me by his foster-mother's social worker because he had been helped so much by his foster-carers that he was considered to be suitable for adoption. The social worker who referred Sammy could see that it would be very painful and potentially traumatic for him to leave his foster-home and accept adoptive parents. She was also very concerned to help the foster-parents, who had not prepared a child for adoption before and who, she feared, might be so upset by parting with him that despite having done so well with Sammy, they might be unwilling to foster other children. The social worker hoped I might help Sammy and his foster parents to work through their painful feelings as constructively as possible.

---

*This paper was first given to a meeting of the Hereford Psychoanalytic Psychotherapy Group, November 2000. Some sections formed part of a paper given to the Study Day for Care and Therapeutic Staff of the Charterhouse Group of Therapeutic Communities, September 2000. It formed part of the symposium on British and Lacanian Approaches to Child Analysis, held by the Squiggle Foundation, with the support of Karnac Books in June 2001.

I was able to work with Sammy, his foster parents, and eventually his adoptive parents, over a period of nearly three years. During this time, he had to cope with the most extraordinary succession and superimposition of attachment, separation and loss experiences. These experiences were happening to a child who had already lost his birth parents after being severely traumatized by them, and who was only five years old when the process of adoption was completed.

Sammy's treatment was an experience that I continue to think about and learn from and in this paper I describe my work with him and another little boy, Harry, during their transition from fostering to adoption. What are striking are the similarities of emotional and behavioural problems these children share. As well as treating children, I also hear about children like these through colleagues I supervise who work in therapeutic communities or out-patient clinics. These children's life histories become predictably and depressingly similar when viewed from the perspective of attachment theory—a succession of broken attachments, often accompanied by escalating aggressive and antisocial behaviour. Clinically, they can be described as suffering from "multiple traumatic loss". If they are lucky, at some point they may be placed with a foster-family or an adoptive family, in a therapeutic community, or with adults who manage to survive their behaviour and gradually establish a secure emotional base for the child (Bowlby, 1988).

The predictability about the emotional makeup of a child who has suffered these external experiences originally drew Bowlby's attention to them and led to his theories about attachment, separation and loss (Holmes, 1993). Children who come for psychotherapy because of other kinds of problems have very varied life histories and have responded to them in their own individual ways, with their own particular symptomatology. But there are few other life events that lead so predictably to such clear forms of emotional and behavioural disturbance as those resulting from repeated disruptions in early attachment relationships. The loss or separation from key figures in a child's life constitutes a major trauma in his or her emotional development.

Because of the paradoxical emotional tasks a child is expected to be able to perform, there is the potential for serious re-traumatization in the process of moving a child from long-term fostering to adoption. This paper illustrates the enormity of these emotional tasks as they can be seen from the perspective of the child in therapy. The transition involves social workers in actions and decisions that require the wisdom of Solomon. Careful thought about how this delicate transition can be nurtured, together with detailed and painstaking case management within the complex network that surrounds the child, is vital in determining how well the child eventually settles in the adoptive home.

The paper describes my work with Sammy and Harry during the transition from foster-parents to adoptive parents. (I have written about Sammy in more detail elsewhere; Lanyado, 1997.) I also discuss the theoretical background of attachment, separation and loss in relation to children in care, and how this helps in understanding some of their very disturbed and aggressive behaviour. Alongside this theme, I emphasize the need to try to create a sense of continuity and transition in these children's very disrupted lives. Although this may seem like a contradiction, I hope to illustrate how, despite the enormity of the external and internal changes in their lives, therapy can enable the child to become more grounded and more able to contain some of his or her anxiety about these changes, which can then be navigated with creativity rather than despair.

Sammy

Sammy was three years old when he was referred for therapy. He had a history of neglect from a very young mother who had not been able to cope with her baby. He went in and out of Care as social workers made many attempts to help his mother to care for him more adequately. Eventually he was placed in long-term fostering with a view to adoption when he was two years old. The referring social worker was concerned about how the loss of Sammy's foster family would affect his relationship with his adoptive family and worried about his generally disturbed behaviour. He had severe temper tantrums and could become suddenly very aggressive. He often expressed this aggression by deliberately wetting and soiling, but he was also able to be loving and sorry for being "bad", and an affectionate relationship had built up between him and his foster-carers.

A treatment plan was set up in which I met regularly with the fostering social worker who had referred Sammy, and she met the foster parents regularly to support the therapy. It was agreed that I would be involved in any major decisions about Sammy, and that when an adoptive family had been found, I would be part of the thinking about how best to organize the transition.

Underlying Sammy's difficult behaviour with his loved foster parents, were intense feelings of being unwanted and unlovable, which led him to feel angry and retaliatory towards his foster-family, the main people (outside therapy) available to express all these feelings to. In addition, not surprisingly, he was enormously confused about his intense feelings of longing for, and rejection by, his natural mother, foster parents, and the fantasized adoptive parents and their families. At times it felt as if he would burst with the intensity of all the powerful, paradoxical feelings that surged inside him. Indeed this was what seemed to happen whenever his behaviour became very disturbed at home. His foster mother had to live with, and survive Sammy's displaced feelings of rejection and anger from his natural mother, as well as his appropriate current feelings of rejection by her and her husband whom, he knew, were unable to become his "forever" parents, however much they cared for him. He knew that adoptive parents were being sought, but waiting for them became increasingly intolerable and unbearable.

Whilst Sammy was struggling to contain his growing desperation that a new mummy and daddy would never be found for him, the fostering and adoption team had found a suitable family who were passed by the adoption panel. Sammy's foster parents and I knew this, but he could not be told as the whole process of his introduction to his new family needed very careful thought and management by all involved. Part of the process involved the foster-parents meeting the adoptive parents and the adoptive parents meeting me to talk about the therapeutic process. While he did not consciously know this had happened, it is very likely that he detected the excitement and tension, particularly that which surrounded the meeting between his foster-parents and his adoptive parents. For several weeks, Sammy continued to yearn for a new mummy and daddy while all the significant adults in his life knew they had been found.

During this time, Sammy would plaintively say that he wanted his new mummy and daddy "now", and that he had been waiting a very long time. But, it also became clear that he was frightened of meeting them in case he didn't like them. He harboured fantasies that he would be handed over to complete strangers who would abduct him from the safety and care of his foster home. It became important to acknowledge these fears and to talk to him repeatedly about how he would move to his new family when the time was right. It would be a gradual process and that he would have time to get used to the idea and to say goodbye to his foster family, in contrast to the abruptness of previous separations and losses. It is hard to know how well Sammy could really understand these rational accounts of what were momentous life events for such a young and understandably confused child.

Sammy used his sessions to work on his feelings about what he was being told. He became preoccupied with transitions and "in-between" states of mind, and started to develop what I came to think of as newly created transitional phenomena and experiences (Winnicott, 1971). For example, a lot of time was spent on the stairs between foster-mum in the waiting area and the therapy room. We talked a lot about how he felt in limbo in his life, not knowing where to "put" himself emotionally and physically. At the end of a particularly painful session, Sammy was desperate to take home a green ball from his box of toys. There was such an imperative expressed in his wish to take the ball that, very much against my better judgment, I let him do this, as long as he brought it back to the next session—which he agreed to do. It was the imperative nature of his wish that changed my mind—and this was after only a brief disagreement. I then said that although I did not normally allow therapy toys to go home, on this occasion I would as I could see how important it was to him, and we would see together what came of this. In other words, I was giving his acquisition of the ball my blessing, rather than letting it feel to him like a theft or a triumph over me. I was also aware of the similarity between the way he had "created" this object for himself and claimed rights over it, and the way a baby will naturally discover his or her own special blanket or soft toy that becomes the classical transitional object as described by Winnicott. This may have helped the ball to become significant for us. Immediately after the session I was convinced I had made a mistake in allowing this, and that I would now have to battle with him as he gradually removed more and more toys from his therapy box to his home!

Throughout the weeks that followed, during which time he was introduced to his adoptive family and left his foster family, the ball came and went from the sessions with Sammy. It was played with and carefully looked after, as well as aggressively knocked about, both in the therapy session and at his foster-home. His foster mother intuitively understood that the ball was important to him. Even when he forgot to bring it to the session he always referred to it. It was very clearly neither his nor mine—and this was a paradox that I deliberately maintained when I realized that, for Sammy, the ball had acquired the properties of transitional phenomena. With hindsight, it is fascinating to hypothesize about how the green ball may have helped him to cope with the paradoxes of moving from foster to adoptive home, in what has been a manageable transition, as opposed to a traumatic discontinuity and loss in his life.

Transitions and play

I would like now to discuss some of the theoretical concepts that underlie my thinking about this work. A capacity to tolerate paradox is at the heart of Winnicott's thinking about the "transitional object"—the special teddy, blanket, rag and so on, that many young children find essential in helping them when they are anxious or in an "in-between" state of mind, such as trying to fall asleep (Winnicott, 1971c). The idea of transitions, and the manner in which they are not "either/or", but are paradoxically "both", is extremely pertinent when thinking about children in Sammy's position.

In addition, I wish to emphasize how therapeutic the kind of play that Sammy was sometimes able to achieve can be to a child who is trying so hard to make sense of his or her life. (The content of his play was entirely unprompted by me.) The value of offering therapy to Sammy at this time was that by providing a facilitating environment, in Winnicott's terms, Sammy gradually became more and more able to play out very painful and complex thoughts and feelings (Winnicott, 1960a). Therapy seemed to help him to cope with everything that was happening in his life because he was increasingly able to express his feelings, however painful and difficult, through play. When I felt most unsure of how to help Sammy with his confusion and intensity of emotion, I was greatly supported by Winnicott's belief that a central function of the therapeutic process is to create and develop a particular facilitating environment where healthy emotional growth can take place. Winnicott sees an ability to play as being central to the individual's creativity and emotional health. In a well-known statement about his view of psychotherapy (for adults and children) he says

> Psychotherapy has to do with two people playing together. The corollary of this is that where playing is not possible then the work done by the therapist is directed towards bringing the patient from a state of not being able to play into a state of being able to play. [Winnicott, 1971c]

In an earlier publication he puts the following view about play as an indicator of emotional well-being:

> Put a lot of store on a child's ability to play. If a child is playing, there is room for a symptom or two, and if a child is able to enjoy playing both alone and with other children, there is no very serious trouble afoot. [Winnicott, 1964]

The therapeutic environment, a real, carefully created physical space (the therapy room, regularity of session times and so on) and mental space (in the therapist's mind) can be thought of as the "transitional space" which exists between internal and external reality in which play and playfulness is the primary mode of expression. This parallels the ordinary developmental process in which parents and particularly the mother at the start of life, create a carefully adapted holding environment in which the baby can discover how to "be" his or her "true" self through the natural unfolding of developmental processes and creative personal potential. Watching the highly relevant play themes that Sammy expressed as they emerged in therapy seemed to confirm that, despite all the pressures, he was able to grow and develop emotionally. This was confirmed externally when he managed to start school with very little fuss, and to enjoy learning in a classroom situation. It was striking that Sammy, and Harry, who I describe below, were able to play in such intense and significant ways at times of great turmoil in their external lives, when they could have gone to pieces and acted out in unacceptable ways. There were still many times when they were chaotic and very difficult to work with, but the periods when the play I am describing emerged, were very valuable and indicated that, despite their very obvious disturbance, some emotional recovery was taking place.

Many authors have suggested that it is extremely difficult to mourn one relationship whilst trying to attach within another (Klaus and Kennel, 1976). Paradox is also at the heart of Winnicott's thinking about transitional phenomena in which the precious blanket for example, is both "real" and "not-real" (Winnicott, 1971). It is both "only a blanket", *and* possibly vital when it comes to going to sleep. A bit of old blanket can be a very powerful thing in these circumstances—it is not a symbol, as other blankets cannot replace its smell, feel and individuality. It has been created to be the way it is, by the child-owner. Where there has been severe early emotional deprivation, many children will not have reached the point in their emotional development where they were able to create their own special transitional object. If they have been able to reach this point, this special possession might in some measure have helped them to cope with ordinary and more extreme anxiety. It will have been an object that has comforted, been loved and hated and precious to him or her. Tragically, where there might have been a transitional object, it has often been lost as children in care move from one placement to another.

Where it is possible to stay with the "here and now" experience of massive change, in this instance, moving from fostering to adoption, with all its paradoxes, it may be more possible to process the memories which contribute so importantly to a sense of continuity in life. The narrative of these events is likely to be more coherent as a result. Sammy's personal narrative about his move from fostering to adoption, and the quality of the memories he retained and could bear to remember as time went on, were hopefully enriched and made more coherent. This was as a result of his ability to keep in touch with, and express, through play and words, how impossible it felt at the time to reconcile his feelings about his natural mother and father, his foster parents and his adoptive parents.

Attachment, separation, loss, and emotional defences

When in 1944 Bowlby first wrote about what he called the "affectionless" personality that resulted from broken relationships at critical periods in childhood, he was very clear that children who had had these experiences were likely to grow up to be psychopathic and antisocial. Sammy and Harry could have been described in this way. Initially Bowlby felt that this was an irreversible condition and that it was pointless, or an unacceptably intense use of scarce clinical resources, to attempt treatment (Bowlby, 1944, 1953). At this stage of his thinking, he might well have questioned the wisdom of my work with Sammy. Whilst Bowlby modified this original stark view, those of us who work with children in Care are highly aware of the manner in which children who have suffered broken attachments carry this painful internal model with them from one foster placement to another, despite the efforts of each foster family to give as much as they can to the child. It is as if the child arrives at the placement expecting to be rejected and it is only with a great deal of perseverance and understanding on the part of the foster-family, that he or she may eventually become able to feel more secure in the family. Even worse, the child may end up seeming either unconsciously or deliberately to wreck the placement, having reached a state of terrible anger and despair about any kind of more intimate relationship with an adult.

Bowlby's views developed over time and he moved from placing too rigorous and simplistic an emphasis on maternal deprivation and separation, per se, as the major causes of antisocial and psychopathic personalities, to a much more complex theory (Bowlby, 1969, 1973, 1980). His detailed and scholarly work form the basis of what is now known as attachment theory. His formulation of ordinary primary attachment proposes that the bond between parents and their offspring is essential for the survival of the species. If human parents do not protect their young from danger they will die. There is now a substantial body of research and clinical evidence that supports the idea that the quality of the attachments that begin in the earliest months and years of life, affects the type of relationships a person makes throughout life.

While the attachments to mother and father in childhood are likely to be the strongest, we all form many new attachments as we go through life (Holmes, 1993). Furthermore, research suggests that the quality of each early attachment can be quite independent—a child may be insecurely attached to his mother but securely attached to his grandmother. Attachments to siblings are also often of great importance. It is probably more realistic to think in terms of a hierarchy of attachments, and this in turn implies that it might be possible to be securely attached to a care-giver to a greater or lesser extent. The question for children like Sammy and Harry is what kind of attachment they are capable of forming. There is a great deal of evidence that suggests that the strength of the template (Bowlby's "internal working models") formed by the earliest experiences of attachment can determine all future types (Holmes, 1993). This is what we are seeing when a child mistakenly perceives kindly, patient foster-carers and adoptive parents as if they were cruel to him or her in ways that his or her birth parents had been in the past. It can be very difficult to shift this perception. An important function of therapy can be to free the child from the ghosts of the past attachments that cloud his or her vision of new relationships (Hopkins,   ).

A child who has grown up surrounded by adults and siblings who care for him has been born into a life of good fortune. The world is a friendly place where he is loved and protected, and any misfortunes and frustrations are made more bearable because of the security and care surrounding him. If, however, when a baby or young child reaches out for protection and help in a very ordinary way, such as needing a nappy changed or being cuddled and patted through a painful episode of wind, the care-giver habitually does not respond for too long a period, or is erratic in his or her response, then the baby is likely to experience greater levels of distress and distrust. This kind of pattern, taken to extremes, is what lies behind the innocent sounding term that a child was taken into care because of "neglect". The child's experience is even worse when expressions of need and protection are met with abuse. When, for no apparent reason, as far as the child is concerned, the care-giver attacks the child physically, sexually or emotionally, and the child has no one to turn to for comfort other than this same adult, emotional defences are built up by the child to protect himself. Fear about his care-giver's attacks, in time may lead, either to very aggressive behaviour, or to an attempt to cut off from any kind of feeling that makes him feel vulnerable. In attachment theory, this type of behaviour is classified as severely insecure, and most children in Care come into this category.

When a child has experienced responses of this kind from his care-givers early in life, there is a fearfulness about allowing anyone close to him. In the child's mind, to do so risks a repeat of the painful rejection, attack, abandonment or uncertainty of past relationships. It took me a while to realize that what often appeared to be sudden aggression towards me from another three-year-old patient of mine, Harry, was related to this fear. A brief excerpt from my work with him illustrates this particularly clearly.

> Harry and his foster parents were less openly affectionate than Sammy and his foster parents, but Harry had gained a great sense of stability and security from his two years of being with the family. Like Sammy, Harry had also been severely neglected as a baby, but the period in and out of Care was shorter. There had been a failed adoption when he was 18-months old, primarily because he had been placed with his older sister, who was extremely disturbed. Just before his treatment started, the difficult decision to separate Harry and his sister was made, because the foster parents could not cope with her very disturbed and violent behaviour. Therapy had been promised for her from the start of the foster placement and there had been pressure on the social services to provide it, but, by the time it was offered, it was too late for the placement to survive. Harry's sister was moved to a specialist residential setting where she did not get therapy. Harry's foster mother did not join the therapy sessions as Sammy's foster-mum had done, but she and her husband were well supported by the fostering social worker. As with Sammy, I was involved in how to help Harry make the transition to his new home.
>
> Harry had coped with his misfortunes by withdrawing into himself, but had gradually come alive, and then thrived, on the attention he got in the foster home when his sister was no longer there. It was as if no one had been able to see him because his sister had had such a massive presence. In therapy, he gradually became able to let me know that he had been very frightened by his sister (who was only six years old at the time), when she was in a violent temper. He secretly felt that she always seemed to spoil good things for him. Harry's defensiveness against painful feelings is characteristic of the way in which many children in Care try to find a way to cope with their difficult lives—by cutting off from a sense of aliveness within

themselves. (By contrast Sammy was much less defended, and much more in touch with his distress.) During the therapy that preceded his readiness for adoption, Harry changed from a toughened, withdrawn, traumatized and unnaturally muscular child, into a sweet, cuddly, but very confused little boy. He had a lot of developmental ground to make up.

In therapy, Harry liked to play a game where he would imagine a monster coming to get him, and quickly urge me to join him in hiding from it under a blanket, or behind the sand pit. We would sit there together, in very close emotional and physical proximity, and for a few minutes it would feel quite cosy and comfortable. His whole manner indicated that he enjoyed this closeness as he could squeeze up to me and feel that he had a companion with him in his game of being in danger. Then, suddenly, he would hit me—often in the face. I would have to stop him, and the game and the experience of closeness would break down. He would be upset, ostensibly because I had had to stop him hitting me but also, I think, because he became frightened by our closeness.

When I had understood this, at an appropriate time, when a similar game developed, I made a point of not getting too close to him as we hid. I said to him that I thought that, although he liked the game at first, it also frightened him, because he suddenly found himself scared that I would hurt him if I came too close. It was as if he felt that I suddenly turned into the monster. At times, over the following weeks and months it became possible to talk to him about how he had been hurt by adults in the past and now could not help but fear that all adults were like this—even though a lot of the time he knew they weren't. It also gave us the opportunity to talk about what felt "too close", and I learned to be respectful of how close he could bear me to get to him. It was also helpful to talk to his foster-parents about his fear of emotional closeness as one factor fuelling his volatility, particularly during the period when he knew he was not going to stay with them forever. When I met his adoptive parents before introductions had taken place, I spoke about how frightening emotional closeness could be for Harry, and how it fuelled aggressive or unpredictable behaviour. It can be very distressing for foster or adoptive parents—and also for professional caregivers—to have their attempts to love and care for such a needy child apparently "rejected".

Broken attachments—the experience of loss

Feeling rejected by children like Sammy and Harry may be an example of the child's projection of intolerable feelings of rejection onto the care-giver. These feelings then have to be contained and understood, but problems of emotional proximity and distance also arise from disturbed attachment relationships from the past. These are based on real experiences, such as being physically uncared for or harshly pushed away and attacked by those from whom the child had sought security and proximity in times of physical and emotional need. Indeed, Sammy and Harry were eventually completely abandoned by their parents. Contrast this with an ordinary secure attachment where an infant, child, or adult seeks closeness with an attachment figure (parent, sibling, friend, partner) when he or she feels in danger or distress, and receives the welcome and care that is needed. It is not surprising to find that emotional (and physical) closeness and distance are central anxieties when children who have suffered disrupted attachments dare to try to form new ones. "Broken or disrupted attachment" is the term to describe the terribly painful experiences of separation and loss that children in Care have to find a way of living with.

Loss and the process of mourning are as much a part of human experience as forming relationships with others. "The pain of grief is just as much a part of life as the joy of love; it is perhaps the price we pay for love, the cost of commitment" (Parkes, 1972, p. 20). Describing the grief arising from the death of a loved one, Parkes states in his classic, *Bereavement. Studies of Grief in Adult Life*, "I know of only one functional psychiatric disorder whose cause is known, whose features are distinctive, and whose course is usually predictable, and that is grief, the reaction to loss" (Parkes, 1972, p. 20). His account of a process of mourning that unfolds along fairly predictable lines in ordinary everyday life, for children as well as adults, was further defined by Bowlby in the third part of his trilogy (Bowlby, 1980).

The key components of the ordinary mourning process (in no particular chronological order, or order of importance) are still viewed as being sadness, depression, numbing, searching for the lost loved one, yearning, anger, disorganization, despair and eventually, with gradual recovery, reorganization. When this process has happened the individual can also be seen to have grown emotionally as a result.

By contrast, when mourning has been compounded and complicated by external or internal circumstances, there are likely to be many developmental repercussions. It is now generally recognized that mourning following a death may take at least a year, with anniversaries of important past events playing a significant part in the process; the age of the mourner also determines his or her ability to fully engage in it. Adults, and children in particular, fare better or worse in managing mourning, depending on how well they are supported by other attachment figures at the time. Many children who have not lost contact with key attachment figures through death, but through neglect, abuse or abandonment, are unable to mourn this loss. Not only are their emotional structures less developed than those of adults in similar circumstances, but they are frequently unsupported by the presence of other known attachment figures. It is also less complicated to mourn the death of a loved one than to cope with knowing that a missed parent is alive and well, living a few miles away, but not wanting to see the child. And, for most children in Care, the ordinary time needed to go through the process of mourning has often been filled with an accumulation of further losses and changes, which become almost impossible for the child to metabolize. A great deal of these children's anger and violence can be understood as being rooted in undigested experiences of loss.

I suggest that children in the Care system like Sammy and Harry are suffering from "multiple traumatic loss" for the following reasons. First, many of their own experiences of loss, in turn become "lost" in the face of their disturbed and disturbing behaviour. Second, the losses they have suffered are not the more ordinary, even necessary losses faced by all. They are traumatic losses of the most important relationships in their vulnerable young lives. These children are alone and unprotected and they have usually suffered repeated traumatic losses without any real chance of recovery from one loss before another takes place. It is often possible to retain an empathic response to young children like Sammy and Harry despite their aggressive and hostile behaviour. It is much more difficult when these children are physically larger and more dangerous. It then becomes easy to forget what has lead to this level of detachment, hostility, and violence. The idea that these frightening adolescents are suffering from "multiple traumatic loss" reminds us of what has lead to such severe disturbance. Both loss and trauma are central for a clinical category that adequately describes their situation.

We all try to defend ourselves from the rawness of the blast of grief. It can often, even in the best of circumstances, feel too much to bear, and some defensiveness is normal, even necessary, to keep going. However, if defences such as anger or detachment become the predominant response to the pain of grieving and are present too much of the time, the healthier emotional experiences of sadness and ordinary depression cannot be sufficiently experienced for the individual to move through the mourning process. As with Harry, this tends to interfere with the possibilities for forming new attachments when they present themselves.

In the next section I describe how Sammy coped with his feelings of attachment and loss at the time of leaving his foster home and moving to his adoptive home. The clinical material relates to the first session after he had met his adoptive parents.

The transition from fostering to adoption as seen in therapy

Sammy

> When I went to fetch Sammy and Sara (his foster-mother) from the waiting room, Sammy's head was down in a very doleful and ashamed way. He avoided my gaze and was wordless and reluctant to come to the therapy room. Sara was exasperated with him, saying that he had been "as high as a kite" since he'd known about his adoptive family. Sammy continued to stand with his head down in a desolate, lonely way when he came into the room with Sara. (All of his sessions started with some joint work before Sammy had some time on his own. This unusual way of working had been decided upon as a means of helping them to work through the impending separation and loss of Sammy's adoption. It had worked surprisingly well, as indeed it did in this instance.)
>
> Sara repeated that she didn't know what had come over him just as he came to the clinic. I asked Sammy if he could say anything about

this, but he stood rooted to the spot and very unusually, started to cry. I wondered if he needed some time on his own with me, so I suggested that Sara go back to the waiting room for a while. No sooner had she done this than Sammy wanted her back, so we went to fetch her, but she had just gone to the bathroom.

As we waited I took the opportunity to say to Sammy that I knew that he had had some very important days since our last session, and I wondered if it was this that had made him upset. He immediately and urgently blurted out, "I don't like my new mummy and daddy". As I was not sure that I had heard him correctly, I asked him if he could say this again. However, he said something quite different, "I'm going to miss Sara and Jim". There was no time for him to say anything else as Sara had just returned and to her surprise he flung himself into her arms. She carried him back to the therapy room, rather overcome by his show of emotion and visibly moved herself. Sammy continued to cry and to cling to Sara. This was one of many occasions when her anger melted, as she was able to see, behind all the bravado and rejecting defences, how upset he was at leaving her. She comforted him and told him that she and Jim would really miss him and that they also felt very sad that he was leaving them.

In the three weeks that followed Sammy brought out his full repertoire of awful confrontational and aggressive behaviour towards his adoptive parents, and was very volatile with his foster-parents. (This was the time the green ball was with him a great deal.) However, as Sammy came to see that his adoptive parents really wanted him and tried very hard to understand his distress, he became more able to accept them and the inevitability of saying goodbye to Sara and Jim. As the day approached he often asked them whether they would cry when he went. They told him truthfully that they probably would—and in fact did. It was very significant for Sammy to know that he mattered enough for them also to be very upset at their parting. This was very different from the separations and losses of the past when he had felt that the grown-ups were glad to get rid of him.

I now describe how Harry negotiated the same transition very differently, with less openly expressed emotion all round, which was very much in keeping with his more defended personality structure. Both clinical illustrations show how play in therapy, during such a crucial time, enabled them both, to some extent, to keep their conflicting feelings in their minds, rather than finding that the whole experience blew their minds. If children experience an environment in which they can safely play out their anxieties and fears, they can use play to express and work through feelings. Without this opportunity, children are likely to become "over the top" (as Sammy was after his first meeting his adoptive parents), or highly defended and out of touch with their emotions, particularly sadness and loss. They may also seem detached or bewildered. During this phase in Sammy and Harry's lives each child found his own way to try to play (think) about what was happening to him.

Harry

I knew that Harry's adoptive family had been found and that the whole process of "linking" was starting. Harry did not know and, because he lived in rather a protective haze a lot of the time, he had not expressed intense feelings about the loss of his natural mother nor any longing for a new mummy and daddy. Even the loss of his sister had not been fully registered, though it had been a mixed blessing for him, as his emotional life seemed to take off after her departure. His foster mother said he did not seem to understand what adoption meant, even though he had heard the word quite often. He did not seem to feel he had ever had a mummy and daddy, nor that he would ever have them in the future.

Harry had been coming for twice-weekly therapy for seven months when this session took place. He had not paid much attention to the wooden trains and track in the past, but, in this session, he started to play with them in quite an unusual way. He connected two trains together and placed them on a single piece of track, running the trains to the end of the track and stopping them there. He then added another piece of track, carefully moved the trains to the end of this piece of track, and so on, until he had built a piece of track with a number of pieces. He was unusually quiet and intent on this play, as if he were trying to work something important out. At the end of the session I felt I was interrupting him and he protested.

At the time I wondered whether the way he had built up his track would be a useful way of talking to him about not knowing where the Harry-train was going, that he was finding out, literally, as he went along. Two sessions later he arrived saying, "Jane (his social worker) is getting me a mum and dad". He was delighted and excited and rather all over the place with this astonishing news.

In his next session he went straight to the train track and spent the whole session playing with it. He had never managed this concentration before. He made up the track in the same manner, piece by piece, moving the train to the end of each piece as he built up the track. He had an idea that when the train came to the end of the track, it risked "falling into the water", which was why more track had to be added. He was particularly fascinated by a piece of track that forked in two directions, and spent a lot of time manoeuvring the train backwards and forwards along the two alternative routes of this junction. I watched this play quietly for about thirty minutes and eventually said that the little train might feel really scared each time it came to the end of the track, that this time it would fall into the water. But luckily, it seemed that some new track arrived just in time. (I think this expressed the level of trust in his emotional environment that he had managed to attain—that everything would turn out all right in the end). He had previously made a big play on the word "*now*"—interspersing some of his play with "*Now*" this is happening, *Now* that is—as if it were a new word for him. The immediacy of his sense of having to live in the present because he could not see the way ahead, was powerfully conveyed. I pointed to the fork with which he had been so engrossed and said that I thought he was trying to work out what it would mean to "fork off" the track he was on with his foster parents, and go on the other track with his mummy and daddy. It was as if he had run out of track with his foster parents and could go no further with them, but there was another track with his mummy and daddy, where there was lots of track. The trains needed a track and he needed a mummy and daddy. This was very moving, especially because he had found the metaphor in his play that I could not find in words.

Between this session and the next, Harry's foster mother phoned to say that he was now convinced that he would have his foster family *and* his adoptive family. At his next session he went straight to the train track and, this time, he could set up a length of track before he got out the train, and seemed to have a better idea of where the train was going. Forks in the track again featured prominently. There were two wooden trains and one carriage in this shared box of wooden train track and, at one point, the little carriage was on its own for quite a while. When I mentioned this, he became very anxious and stopped playing. I spoke of his worry that he would be all on his own without his foster parents. I then added that he wouldn't actually be all on his own because he would only leave his foster parents when he was ready to go and live with his mummy and daddy. I also stressed that it wasn't any mummy and daddy that he would have, but the right mummy and daddy who his trusted social worker had helped to find, and who had also been looking very hard for him. He listened very carefully but could not return to the train play for the rest of the session. I decided to buy him two more small wooden trains for his personal box of toys, to deliberately represent his mummy and daddy. I would not normally be so directive with a child. However, the circumstances suggested that he might find it helpful and there was a time pressure to work as much as we could on these issues before he was introduced to his mummy and daddy.

Harry was delighted to have his own mummy and daddy train and spent the whole of the next session playing with them and the other shared trains on a track that he made up in sections, including the fork. There was no longer any play about the train falling off the end of the track, but there were lots of couplings and de-couplings of the carriage to the different foster parent trains or the mummy and daddy trains. Again it was the intense concentration of this play and the fact that it was so sustained that was impressive in a little boy who prior to this had been so unable to settle to any sustained play. The little trains in his box meant a great deal to him, although he never wanted to take them home with him. They were a predominant theme in his play in the next two months during which he met his adoptive parents and moved to live with them.

This was a very positive adoption to observe and, although Harry has now stopped therapy, we keep in touch. He could often be boisterous and disruptive in his sessions but there was no other theme of play that was so sustained and important to him. This increased my feeling that the train play served a particular function in helping him to think and feel about what it meant to leave his secure foster home and live with his mummy and daddy.

Harry's sister is still in her residential unit and unlikely to be placed for adoption now. Unfortunately, she has still not received the therapy she so badly needs. She and Harry meet once or twice a year, but the meetings are very disturbing for him and his adoptive parents are very unsure of the value of this contact at this time in his life.

Conclusion

By discussing Sammy and Harry from the perspective of their efforts in therapy, I have showed a particular view of their difficult life experiences that is not ordinarily available for thinking about in such detail. Therapy can make it possible to see the minutiae of the child's inner world, while everyday social work practice provides the broader picture of these heartbreaking child care issues. Taken together these perspectives can inform each other in the productive service of the child in Care.

CHAPTER SIX

Prince Blackthorn and the Wizard: fantasying and thinking in the psychoanalysis of a ten-year-old boy

Angela Joyce

"There is nothing good or bad but thinking makes it so"
Hamlet, Act II Sc. ii. Shakespeare

"Yon Cassius has a lean and hungry look:
He thinks too much: such men are dangerous"
Julius Caesar, Act I Sc. ii. Shakespeare

This paper explores the relationship between fantasying, imagination and thinking, as they have been evident in the psychoanalytic treatment of Peter, a ten-year-old boy. The capacities to think and to imagine accrue developmentally and are profoundly shaped by the interplay between the child's environment and his response to it.

Shakespeare reminds us that thinking is dangerous and frightening; it is the harbinger of the discrimination of good and bad, it faces us with complexity, including the probability that there are other perspectives apart from our own, and it challenges us not to fall for simplistic solutions. Enriched by unconscious derivatives that emerge through the imagination and fantasy, these processes contain our internal psychic reality, and the substance of knowledge of ourselves and, ultimately, of the external world.

In this account of the first fifteen months of Peter's five-times-a-week analysis, I will show how, in his development, difficulties in his early relationship with his mother were accentuated by a degree of absence of the paternal function, at an inter-generational level. I see this paternal function bringing complexity to the mother–infant dyad (Lacan, 1958), and promoting perspective-taking (Britton, 1998) and the development of a self-reflective capacity (Fonagy and Target, 1996) already begun in the mother–infant dyad. Ultimately it allows for the creation of the oedipal situation. In the absence of a capacity for self-reflection, fantasying as escape (Winnicott, 1971) risks becoming the primary quality of the child's imagination. This undermines the imagination as a psychic space where the child may use play and fantasy to elaborate and integrate his internal predicaments and promote the capacity to think reflectively.

From the outset of his treatment, Peter made it clear that anything I had to say about him, his play, and his relationship with me was unwelcome. It quickly became an established feature of the analysis, and it was often returned to at a later stage, when Peter was facing situations he found unbearable. He insisted that thinking with me about himself was not what he was in the consulting room for: thinking only made things worse. Sometimes his extreme resistance to my verbal interventions manifested itself in violent ways—shouting at me, kicking the furniture, attacking the walls and, very occasionally, directly attacking me. However, he also played in a very complex and detailed way, elaborating dramas both fanciful and reflective of his interests. Sometimes, and then increasingly, he included me in assigned roles. It seemed that he wanted to play, and gradually he wanted me to play with him.

I was faced with the dilemma of how and when my analytic thinking might be conveyed to my patient in such a way as to promote his understanding of himself, rather than fuel his resistance. Analytic "thinking about" the patient often has to be held in the analyst's mind for a long time before it can usefully be put into verbal interpretations. This does not mean that it is not part of the interaction between the two participants and, in this case, it presented me with a paradox in which the resistance was also a communication about Peter's fundamental dilemmas. To see his resistance to my thinking and talking simply as a destructive attack on the analysis and the integrative function it embodies, risks falling into a split that can hamper analytic work.

This paper discusses how, over the course of fifteen months, the quality of Peter's play changed from an essentially narcissistic and uncommunicative "fantasying" (Winnicott, 1971) to imaginative fantasy. This shift was connected with a subtle change in my approach to him. I largely gave up attempting to address his play and his way of being with me in the usual psychoanalytic way, what Ferro has called "saturated interpretation" (Ferro, 1999), and allowed him to co-construct an action narrative in his play with me. Through his introduction of the story of Prince Blackthorn and the Wizard, and my response to it as described here, Peter changed my relationship with him from one where—if I figured at all—I was an audience in his intra-psychic drama, to one where I *could be* a participant. We were thus able to effect a degree of developmental progression that had not been possible before.

After a description of Peter's family background and the clinical process that shows the progression I wish to highlight, I explore some theoretical aspects of development in order to elucidate these processes. I then apply them more specifically to the material.

Peter's family background

Peter was referred by his parents and recommended for analysis when he was nine and a half years old. His principal presenting feature was violent outbursts of rage at home, which showed no sign of abating. He was a bright boy who was doing well enough at school although his teachers thought he was underachieving. Mr and Mrs W. had a rather diffuse feeling that things had not been right for him since he was very small. Although they both had a tempestuous relationship with him, they each got on with him better on their own. They felt he had very poor self-esteem. As a very small child Peter used to hate being picked up or helped if he fell or had difficulty with anything. His mother said he seemed to find it humiliating and to be somebody who did not want ever to need any help with anything. His parents were concerned that in the long term he would find relationships difficult and his life would be impoverished. Peter himself was sometimes miserable about his difficulties and would say that because of his temper nothing would ever go right for him. His parents conveyed a sense of his being very special, extremely talented, and intelligent; it was as though he embodied an idealized child about whom they harboured an ambiguous wish that he would both stay a baby and also grow up. They described him as an extremely nice boy when he was not being difficult. Peter was a lively child, on the small side for his age, slim, almost wiry, with an engaging smile. He had an older sister. Unlike his father he was a talented sportsman, and he had resisted his family's attempts to encourage him to be like his father in other ways.

This family has a marked inter-generational feature, the position of the father, that I have come to see as a very significant issue in Peter's development and in his difficulties. Both Peter's parents had troubled childhoods with absent fathers and difficult relationships with their mothers. His maternal grandfather, who had left home before Peter's mother was born, had remained interested in his daughter's life, but she said she loathed him when she was growing up. Peter's father had never met his own father. Mr W. was born just after the war and brought up by his grandparents, Peter's great-grandparents, until he was eleven years old. He then went to live with his mother, who was living a single life with boyfriends, of whom Mr W. was very jealous.

When Mr and Mrs W. created the new family together, they each brought their own difficulties about the place of the father in the family. This made it hard for them to situate themselves as a functioning parental couple in relation to Peter. They found it almost impossible to be with him together, and they seemed to organize their lives to take it in turns to be with him. Neither could be firm with Peter without the situation deteriorating into a row. Father's closeness had the quality of a brother or peer—he preferred to play football as one of the lads rather than being referee—while his mother's claim to understand her son felt like an over-close seduction.

Peter's proneness to shame and humiliation, his eschewing of his need of his objects, seemed to be of a narcissistic nature, located in a family culture where the triangulated oedipal space was hinted at rather than securely established in the minds of his parents. The inter-generational failure to establish an oedipal space compounded a feature of Peter's early development, and became a significant element in his difficulties. It was played out in the analysis partly through his repudiation of my psychoanalytic thinking and it was contained in the fantasy of Prince Blackthorn and the Wizard.

Clinical material

The shifts that Peter and I were able to accomplish in the first fifteen months of his analysis were evident in his play, which at first had seemed rich and full of symbolic and narrative interest, but in the interactions with me emerged as essentially narcissistic. In the counter-transference I felt that rather than being "used" (Winnicott, 1971) as a separate object, I was an extension of Peter himself. There was little, if any, sense of being communicated with and, insofar as I was separate, I was to be an audience for his display.

> From the outset Peter differentiated between the reality of his day-to-day life and that of his "vivid imagination". He very rarely spoke to me about his life, his friends, or his family, and, if I enquired, he would answer monosyllabically. In his play there were wishful compensatory fantasies, but also evidence of a dangerous world of capricious events, a world over which the characters had little control, often with powerful, violent emotions exploding in uncontainable ways. He spent many sessions using the doll figures, repetitively playing football, endlessly going through a replica of the World Cup football tournament happening at the time. Authority figures were frequently ignored or swept aside, occasionally attacked and rendered impotent. I was usually cast as the observer of these played-out events, but eventually I was assigned a place as the referee, or, sometimes, as the opposing team. He ignored any attempts to link the themes in the play to him or to us, and on many occasions he shouted his own commentary on the game at such a pitch that it drowned me out.

> His play with the animals was more characteristic of a younger child, and here an intensely ambivalent relationship between maternal figures and sons emerged as a recurrent theme. The

mother animals were often in mortal danger, apparently precipitated by the son's departure; they had to be restored to health either by magical solutions, or by the son's return. In one game, the young panther challenged and won, a fight with the old lion king. He then went off victorious with his friends, but, suddenly, over the airwaves, the mother panther sent a message that she was injured and dying. The young one returned home and got his mother to the vet, but she died, and he was distraught. Peter protested that it was not his fault. I said that the young panther felt very bad and perhaps rather guilty about leaving his mother and now she had died. He insisted that it was not the young panther's fault and made him hug the mother until her heart started beating and she came back to life. Then the young panther had a fight with the vet. My comments about his being angry with me for voicing the panther's guilty feelings were shouted down and the session ended in confusion.

A first sign of change came after the summer break, three months into the analysis, when Peter seemed to be more open with me. He told me a little bit about the holidays and even responded to some humorous teasing about his not allowing me to know much about him, what he enjoyed or hated. He told me that what annoyed him most was that when he wanted to talk to his mum, someone like his dad or his sister always interrupted. For the first time we were able to link his rages and tempers to his hatred of his father muscling in on his relationship with his mum. He liked to have her to himself. He added that he liked talking to one person at a time and when it was not like that at home he got fed up. I linked this to his sessions where he did not get interrupted except when I said it was time to finish or when the holidays came. He mumbled something in response, but he did not shout me down. Later in the session, when he created a football game with the dolls where all the referee's actions were opposed, I was able to comment on his dilemmas with paternal authority. I talked about how he enjoyed breaking the rules, and wondered if he would prefer to be the rule maker. Without answering he took the part of the referee and assigned me to be the players. As referee he tried to impose red and yellow cards for fouls, but when I played as he had, opposing the rules, he caved in as referee and could not sustain his authority. I interpreted that he really did not want to be the grown-up boss referee, but wanted the boys/players to be allowed to make the rules. He grinned in agreement.

Some sessions later, this issue of where adult authority resided and how it was exercised came right into the interaction between us, when he assumed he could change the agreed rules of a game in the middle of it. When I protested he tried several different ploys to get his own way. They included tyrannical domination and seductive persuasion, but not negotiation. In the following sessions, his play frequently included a child character who felt very little, wanted to have lots of power, have his mummy to himself, and get his dad out of the way. This character would get upset and angry when he did not get his own way. I largely interpreted this as displacement in the play, but I also linked it in the transference to his hating my challenging his claim to power, and my comings and goings over which he had no control. He appeared to ignore much of what I had to say but he did seem more able to tolerate the fact that I wished to say these things. In fact I felt that Peter was beginning to locate me somewhere in his world, that his play was becoming more object-related, and that, unconsciously I was beginning to be experienced as an object to whom he could communicate his internal predicament, and with whom he could begin to work it out.

Gradually Peter began to let me know that he was registering his relationship with me, that he was curious about me and my life, especially whether I had children. In a Friday session half way through the autumn term, he revealed a fantasy that I had a boy the same age as him. When I would not confirm or deny this, but talked about his feelings about my not seeing him over the weekend, he became enraged, declaring that everything I had told him was lies, that he didn't like me anyway, and that he bet I wasn't really married; I had just bought a ring to pretend. All the time he was kicking the small football very hard, straight at me, hitting me, and hurting me. I talked about his sense of humiliation at letting me know his interest in me, and that, because I would not just tell him what he wanted to know, but wanted to help him understand his feelings about it, he felt I was a horrible person that he wanted to hurt and humiliate. He replied that I was horrible and he didn't like coming here. When I interpreted his wish to turn away from his jealous feelings about having to share me with my husband and children, he aimed the ball right at my legs and kicked, hitting me with great force. I picked the ball up, and he jumped up on the window ledge, taunting me and shouting his dislike of me. He only calmed down after I made some links with his feelings of wanting his mother to himself and hating it when he had to share her.

About ten minutes before the end of the session he decided to get ready for his football match after the session, and he took off his tracksuit bottoms to reveal his shorts and kit underneath. He then asked me, apparently innocently, but replete with innuendo, if I thought he had muscled legs. I said he wanted me to admire him, which he denied but then showed me his Arsenal football shirt, and said he was known throughout the school, and was very popular. I said he was afraid I would not like him after today, but would feel he was horrible just as he had felt I was. He wanted me still to like him. He did not respond, and that was the end of the session.

Interpretations of this kind are what Ferro (1999) describes as "saturated", that is, they are interpretations that decode meanings and reveal truths about the patient rather than help the patient develop and strengthen his capacity to think about himself. In Ferro's view this is the analyst's task, which is in the Winnicottian tradition of enabling the patient to arrive at his own understanding of his unconscious predicament through the analysis.

This session was followed by weeks of provocative, aggressive behaviour, with Peter calling me all sorts of insulting names, and likening me, and my putative family, to the animal pictures on the walls of the consulting room. When I talked about his feelings of rage and humiliation, this only seemed to provoke him into more contempt and insults. He told me my thinking was rubbish, a waste of time, and insisted that he did not need my thoughts; they were rubbish, and I was rubbish. There were lots of provocative actions, attacking the plaster walls, jumping up on the window ledge, throwing water over me from the basin, and I was much provoked. But I also felt that something central had been touched and he was retreating in the face of it. When I gave him the dates of the Christmas break, it provoked a further outbreak of attacks on his time with me. His play seemed to disintegrate as he became consumed with determination to leave the analysis, convinced that I had ruined his life by isolating him and interfering with his friendships. He was quite unable even to use the narcissistic retreat familiar at the beginning of the analysis; he was agitated and aggressive, and very frightened to go on.

He declared he did not need help, he could look after himself just like his dad, and if he ever needed to talk to anyone, he had his mum. At one point he suggested that she could join us in the sessions and I could listen to them talking to each other. I commented that no one was allowed to get in between him and his Mum and he vehemently agreed. I took up his feelings of being shut out by me and wanting to turn the tables so that I now felt shut out, and that the Christmas holiday dates had upset him, and provoked his wish to escape from horrible feelings by leaving his analysis. This was met with derision and further physical taunting. At the same time as talking about his wish to leave his mark on the walls and on me, to make an impression, I was pushed to take control of the situation, to physically restrain him. It was in this context, eight months into the analysis, that Prince Blackthorn appeared in his games.

Slowly he turned his taunting into a game. Initially, he was going to see the Wizard of Oz and I was assigned to be various impediments on the way. This was elaborated into his being a king who knighted me as the "highest psychoanalyst" (strikingly in contrast to his overt denigration of me!), then his dad was the king's father, his mum the queen mother, changed to king mother, and his sister the maid. By further metamorphosis his parents became king and queen, and his sister the princess, and he was transformed into the prince, with a magic sword whose task it was to defend his father's kingdom against the threat posed by me. I was any one of various vile animals and goblins that he would zap with his magic weapons. What was most revealing about this wonderfully creative transformation of the conflict between us was his equating the characters assigned to me with his mother, when he shouted at me at one point, "Go away, mother!!"

The story of Prince Blackthorn developed gradually over the next six months. All manner of magical manoeuvres were available to us, using "props" such as a ring (not my wedding ring) that I habitually wore on my finger, the keys to his locker, a pen, all the furniture in the room, tables, chairs, the couch, covers, and cushions. I was given the role of many characters who threatened his father's kingdom, but principally I was the wizard who had stolen it and killed the parents sometime in the past. Peter's task as the prince was to reinstate the hereditary line of descent. The essential theme of the prince being deprived of his birthright to inherit his father's kingdom was worked over time and again.

The whole story was located deep in the mists of time, as though a fantasy of events in an archaic past were being elaborated in Peter's mind. The imagery was replete with symbols of developmental time, with magical poos, and genies whose power leapt out from the ring. The wizard was a cruel and tyrannical figure. The guards to his castle (to which roles I was also usually assigned) were prepared to kill anyone who dared to challenge his power, but Prince Blackthorn killed many of them. One particular theme was that those who came under the power of the wizard were not human, and the greatest gift Prince Blackthorn could tempt them with was to give them their humanity by freeing them from the wizard's captivity.

In another theme the wizard possessed a secret, and it was Peter's task as "secret squirrel" to track him down and find out the secret. The secret was not revealed in the Prince Blackthorn narrative, but it was associated with one he told me at around the same time, about his father. When his father was 18 years old, he was going to have a party, but his mother (Peter's grandmother) had had a party for herself instead and his dad was so upset that he went away for three days. Peter found it very difficult to elaborate on this story but, together, we were able to talk about his father's anger and upset at his own mother for putting herself in his place and preventing him from having his own celebration of his birthday/birthright. It was one of the rare times that Peter talked to me spontaneously about his family.

For most of the time Peter was elaborating this drama I played the roles assigned to me in the way he wanted. The few comments I did make were usually to do with the wishes and feelings in and between the characters, and I made very little attempt to link them to Peter's life, or to his relationship with me. The exception to this was that I would sometimes remark on how he put me in a role where I was bound to be violently killed, while he survived. In this period I abandoned the "saturated interpretations" of the earlier sessions and allowed Peter to place me in the unfolding story as he needed.

Some theoretical considerations

A central question in the psychoanalytic theory of fantasy is whether it serves the function of integration of the different levels of the mind, or whether it is used to escape psychic reality. I am proposing that in this material, Peter shifted from using his imagination in a way that is essentially dissociative, "fantasying" (Winnicott, 1971), to what I will call "imaginative fantasy", where he drew upon his unconscious and preconscious knowledge of himself to communicate his predicament. I want to distinguish between "imaginative fantasy", which is integrative, and "fantasying", which promotes escape. Winnicott described "fantasying" predicated on dissociation as an escape from psychic and actual reality. Imaginative fantasy, however, gathers together material from the outside world with new ideas, concepts and images often arising from conscious and unconscious conflicts and wishes. Both "imaginative fantasy" and "fantasying" utilize thinking, a property of mind in which ideas are connected together in sequence. Thinking involves experimental action: things can be tried out in the mind through thought instead of enacting them in the outside world. It also involves consideration of the qualities of the ideas, judgement and evaluation. Thinking about the self, or self-reflection, I suggest, arises out of the integrative function of imaginative fantasy, through which the person comes to know his or her psychic reality through this mental activity. Developmentally, these phenomena arise in the context of the different qualities in the child's relationship with his primary objects.

Psychoanalytic theories of thinking locate its development in the space opened up by the mother's failure to satisfy the infant constantly. For Freud the infant hallucinated the breast that did not feed when he felt hungry. For Bion, the absent breast, a "no-breast", meeting what he saw as an expectation or preconception of a breast, gave rise to thought if the infant could tolerate the frustration inherent in this situation. However, it is Winnicott's ideas that I have found particularly helpful in understanding the relationship between the imagination, fantasying, and thinking.

At the heart of Winnicott's theories of psychic development is the importance of sustaining paradox. The mother's role at the beginning of the baby's life is to sustain the baby's illusion of omnipotence. Through her graduated failure, her disillusionment of the baby, the paradox of the baby creating the breast that is there to be found gives way to that of transitional, or potential, space. Winnicott described this as "The intermediate area ... that is allowed to the infant between primary creativity and objective perception based on reality testing" (1971a, p. 13), and adds, "unchallenged in respect of its belonging to inner or external reality, [it] constitutes the greater part of the infant's experience, and throughout life is retained in the intense experiencing that belongs to the arts, religion and imaginative living" (1971a, p. 16).

Graham Lee (1977) has developed Winnicott's theory of potential space, differentiating the dyadic from the oedipal. In the dyadic potential space the paradox is of one-ness and two-ness, based on the infant's experience of being both not separate and separate from the mother. A sense of being separate is also a healthy developmental progression and, for Winnicott, it was the outcome of a further paradox, of the infant coming to recognize the otherness of the object through its survival of his or her destruction in unconscious phantasy. In the oedipal potential space the paradox is of two-ness and three-ness, encompassing the child's experience of exclusion and non-exclusion from the primal scene.

In the dyadic potential space the paradox of separateness and non-separateness allows for the development of the capacity for symbolic functioning, the beginnings of a triangulated space in the mind between the symbol and the symbolized, mediated by the interpreting subject (Ogden, 1993). If the paradox of separateness and merger in the mother–infant dyad is "resolved", in Winnicott's terms, it can go two ways. In the direction of merger, there can be no symbolic representation, and in the direction of separateness, pseudo-independence and a split between thinking and feeling follow. In either case the child remains in a state where the paradox of its primary relationship in the dyad has collapsed, and the capacity to be alone in the presence of another is foreclosed. Winnicott links this capacity to be alone with the child's first apprehension of the primal scene, and thus with the early precursor of the Oedipus complex (Winnicott, 1958a). In this situation of collapse, the primal scene cannot be countenanced and the paternal principle, as the agency in the mind that disrupts the mother–infant dyad, is denied. In this circumstance the paradox of exclusion and non-exclusion in the oedipal potential space cannot be broached. As Winnicott stressed, the absolute dependency on the mother of the infant at the beginning of life, one of the features of the "good enough mother", is to provide the conditions where these paradoxes can be sustained.

The failure to develop a triangular psychic space in which this paradox is sustained has consequences for the imagination, fantasy, and thinking. The dyadic potential space, held in its paradox of oneness and two-ness, uncompromised, is characterized by "an absence of a sense of boundaries, a lack of real-world constraints and a potentially infinite, free flow of images and ideas" (Lee, 1997, p. 80). But, in the oedipal potential space, creativity and thought are more bounded, "linking together ideas connecting them to a cultural and historical context and generally taking account of how ideas can be applied in the real world" (Lee, 1997, p. 80). If these paradoxes collapse, the integration of primary process qualities with those of the secondary process is disrupted. For thinking and imagination to have the possibility of enriching life that Winnicott describes, these paradoxes have to be sustained. It necessarily involves the integration of different levels of the mind, where aspects of primary process can co-exist with secondary process, where states of unintegration and integration (in Winnicott's terms) are available to be experienced.

Ron Britton (1998) and Michael Feldman (1989) have both linked disorders of thinking, the incapacity to gain perspective and link together ideas and thoughts in a creative intercourse, to the failure of an oedipal triangular mental space. I would add that the spurious resolution of potential space in the mind of the child inhibits the development of reflective-self functioning, that is, the capacity to "think about" the self and the experience of living (Fonagy and Target, 1996). The pathology arising out of the resolution of paradox in the area of dyadic potential space (Lee, 1997) contributes to the child being unable to use his imagination for integrative elaboration. Instead, it becomes fantasying, a form of escape from psychic reality and, ultimately, a refusal of the primal scene. This refusal represents a foreclosure of the oedipal situation, one consequence of which is to interfere with the child's capacity to think creatively about himself and his life. This is what Peter was struggling with in his analysis. It was exemplified by his determination that there was no space for a third who would disrupt the dual unity with his mother.

What are the factors that influence the fate of paradox in the area of dyadic and oedipal potential space? It is a truism that we always have to take into account both the child and his environment. There is a large psychoanalytic literature (S. & A. Freud, D. W. Winnicott, M. Balint, S. Fraiberg, M. Mannoni, etc), more recently added to from attachment theory (J. Bowlby, M. Main, M. & H. Steele, P. Fonagy etc), which chronicles the inter-generational transmission of family and individual characteristics, as well as phenomena such as trauma. The family that the parental couple establishes for the child is his first environment and essentially is comprised of the admixture of their internal worlds. Their particular strengths and weaknesses, together with the compromises they have made in order to accommodate their own family inheritances (what M. Mannoni calls "the parental discourse" 1970), all form part of what the child has to grapple with in the construction of his own internal family in his mind. This "family in his mind" has a profound effect on his psychic life, as the child struggles to risk the knowledge of that psychic reality (Davids, 2000). Aspects of mental functioning such as thinking and imagination can be used in the service of such knowledge, or distorted into a more dissociated form, which serves a flight from that knowledge. The direction the child "chooses" is linked to the complicated interplay of the external and internal family in his mind. The extent to which his parents have, in their own minds, triangulated space where thought and perspective-taking is intermixed with the dream and imagination, enables the child to risk the inevitable pain of disillusion and acceptance of his place in the generational order.

Discussion

Peter's repudiation of the analyst's thoughts allowed him to use his "vivid imagination" to escape the complexity of thinking about what those creations might mean. Since the material discussed here derives from the early part of Peter's analysis, it might be said that this is the rather ordinary problem of how the analyst engages the child. That is certainly part of the story, but I have been describing a mode of relating which is typical for this child, and to which he has returned whenever he has felt under too much emotional pressure. It is a mode of relating consonant with his psychopathology, and not just to do with the problem of how to engage him in the analytic process.

It is also of some consequence that Peter was a boy of latency age when fantasy, and the use to which the child puts it, is most revealing about psychopathology. The latency child uses fantasies as part of the defensive structuring of the ego, to further the developmental process. Fantasies "serve as a safety valve and preserve latency" (Sarnoff, 1987), and help the child to deal with unbearable wishes through the mechanisms of repression and displacement. As a consequence of the impact of pre-existing disturbance, these processes sometimes fail to create sufficient equanimity for latency to fulfil its function of allowing the child to get on with the business of growing up. Clinically, we then have to try to understand the complexity of the child's use of fantasy as a way of facilitating the developmental process. Peter's internal life was in turmoil, as his relationship with me also came to be.

From a technical point of view, the critical question in this analysis was whether it was useful to try to help Peter become conscious of what his fantasy and play showed me, or whether it was more conducive, in the long run, to his engagement in the analytic process, to allow him to use me in the way he needed to and not to interpret. There is no easy answer to this, and it is a pervasive dilemma in the analysis of both children and adults. It seems to me there can be no hard and fast rule. In the case of Peter, his humiliation about feeling I knew something of his internal predicament overrode any potential benefits of its recognition. The violence of his response to my interpretive attempts to make contact with him reflected just how mortified and wounded he was feeling. "Saturated" interpretations that sought to show him my understanding of the meaning of what I observed only made things worse for him. My problem as his analyst was to find a way of making contact with him that did not exacerbate these feelings. He showed me the way through the creation of the Prince Blackthorn story.

In the first six months of treatment the football games were both boring and illuminating. Although they felt like time fillers, they also showed me the explosiveness of his inner world, the lack of emotional containment, the preponderance of destructive jealousy, and the absence of an effective and benign paternal presence with whom he had to reckon. The play with the animals, where the mother invariably died and could only be revived through magic or the son's return, demonstrated the terrible consequences of the son's attempts to be himself.

In those early months I felt Peter was telling me that he had no objects outside his own omnipotence. Winnicott's meaning for this term was typically idiosyncratic. He used it both to describe dependence (the developmental experience of omnipotence) and also hopelessness about dependence (omnipotence). For Peter, I think there had been a distortion of the developmental experience of omnipotence as a consequence of something malign in the dependency. There had been a collapse of the paradox of potential space so that understanding him (as his mother claimed she did) felt like a claim for merger, which precipitated the opposite resolution, spurious independence. His parents had described Peter as hating help from a very young age, and certainly he let me know many times just how humiliating he found recognition of his need. My wish to communicate my thinking about him also seemed to have these connotations. His insistence that I play with him and forgo, at least for the moment, the satisfaction of being his analyst, who could think and speak of this understanding, appeared to shut me out. But it also invited me to be a different object, one that could tolerate the paradox of the dyadic potential space, and not challenge too quickly the way he was relating to me.

It was in the area of the fate of the paternal function that he first began to allow me to speak my thoughts, when he grinned at my comment that he did not want to be the grown-up boss referee, but preferred the boys/players being allowed to make the rules. This provided a link between his previous repudiation of my analytic stance and this paternal element. When dyadic potential space is spuriously resolved, the beginning of a triangulated mental space, in which the interpreting subject mediates between the thought and that which is thought about, is attenuated. When this is then linked with the paternal element that breaks up the mother–infant dyad, "thinking about" the self and one's experience together with the father may be similarly repudiated. The analytic function of "thinking about" seemed to be connected with the paternal function of making the rules and ensuring they were kept. In addition, facing out Peter's challenge to the rules when he wanted to change them in the middle of a game contributed to a sense that he might be able to tolerate my presence in the paternal transference, and be relieved by it. This was connected to a sense that his omnipotence could be disillusioned in a way that did not fuel his despair about dependency, but could give him some hope of a more complex, now oedipal, potential space.

Gradually it became clear that there was a contradiction between what Peter consciously claimed and what he unconsciously experienced. As his curiosity about me emerged, so did the idea that he recognized my existence whilst I was away from him and thus was not identical with him; I was with somebody else. This interpretation provoked the most violent of Peter's responses and his humiliation became most apparent. The hope that seemed to be emerging disappeared in his rage and despair about not being the son of the same age he imagined I had at home—and my exposure of it. Theoretically, this is complicated: did Peter's despair reflect the shortcomings of the dyadic relationship with his mother, or was this essentially a primitive oedipal situation? I think that both were contained in his response, and they became manifest in the narrative of Prince Blackthorn and the Wizard.

The figure of the Wizard was, in several ways, a paradoxical one. He was created out of Peter's projections of his murderous wishes towards his parents, and a representation of his family, where the parental couple could not function effectively in the oedipal situation. He was both a female and a male figure: the wizard as woman who stole the Prince's birthright of his father's kingdom (as in the father's birthday party secret): the wizard as male magician, a projection of the child's omnipotence, who steals the place of the parents and puts himself there; the wizard as mother who lures the child and deprives him of his freedom and, therefore, his humanity, a projection also of the child's wish to remain embedded in the mother's realm. Consciously, he was the thief who had to be found and killed. Unconsciously he had to survive, for as the mother has to survive her child's destructive attacks to be used as an object in her own right, so did I, the analyst, have to survive for Peter to move on developmentally. Peter's unconscious desire was that the old order be disrupted. To remain in its grip was to remain not human. To become fully human is to be released from the maternal realm into the complexity of difference. As a consequence, he could begin to move into the triangulated oedipal space where there could be complexity of thought, and imagination. In this realm fantasy could integrate the different levels of mind rather than be the route to escape.

The signs that Peter might sometimes, albeit not reliably, be able to use the analytic space to think, to think aloud with me, and to let me think, gradually became more apparent. I tried to be sensitive to his tendency to feel humiliated by my thoughts about him by following his lead for much of the time. Some of his capacity for spontaneity could then be brought to bear in relation to his mind and to the analysis. After about 14 months of analysis there was another disruption when I cancelled a session. This led to the familiar declaration that he was going to stop coming, and a long incoherent story about what he had done the day he did not see me. Then he stopped suddenly, commenting to himself, and to me, that he was not telling the truth, that he lied all the time, just did it without thinking and, when he did realize what he was doing, he usually allowed it to continue. He then linked this to his imagination, and we talked about how he used his imagination in his analysis, both to show me what goes on inside him and, also, to hide. He said there was a difference between the wars and killings in his play and in his life. I agreed that he could try out all kinds of things in his mind and imagination, knowing that it was not the same as doing them in real life, although sometimes it might feel they were. He clearly felt tremendous relief that these aspects of his mind could be understood and spoken about, something that had not been possible before. This emerged spontaneously from his preparedness to speak to me of what he had thought about himself; it indicated the appearance of his self-reflective capacity.

Conclusion

In this paper I have explored how the emergence of imaginative fantasy in the analysis of a ten-year-old boy reflected and contributed to significant development in the integration of his psychic reality. Initially, his play had the quality of "fantasying", essentially an escape, but through his construction of the narrative of Prince Blackthorn and the Wizard, it changed to one where his unconscious concerns could be expressed and elaborated. I have connected this to a change of interpretive style, from one where the meaning of the play was interpreted, to one where I allowed my patient to place me in the narrative as he needed me to be. As a consequence, Peter was able subsequently to engage his analyst in a reflective conversation about his state of mind in a way that had been impossible. He moved from feeling that thinking only made things worse to spontaneously thinking together with the analyst about his predicament. I have suggested that these are external manifestations of internal change in the area of potential space, both dyadic and oedipal, to reflect a triangulated space in the mind where thinking about the self in relation to others can be countenanced.

CHAPTER SEVEN

Some remarks on adolescence with Winnicott and Lacan

Alain Vanier

Referring to observations on adolescence, notably those of Winnicott, as well as the work of Lacan and a clinical case, the author advances several propositions concerning the relationship of adolescence to time. The consequences of this relationship are then examined in terms of the Oedipus complex as theorized by Lacan in his discussion of the paternal metaphor.

The word *adolescence* rarely appears in Freud's work and was almost never used in his day in the way it is today. Etymologically, the term comes from the Latin *adolescere*, which means "to grow up to maturity". An adolescent is someone who is growing into adulthood; thus, the very meaning of the word inscribes the adolescent in time. Up until the seventeenth century the word "adult" meant very much what "adolescent" means for us today. More recently, a shift has occurred and there is now a discrete time period assigned to adolescence. The term that Freud uses, especially in his *Three Essays on the Theory of Sexuality* (1905) is "puberty", a word that stresses the physical aspect of this period of development. Since psychoanalysis has no ready definition of what an adult is, it may be more consistent for us to say that adolescence is not so much a prelude to adulthood as the necessary sequel to infancy after the latency phase.[1]

How should we view this return to infancy, or the return *from* infancy with its reactivation of oedipal impulses? How can we speak of a return while avoiding any idea of a reversibility of time? The solution lies in the realization that this "return" is not the return of the same thing. Entry into the latency period (which corresponds to the decline of the Oedipus complex and its apparent desexualization) occurs against a backdrop of impotence, an impotence based on organic factors. There is, of course, the father's symbolic prohibition, but there is also an organic impotence of the sexual organ in respect to the *jouissance*[2] the child may seek. What corollary significance should be given to the reality of the body and the sexual drive at adolescence?

For a number of complex reasons, (the simplest of which is not the most obvious), puberty reactivates what has earlier been blurred. The child becomes capable of acting on impulses repressed in childhood and marked by impotence. For the adolescent, the issue arises of a potential passage from impotence to the possible. In this respect, we should note that in analyses with a child, one encounters the limit of their genital impotence. However, in adolescence, sexual energy goes on the rampage or, as Dolto (1968) once remarked, "the libido blows its lid".

Adolescence and time

Although the adolescent experiences a return to an earlier phase that might appear to be a kind of time warp, because of the reality of the body, he or she is faced with a number of irreversible consequences. The threshold of adolescence, namely puberty, and its termination—the "crisis of adolescence"—both mark the irreversibility of time. And, since young boys and girls are then forced to position themselves in terms of gender, adolescence also functions as the culmination of the process of sexual identity, begun in infancy.

Clinical vignette: Pierre

I once treated a very young psychotic child, Pierre, over a long period. His parents had consulted me because he constantly courted danger and had had a number of accidents. At the time Françoise Dolto was my supervisor and she ended her supervision of this patient with these words: "You've cured him of his psychosis, so we don't need to talk about him anymore".

At the time, the meaning of her words was enigmatic, (although apparently she made similar remarks fairly often). What did she mean by "cured", since the boy had just entered a specialized institution, and the analysis would in fact continue for a long period after her comment? True, Pierre's behaviour had changed considerably: he no longer sought physical danger and he was neither delusional nor incoherent in his speech. The institution that had admitted him later discharged him claiming that he did not belong there since he was not psychotic, but rather "pre-delinquent". While it was true that he still had a propensity for acting out, what happened later showed that he was not really on the road to delinquency.

When Pierre reached puberty, he experienced major anxiety attacks and returned to see me. He told me he was terrified—and indeed, I could read the terror in his eyes—by the idea that he was going to grow pubic hairs. It was very hard for him even to leave his home and he had developed a considerable number of ritualistic behaviours. He slept fitfully and spent hours in the bathroom meticulously examining his body, on the lookout for the first dreaded hair.

Winnicott's view of adolescence

Adolescence is time. It is often said that this period constitutes a difficult moment in life, and that teenagers "just have to get through it". Winnicott (1961) did not disagree in his well-known essay on adolescence; the problem, he believed, is that in adolescence, "each individual is engaged in a living experience and a problem of existing" for which the only remedy is "the passage of time" (p. 79). Winnicott's text begins with the remark that the adolescent boy or girl does not really want to be understood. This is a good thing for analysts to remember when dealing with adolescents, since here, more than elsewhere, sympathetic understanding can be counterproductive. We should not seek to "understand" the parents, the school, or other aspects of the adolescent's environment. Nor should we try to show understanding for the adolescent's self, since the patient is not looking for this.

However familiar one might be with Winnicott's essay, rereading it is rewarding. It is interesting to note, for example, that Winnicott does not privilege the sexual or genital aspect of the changes of puberty. From the very beginning, he invites the reader to understand the word "libido" in a more complex manner. Although acknowledging that the adolescent has the physical capacity to possess the sexual object, since he or she is no longer faced with the impotence of the past, Winnicott insists that the adolescent also has the physical power to destroy. Thus, emphasis is placed not so much on incestuous desire as on the imaginary figure of the depriving father. The adolescent's predicament revolves around the status and function of prohibition, and this becomes the starting point for the relationship to the object. The issue is not so much that of "killing the father" as of accepting the fact that the father is dead and that it is the adolescent's self, not the imaginary father, with whom the adolescent must come to terms. However, to succeed in doing so, certain conditions must be satisfied.

"How shall the adolescent boy or girl deal with the new power to destroy and even to kill, a power which did not complicate feelings of hatred at the toddler age? (Winnicott, 1961, p. 80). In a later text, Winnicott (1971) reconsidered the issue: "In the total unconscious fantasy belonging to growth at puberty and in adolescence, there is the death of someone" (p. 145). Winnicott advised parents that the best they can do during this turbulent period is to try to survive without relinquishing what is important.

The death drive is thus seen to be especially manifest in adolescence. Sex, in Winnicott's opinion, is possible before adolescents are ready for it, and he argued that their sexual behaviour actually serves the purpose of getting rid of sexuality. On the other hand, Winnicott observes that adolescents are deeply involved with their environment. The violent games in which children engage, particularly those privileging death and the survival of the fittest, sometimes surprise, or even worry parents, and their prevalence is often attributed to cultural influences (television, for example). Participation in such games usually ends with adolescence but if this is not the case the fantasies are acted out.

For Winnicott, adolescence is primarily a social phenomenon, that is, a phenomenon of discourse, and it is one that now exists in all modern societies. Moreover, our clinical experience shows that adolescent breakdown can occur very late, and that it sometimes plays itself out in an analytical setting. By considering adolescence as the return to infancy, one can also see it as a moment when the primal illusion is revived. The idealism often observed in adolescents is a way of keeping at bay the disappointment that is the inevitable counterpart of this illusion. Such disillusionment is linked to a modification of the status of both the ideal and the body—an ideal that keeps the group together and makes it a "body". If adolescence is above all a social phenomenon, Winnicott is right to consider the mutual relationship between adolescents and social changes. In 1961, when he published "Adolescence: struggling through the doldrums", Winnicott believed that the existence of the atom bomb had altered the whole climate of adolescence. (Similarly, Lacan thought that the death drive was lodged in modern physics). For Winnicott, the atom bomb's existence meant that "we know that we can no longer solve a social problem by organizing for a new war" (1961, p. 83). Before the bomb, adolescence had a social solution for its problem. Winnicott speaks of a "social" solution because adolescence is a problem that directly affects the social bond and the cohesion of the group. However, with the bomb, things had changed radically.

> Here comes the effect of the atomic bomb. If it no longer makes sense to deal with our difficult adolescents by preparing them to fight for their King and Country, then that is another reason why we are thrown back on the problem that there is this adolescence, a thing in itself. So now we have got to "dig" adolescence. [1961, p. 83]

In many ways, it is society's, and the group's failure to deal with adolescence that reveals the face of adolescence to us.

Winnicott goes on to say that the difficulty experienced by the male child or adolescent in his imaginary life is linked not so much to potency, but rather to the confrontation with another male and the admiration of a girl who, *looking on*, admires the victor. Here we should note the importance that Winnicott ascribed to the gaze. Approaching the issue from another angle, Dolto (1968) saw the adolescent problem as "a particular form of the conflict between heterosexual genital drives and genital drives which have remained homosexual" (p. 241).

Adolescence should be interpreted, of course, entirely along the lines of the oedipal dilemma. But it also represents a return to primal elements and to the issue of illusion mentioned above. Dolto believed that with the "birth pains of puberty" the individual "returns to the level of structuration before the oedipal crisis" (p. 239). Lacan's paradoxical expression, "the pre-oedipal triangle", seems appropriate to this time of life.

I would like to provide another clinical vignette in the context of Winnicott's belief that in psychoanalysis we need time (see also Lacan, 1970). As analysts, we become acutely aware of the time factor whenever we attempt to give an account of one of our analyses and describe how the treatment ran its course. We soon realize that it is impossible to provide a full description for the simple reason that we cannot give an account of the "time" of the treatment. In the following account, I limit my comments to a few clinical elements in order to highlight what I believe to be two essential phases in adolescent analyses.

Clinical vignette: Bastien

The patient, whom I will call Bastien, was fifteen when he came to see me. "He's been in adolescence for two years", was the first thing his mother told me during our interview. "In the beginning, it went fairly well. Then things took a turn for the worse". Two events had occurred at practically the same time: his father had left home, separating from his wife, and Bastien's grandfather, to whom he was very attached, had died. Bastien thus felt abandoned by his fathers. He had earlier been a "good boy", as he himself put it, an above-average student who liked "classical music", but he had radically changed his life-style. Analysis had been tried twice before. Without going into the details, it is quite probable that these two attempts had failed because of the inability of the parents to occupy the position that was being challenged. (It should be noted in passing that the father's activities brought him into frequent contact with adolescents.) The parents described their worry over Bastien's failure to apply himself at school and noted that he had started to truant, writing his own excuse notes and faking the signatures. He had become very aggressive with his mother, and even more so with his father, whom he scarcely wanted to see at all.

Bastien told me in our first interview that shortly after his father had left home, he had become friends with another student with whom he had a "hate relationship", as he put it. The other boy "won all the time" and hung around with people from outside the school, questionable characters. Bastien's new acquaintance was "a *batard*", he didn't "respect other people. He wasn't tolerant". But at least he wasn't "racist", because he was of Algerian descent. Bastien told me he did not know why but he had begun to act like the other boy, skipping classes and keeping company with delinquent types not from their school. He had even started "shaking down" younger kids and finally had run into trouble with the police. He had also changed his dress habits, had started listening to rap, and had covered the walls of the neighbourhood with graffiti.

He told me later in the treatment that he used his body as a sign of his own delinquency, since he had experienced the departure of his father as a delinquent act. I will not insist on the provocative nature of these actions through which he sought to encounter the law as something real. The result was that Bastien kept not only his mother and father but also the local police, very busy.

As mentioned above, I use this clinical account to highlight two phases of the analysis. In the beginning, it was a treatment marked entirely by actions, as is often the case with adolescents. The acting out bore witness to fluctuating ideal egos that became extremely mobile almost immediately. There was very little reminiscing during the sessions. All this reminds us of what Winnicott wrote of certain patients who are not integrated in time and who are incapable of relating *now* with *next*. Bastien, for example, had no plans and had stopped going to school. In such cases, the analyst is not a point of reference, nor can he or she embody the father figure. Indeed, I caution any analyst against trying to occupy what may appear to be a faltering position, since the latter constitutes, in many respects, the very nature of adolescence.

Shortly after beginning his analysis, Bastien tried unsuccessfully to be admitted back into his high school. He then asked to take correspondence classes, but his parents were worried about his being left alone all day. I pointed out to them that Bastien was already alone anyway, since he no longer went to school, and I encouraged them to let him choose his own direction. As it turned out, Bastien enrolled in and kept up with the very demanding programme.

He was living with his mother at this point. Little by little, he built up in his imagination the idea that he was the leader of a small gang of three or four members whose main territory was the street in a relatively quiet part of Paris where Bastien lived. His fantasy transposed the whole mythology of the inner cities (actually, in France, the "inner cities" are the suburbs). He organized a defense of the staircase in his building, marked out the perimeters of his territory and invented a legend around it. He recounted with great enthusiasm the history of his *demesne* and the high deeds of heroism that had been performed to protect it. In short, he stood watch over the carefully mapped-out maternal body, the motherland that his father had deserted.

Such behaviour can be likened to what Winnicott (1961) wrote about the usual fate of adolescent boys when they are drafted to defend the national territory, the fatherland. This solution helped channel the impossible death drive linked to that time of life, just as the narcissistic question is linked to signifiers and symbolization.

Bastien's territory was marked with signs and graffiti, as if he wanted to inscribe something on the body of the area he had mapped out. Signs also appeared on Bastien's body at this time in the treatment, as he experimented with a wide range of clothing and hairstyles. In societies different from our own, rites of passage always involve marking the body with initiatory signs. Perhaps in adolescence, more than at any other time in life, we are given notice that we have a body, since this is when it undergoes so many transformations and becomes singularly alien. Indeed, we can say that in adolescence our body often *possesses* us.

Gradually, Bastien abandoned the idea of defending his imaginary territory. Instead, he became attached to a real country that he claimed as his own but which, in fact, was his mother's country of origin. Bastien had never been there but he recalled some phrases of the language his mother and her father spoke with each other. He remembered meeting his maternal grandparents on a few occasions, although at first he said little about these meetings. However, he began to feel great nostalgia for his grandfather, talking about him more and more. Finally he decided to learn his grandfather's native language. He chose it as an optional course in his correspondence course and was soon able to read newspapers from the "homeland". He went to visit his maternal uncle, who lived in Paris, and came back elated. He spoke about his mother's country in glowing terms, a marvellous place, he said, devoid of all conflict. His behaviour began to improve, along with his grades. It was around this time that Bastien began to talk about his parents' divorce and to wonder openly what it might have meant for him. Then, little by little, he lost interest in this topic.

He often talked of the need for rules that would assign everybody a place in society—an attitude prevalent among inner-city gangs. His opinions became somewhat reactionary, and he often claimed that certain deviant types of behaviour scandalized him. His call for law and order alternated with radical protests against society. He dreamed of an ideal country. He expressed his passion for his mother's country by becoming an avid supporter of its national soccer team, although in the past soccer had never interested him.

Bastien was going too fast, and his body got in his way and disturbed him. He bumped into things and felt awkward. In the end, however, his good grades and his interest in a girl in the neighbourhood, a former classmate whom he met by chance, coincided with a felicitous turning point in his life.

Acting out

As mentioned earlier, Bastien's analysis—although he was very much involved in it—was marked by more than a few instances of acting out. Can we really speak of it, therefore, as an analysis? As we have seen, with adolescents, some degree of acting out in the initial phase of the treatment seems inevitable, and I think that analysts should be tolerant and recognize that such acting out may reflect major inner changes. There is, of course, a risk involved in such an attitude, but it outweighs the disadvantages of becoming identified with a repressive authority or of trying to put the patient's problems into some kind of new framework. However, the analyst's tolerant attitude does not mean that he or she should condone acts of delinquency.

The first part of Bastien's treatment provided him with a forum in which he could talk about what had been acted out. Caught in the currents of an overpowering and imaginary flood, he had found a haven where he could feel that he really existed, a feeling that was reinforced by the analyst's ability to listen. Winnicott (1961) argues that adolescence is a problem of existing, and we should keep in mind that the word "exist", which Lacan liked to write ex-ist, means, "to take up a position outside of". Existing in adolescence calls to mind the themes of separation and exile upon which individuality is ultimately based.

Acting out reveals an aspect of the treatment of adolescents that is ubiquitous, albeit in various forms. It is part of what Winnicott calls "the paradox of adolescence", namely that the only real remedy for psychic pain is "the passage of time" (Winnicott, 1961, p. 79). This, of course, is the last thing adolescents want to hear, since they are looking for an immediate cure. However, even when adolescents consider themselves to be in an emergency situation, they are not necessarily in a rush. This is why I believe that, despite their complaints about how long an analysis takes, getting adolescents to accept the fact that time will be needed and that this cannot be otherwise, is an important part of the treatment.

The contradiction between the emergency situation and the need for time to pass is sometimes the cause of what Winnicott calls the adolescent "doldrums". The doldrums is a name given to an oceanic region near the equator, where the weather is characterized by dead calms and baffling light winds, where ships make very little headway. For people on board every minute seems like an eternity. The analogous unhappy listlessness of adolescence, caused by the disharmony and disjointedness of time, is another, very important factor to keep in mind when treating adolescents.

Following on Winnicott, Jean-Jacques Rassial (1990) addressed the importance of time in adolescence. In terms of the real, Rassial sees adolescence as a kind of "precipitation" (pp. 204–205), noting that adolescents are not in control of the changes occurring in their bodies. On an imaginary level, however, they may view life as something that is "not going fast enough". Finally, on a symbolic level, Rassial argues that the time of adolescence is ordered by repetition, reproduction and invention. There is a repetition of a primal scene, but the repetition is not a real one, and thus the adolescent is forced to merely repeat the repetition. Rassial also notes that adolescents are in a period in which reproduction becomes possible and reproduction often appears to be an alternative to repetition. This is why some adolescents rush into parenthood.

Influence of the rhythm of speech

Our relationship to time, speed and motion is often taken for granted. In order to listen to someone, for example, we have to adjust ourselves to the speaker's flow of words and speed of delivery. Sometimes we get annoyed at a person who talks too fast or too slowly, because we know that this can make us lose the gist of what is being said.

But how do we actually adjust to the time and rhythm of speech? In *Une Âme Prisonnière (A Captive Soul)* (1994), Birger Sellin used a computer-assisted method of communication to quote texts he had written as a young man suffering from autism. The results of this technique have been hotly contested: could an autistic patient really be the author of these texts? For us, this is not the issue. Whether the texts come from Sellin or an assistant, their relevance lies in what such a clinical relationship reveals about the difference between speech and writing, since Sellin is reported to have begun to write before he could speak.

Here is an example of the (unedited) text:

> It's absurd to think that autistic people are less intelligent than other extraordinary mutes we cannot speak because our internal agitation is extraordinary, even annoying the agitation is indescribable and must remain without appropriate expression because outside-men haven't experienced it and weren't able to give it a name I call it the-depths-of-the-power-of-agitation. I hardly ever have moments without this agitation [p. 64, trans. J. Monahan]

Writing in the same way, Sellin, like other autists, later describes words as coming at him "as fast as a bullet train". Most of us probably have an innate capacity to isolate and delimit the voice, much as we do when we look at a precise point of space and isolate it from the surrounding area. But how do we manage to select relevant *auditory* elements? How do we enter into the tempo of sentences and adjust ourselves to what the Other is saying? Are we already inside the rhythm of the Other's speech, or do we adjust to it from the outside? Some autists and psychotics (who decompensate late) are capable of astonishing intellectual performances and demonstrate a singular openness to signifiers and language.

These questions can be partially answered by noting that the ability to differentiate requires both a degree of inhibition and a paraexcitatory function which allows us to record, on a temporal level, certain incoming stimuli while discarding others. In some cases, this capacity to screen and register can be missing or, in other instances, an apparently ordinary object becomes the centre of attention. The result is a short-circuiting of instinctual drives. I remember one young psychotic patient who was fascinated by French Brittany and everything related to it. He could recite from memory the arrival and departure times for trains over an entire year, including rail connections from one town to another.

Other viewpoints on adolescence and time

Adolescents in trouble, like Pierre and Bastien, are inscribed in time, a time that begins with the signifier. If, as Hegel (1807) wrote, the concept is time (p. 305), then the signifier is what produces and deploys time, a time which is the real refusal of what occurred in the beginning and which later unfolds on the level of imaginary "lived experience". Psychologists have observed that the idea of infinity, the passage of time against the backdrop of eternity, is inconceivable for a child. Only in adolescence does infinity become something imaginable. This is why adolescents seek an inviolable truth. What is special about truth, for otherwise it could not *be* a truth, is that it is eternal. Faced with the apparent failure of what once seemed certain, the adolescent has to return to the initial period of symbolization which introduced him or her to time. This is why adolescents have trouble dealing with time and why they act with such impulsive haste. Freymann (1992) stresses this point when discussing anorexia, an affliction that affects girls mainly during adolescence, and argues for a relationship to primal symbolization.

The disconnectedness that adolescents experience between eternity and time is due to the function of the signifier. This disconnectedness leads to a re-examination and reinvention of time, because adolescents need to re-inscribe themselves and position themselves anew as subjects. In order to subjectivize time once again, the adolescent boy or girl must find a position that satisfies both the demands of the species and the particularities of genealogy. If, as Winnicott suggested, the remedy for this troubled period is indeed the passage of time, then the best thing psychoanalysis can do for the adolescent is to allow time to go by.

Freud posited that the relationship to time is first experienced as a rhythm which later recurs in the alternating absence and presence of the mother, inscribed in language, as shown in the well-known Fort-Da description (Freud, 1920, pp. 14–17). The same rhythmic pattern of time permeates the *paternal metaphor*, the structure that Lacan uncovered in the Oedipus complex (1966, p. 557). The paternal metaphor consists in the substitution of a signifier, the Name-of-the-Father, for the signifiers of the desire of the Mother that are linked to the desire to be the maternal phallus (which is missing and thus causes the mother, in turn, to desire). This constitutes the first phase of the Oedipus complex. The paternal metaphor is a prerequisite to all later forms of metaphorization. It manifests itself as something that emerges in the desire of the mother. Non-deployment of the paternal metaphor corresponds to psychosis.

The Name-of-the-Father replaces what was first symbolized by the absence of the mother. Thus, primal repression involves a signifier attached to the other as a body, as *"jouissance"*. Afterwards, the phallus performs its task of separation, and the repression of other instinctual representatives is correlative to this. The result is to make phallic, or sexual signification pre-eminent, since it is linked to castration, and thus to introduce the Law and symbolic order. Desire in the individual is maintained by being carried over on to any object other than the mother (Vanier, 1998b).

However, the implementation of this structure has a primal function. The Name-of-the-Father is a signifier that can be represented by the Freudian myth of *Totem and Taboo* in which History begins with the death of the father and his totemization— that is, the reduction of the father to a signifier. In this way we can say, paraphrasing Saint Augustine, that time is a function of the father. Nevertheless, in both the Fort-Da episode and the paternal metaphor, yet another dimension is involved, that of *jouissance*. In adolescence, all the terms of this structure are redeployed. Bastien's story, for example, can be read as the attempt to circumscribe or contain maternal *jouissance*.

Winnicott's remark about a confrontation with the look-alike under the gaze of a young adolescent girl leads us to believe that it is only with adolescence that the subject *begins to see himself or herself*. This suggests the termination of an instinctual cut, the completion (or possibility) of a sublimation needed for a symbolic qualification of the gaze, or the voice—the completion of a signifying definition that was only half-formulated when the child entered the latency period.

In his observations concerning little Hans, Lacan (1975) stressed how the child's first erections represent for the body a kind of breaking and entering of the real of *jouissance*. Could not the same be said for what happens to the body at puberty? The *jouissance* that breaks into the real of the body must be restructured by the adolescent in his or her own image and attached to a signifier.

As we know, most childhood phobias occur around the age of two or three years. These phobias probably correspond to the initial period of the Oedipus complex when what is involved is a loss or a renunciation of *jouissance*—that is, castration. Other phobias may occur around the age of nine, and Dolto saw them as linked to the imagined death of the parents, in other words, once again, to a loss, a "letting go". I tend to think that early and late cases of phobia are not radically different. Obviously, both periods can be linked to Freud's initial theory concerning traumas and the ensuing transformation of this theory into two periods separated by a latency phase. The second period, later elaborated by Freud, is, of course puberty.

All this causes us to suspect that there is a *revival*, or a "*replay*" of *the paternal metaphor* during adolescence. There seems, therefore, to be an initial anticipatory phase, and then a second retroactive one in which Freud (1905) observed a decisive moment: "the irruption of an intense mental erotic impulse (*Liebesregung*)" (p. 235), leading to a testing of the authorized limit of *jouissance*.

Love, as Lacan (1953–1954) observes, is not only imaginary, not only *Verliebtheit*, it is also symbolic and requires that the individual take a gendered position with respect to the other sex. Maintaining such a position also means "entering oneself among fellows" (Lacan, 1974, p. 11). This is made possible when, in adolescence, the concept of castration takes on new significance and the real body image is correspondingly revised. This leads to the necessity of a discursive re-inscription, for which, this time round, the individual will be responsible.

As in any treatment, the analyst, when dealing with adolescents, becomes the embodiment of the fixed point of a repetition which always returns to the same place (Perrier, 1968). The analyst is thus situated in the Real.[3] The analyst is the depository of the deadly aspect of repetition and, at the same time, the place where transference can be deployed. Thus, the analyst's place is not just that of repetition, but also of invention. This point of certitude, the "eternal truth" which the adolescent needs in order to renew himself or herself, reminds us that, as an adult, each of us is a person with one idea or discovery which we re-examine and develop for the rest of our lives. This idea or discovery often dates back to adolescence.

Conclusion

By providing a point in the Other on which the adolescent can rely, analysis allows a boy or girl to go beyond the traditional dilemma of adolescence, that is, the protest against an established order that ultimately ends in the establishment of yet another order, or the abandonment of worthy dreams resulting in total conformism. Here, we might do well to think of analysis as a place where a conflict can be resolved in the subject's own terms. With a fixed point in the Other, a point which remains an enigma and a question, but which, at the same time, allows the adolescent to form a conviction, the analytic setting enables the individual to find sustenance in something after the crisis has unfolded. The term *adolescent crisis* is indeed reminiscent of the *krisis* of Hippocratic medicine during which the doctor waits for the passage of time to provide the remedy and to decide the fate of the patient who is balanced between life and death.

In a setting such as analysis, the adolescent may even be able to give language a little help—the kind of help that adolescents love to supply, since it is they who invent the new idioms that reshape and redirect the language in which we live.

Notes

1. Lacan (1953–1954) proposed alternative factors to the idea of a unification of partial drives in adolescence. He noted that the "child's admirable way of speaking ... does not commit it to anything" (p. 255), unlike the speech of an adult. Children lack something that would allow them to take responsibility for what they say and accept the consequences in terms of interlocution. Lacan (1967) defined the modern era as a *generalized childhood*, which he linked to the present day increase in segregation—that is, the status of the child in respect to *jouissance*.
2. *Jouissance* is a term introduced by Lacan to designate the satisfaction procured in the use of a desired object. The problem is that this type of satisfaction, which must be thought of as complete, supposes an object that is fundamentally forbidden. All other objects that attract desire are so many substitutes for the first one, and can only be partially satisfying; thus, a distinction must be made between satisfaction and jouissance. Moreover, jouissance seems to contradict the pleasure principle, since it apparently corresponds more to an increase in excitation than a return to the lowest level possible. Although strictly speaking, the term is not found in Freudian theory, Freud often referred to such a concept, and in several Freudian terms we can find something approximating the idea of *jouissance* linked to sexuality, but Freud also linked *jouissance* to pain, correlating it with an increase in psychic excitation. Moreover, when Freud posited the idea of a death drive, he suggested a link between *jouissance* and death, a mythic experience of satisfaction in which Eros is always coupled with Thanatos. Lacan later distinguished between several types of *jouissance*. There is, on the one hand, what Lacan called *phallic jouissance*, accessible to the subject due to castration. However, Lacan also posited a *jouissance* outside language, which he called the *jouissance* of the Other, (1972–1973). Such jouissance, he wrote, "thrives only on infinity" (p. 94) as opposed to sexual *jouissance* which is finite (see also Vanier, 1998a, p. 46, 1998b, pp. 65, 77, 88).
3. The real is a term introduced by Lacan (1953–1954) to denote one of the essential registers of analysis, along with the symbolic and the imaginary The real is not reality the latter being a consequence of the symbolic and controlled by fantasy. The real is rather a category produced by the symbolic that corresponds to what the symbolic excludes when it comes into play. Although Lacan located the real in psychosis and in hallucinatory phenomena he approached this concept in a more precise manner when he re-examined Freudian sexuality and

the relationship between the sexes based on fantasy. Because of the non inscription of the differences between the sexes in the unconscious, and the position of fantasy in relation to the status of the phallus for both sexes, Lacan (unpublished) later stated that there is no sexual relationship; this represented a reformulation of the Freudian position regarding the difference between the sexes and the way in which the child is introduced to the issue of sexuality by the parental couple which is what constitutes the real for the subject. This non-relationship is a consequence of language and speech. Due to its position in relation to the symbolic, the real is that which is unnameable. As Lacan once wrote (1970) the real is the impossible (p. 74) (see also Vanier, 1998b).

Response: Jenny Davids

I found Vanier's paper stimulating and thought provoking and I particularly appreciated the integration of theory and practice.

Some general comments and complementary theoretical views:

Vanier reminds us of the distinction between puberty and adolescence, and we know that adolescence as a phase came to be widely recognized as such in the 1950s and 1960s. A more clearly defined teenage group culture reflected through the radio, television, music, film and drama became more evident. Over the past decade the phase of adolescence seems to be stretching—it needs and takes time. Inge Wise (2000) writes in her introduction to a recent book on the subject: "The age from 12/13 to 20 years used to be defined as adolescence. It seems to take longer now; 12 to 25 years of age (or even later) is not an uncommon time span in today's uncertain and complex times" (p. 7).

Van Heeswyk (1997) provides a colourful if somewhat ironic definition of adolescence: "Adolescence begins with biology and ends with psychology. It is kick-started by puberty and cruises slowly to a halt at adult identity, the point at which the petrol is getting low and we need to think about saving it for the long, straight road ahead" (p. 3).

Vanier places much emphasis on the relation of adolescence to the sense of time, where time refers to both psychic time and the clock of the body. I would like to add the concept of rhythm with its harmonies and clashes, a kind of music of adolescence, where the young person has to find his or her own tune to negotiate this crucial voyage in a meaningful, authentic way.

Vanier reminds us that "puberty reactivates what has been blurred" and of Dolto's description of "the libido blowing its lid". The adolescent is all dressed up and ready to go, but where and when and how are the questions. So much is changing, both at a bodily level and psychically as well in the realm of object relations, that there seems to be a crisis of self, of who "I" am.

The development of self has drawn much attention in recent books on adolescence and perhaps this notion of self may be linked to "existence" in the sense in which Vanier speaks of it? There is a Lacanian play with the word "exist", ex -ist, which can be read as "taking a position outside of". It is this capacity to separate and to develop an individual perspective that is one of the fundamental tasks of adolescence. To find a place and identity in relation to the family, to the peer group, society and history.

Much has been written (Blos, Tonnesman) about adolescence as a time of mourning where the adolescent is preoccupied with the loss of his infantile objects and childhood objects. Others view adolescence as a second chance when the separation–individuation phase usually associated with the toddler period is re-experienced. With such revisiting come the strains on object relations, not only on the Oedipal level, but other earlier levels. In her developmental line from dependency to emotional self-reliance and adult object relationships Anna Freud (1966) describes an important, earlier phase, preadolescence, which is a prelude to the adolescent revolt, a return to early attitudes and behaviour, especially of the part-object, need-fulfilling and ambivalent type (p. 62). She reminds us of the passionate and savage nature of the adolescent in relation to her/his objects in her description of the central task of adolescence: "the adolescent struggle around denying, reversing, loosening, and shredding the tie to the infantile objects, defending against pregenitality, and finally establishing genital supremacy with heterosexual objects outside the family" (p. 62).

It is this breaking away that is so crucial and yet so painful, perhaps a necessary joy and heartache as Lanyado (1998) has written.

This leads me to comment on the role of the parents during adolescence, an issue Winnicott addresses when he talks about the need to meet the challenge of the adolescent, when understanding is replaced by confrontation. He uses the term "confrontation" to mean that "a grown-up person stands up and claims the right to have a personal point of view" (1968a, p. 147).

Sometimes the parent needs to present a different point of view while allowing the adolescent his or her own perspective. The need for diversity of expression is precious. I think that not only the attitude of the parent to the adolescent but also *to adolescence itself* is one which invites discussion. Winnicott reminds us of the envy of the parents and we know how some parents wish their adolescent daughters and sons to have the adolescence they themselves did not have. The big challenge from the adolescent, he writes, is to the bit of ourselves (and I think this applies to both parents and analysts) that has not really had its adolescence, that has been defrauded thereof.

Much is contained in Winnicott's elusively simple statement— how to be adolescent during adolescence. It is a crucial developmental achievement to experience adolescence at the right period, not prematurely, or as a delayed experience years later, or never. The parents too have to grieve their younger child and learn to live with paradox, with their adolescent who wavers between defiant independence and regressive dependence.

I now want to propose Winnicott's concept of the *false solution* as vital to our understanding of adolescence and as a way of extending Vanier's account.

The cure for adolescence is the passage of time. Yet the adolescent grasps for a quick fix solution; but rejects one so-called cure after another as a false element is detected. The need for authenticity and for the need to feel real is paramount. There are many common solutions; hasty identifications with parents or peers; escapes into the intellect or sublimation and jumps into sexuality. These are all false solutions however. Instead there is a passage through a doldrums area in which they feel futile and without a sense of having found themselves. *They have to go through whatever has to be gone through.*

I now turn to the case of the fifteen-year-old Bastien and raise a series of questions about his case material. I was surprised by Bastien's good attendance of sessions as this is not something many adolescents can manage. Bastien searches for solutions—is his identification with the Algerian boy a false solution? Do his own delinquent acts signal his need for control, even perhaps containment? Does he seek punishment as a way of dealing with his guilt? Through his behaviour and particularly the concern it evokes, he brings together his mother and father. Is this part of the hope, that all has not been lost or destroyed?

Vanier talks about the role of the body and the ownership of the body as a crucial issue in adolescence. One may well ask whose body?

On the issue of acting out and the analyzability of adolescents, it seems important that the analyst does not collude with enactments but that the communication value of the enactment and/or re-enactment is received in a process of being understood.

Finally I raise M. Laufer's interesting view on the question of analyzability:

> It is most appropriate and most possible to enable a treatment process to develop with adolescents from the age of 16. The younger adolescent is still too absorbed in his efforts to begin to remove himself emotionally from the oedipal parents, and the time up to the age of 16 is one which is characterized by the adolescent still feeling that his body does not yet belong to him, but is still the property of the oedipal parents, especially the mother [in Wise, 2000, p. 8]

CHAPTER EIGHT

A Winnicottian view of an American tragedy

Richard Frankel

Introduction

On April 20, 1999, two American teenagers, Eric Harris and Dylan Klebold, stormed into their suburban high school at lunch time, firing semi-automatic weapons and tossing explosives at students and teachers. Before turning their guns upon themselves, Harris and Klebold killed thirteen students and one teacher, and wounded twenty-four others, making it the deadliest school massacre in America's history.

Although reconstructing the lives of the perpetrators in the effort to make such a tragedy intelligible can provide an important piece of psychological reflection, my intention in this paper is to broaden the inquiry by bringing individual psychodynamics into dialogical play with the wider, collective forces at work in the culture. I discuss the lives of Eric Harris and Dylan Klebold by offering a possible account of the psychological space that they inhabited in the year leading up to the shootings, rather than in terms of how their early histories may have contributed to their becoming teenage killers. Given that the move out of the familial realm that marks the passage from childhood to adulthood places the adolescent squarely in the hands of the collective, by probing the psychological space of Harris and Klebold, I aim to show the impact of culture on adolescent development.

Adolescence marks that period in development when the membrane between psyche and culture is most porous. The adolescent psyche is swept along by the tides of cultural forces, giving voice in personal style, dress, and comportment to what is unconscious at the level of the collective.[1] In this regard, I will be asking what the school shootings at Columbine reveal about the permeability of the border separating the internal life of the individual from collective, external forces. By catching sight of how these larger collective forces speak through their actions, Columbine emerges not only as a personal tragedy for Klebold, Harris, their victims and families, but as an event that can reveal some of the cultural dimensions of the distress of the contemporary experience of adolescence.

The capacity of adolescence to reveal the porousness of the border between the individual and the cultural has not been given enough serious attention in psychological explanations in which an individualistic perspective tends to predominate (Frankel, 1998). Winnicott's writings on adolescence broaden the perspective because they allow us to see an event like Columbine, not only as the play of individual psychodynamics, but also as a cultural enactment. He extends psychoanalytic theories of development through his emphasis on the intricately interwoven network of the maturational processes and the facilitating environment. Psychopathology is seen as the result of a failure of an environment that negatively impinges upon individual development. For Winnicott, the environment is, at the beginning, part of the infant, and he uses the idea of the infant–mother dyad to express this delicate interplay between self and world, where mother is equated with environmental provision (Winnicott, 1967, p. 580).

In theorizing about adolescence, Winnicott offers an expanded conception of the facilitating environment, where the individual–culture dyad replaces the infant–mother dyad of early infancy and childhood. The self who once found recognition in the eyes and facial expression of the mother, and in the mirror which came to represent her face (Winnicott, 1970, p. 271), now seeks reflection in a wider social context.

Young people can be seen searching for a form of identification which does not let them down in their struggle, the struggle to feel real, the struggle to establish a personal identity, not to fit into an assigned role, but to go through whatever has to be gone through. [Winnicott, 1961, p. 84]

The adolescent seeks a holding environment that goes beyond the family to an extended network of social groupings. This broadening is most clearly addressed in his 1961 essay, "Adolescence: struggling through the doldrums". There, he shows how social changes in the culture affect the maturational processes of post-World War II adolescents. His analysis of the impact of the end of venereal disease, the development of contraceptive techniques, and the advent of the atom bomb on the possibilities for living out one's adolescence demonstrates that adolescent maturation is always shaped by a specific cultural context. He indicates a new direction that emphasizes how changes in the social and cultural environment can facilitate or impede the progressive developmental energy of the adolescent.

With this turn to culture, Winnicott offers an important revisioning of how adolescence in psychoanalytic developmental theory came to be seen as a recapitulation of childhood. The theory of recapitulation, espoused in one form or another by all of the major psychoanalytic theorists of adolescence, states that some portion of early infantile and childhood development gets played out again in a repetitive manner during adolescence. For Freud (1905) and for Jones (1922), individual impasses in adolescence are seen as fixations in the early psychosexual stages of infancy. Anna Freud (1958, 1966) describes how, in adolescence, the defences protect the ego from being overwhelmed by the anxiety caused by the id impulses and love objects of the individual's oedipal and pre-oedipal past. Blos (1967), who refers to adolescence as the second individuation process, writes of how early ego organization is the prime determinant for how well the adolescent is able to negotiate the developmental crisis of ego regression that occurs during adolescence. Each of these theorists gives voice to the maturational processes of adolescence from the perspective of intrapsychic development.

In "Struggling through the doldrums", Winnicott follows this tradition when he states:

> ...the general problem [for the individual adolescent] is the same: How shall this ego organization meet the new id advance? How shall the pubertal changes be accommodated in the personality pattern that is specific to the boy or girl in question? [Winnicott, 1961, p. 80]

But in his very next sentence, we find him offering something new:

> How shall the adolescent boy or girl deal with the new power to destroy and even to kill, a power which did not complicate the feelings of hatred at the toddler age? It is like putting new wine in old bottles. [*ibid.*]

The metaphor of new wine in old bottles speaks to Winnicott's awareness of the residues of infancy and early childhood in the adolescent together with the recognition that there is something dramatically different taking place. He gives attention to that difference by staying attuned to the phenomenological contours of adolescence as a world unto itself, with its own unique and originary dynamics which cannot wholly be understood by reference to infancy. He makes an important distinction between the antisocial tendency, which, at root, is caused by an early deprivation, and the disruptive nature of adolescence, which, though clinically very similar, is not the result of early experience. As he puts it: "There is adolescence, a thing itself, with which society must learn to live" (Winnicott, 1961, p. 83).

He goes on to describe what traditional psychoanalytic accounts of adolescents leave out, namely, the cultural context for adolescent maturation. He sees the wider culture as the facilitating environment for the developmental renegotiations of early infancy and childhood that the adolescent must face. Whereas a careful analysis of the mother–infant dyad was necessary in early childhood for understanding the formation of psychic structures, a careful analysis of the individual–culture dyad is necessary to understand the psychic restructuring that happens during adolescence. In infancy, we trace the opening of the psyche to the mother, whereas in adolescence we trace its opening to the wider world.

Following Winnicott, who understands the outbreak of violence and extreme defiance in adolescence to be evidence of an environmental failure (Winnicott, 1962a, p. 66), I want to examine how current changes in cultural practices, specifically the revolution in information technology, which in the short span of a decade has dramatically altered the cultural landscape, may have contributed to the environmental failure that led to the deadly actions of Harris and Klebold.

Heuristically, this focus on the facilitating environment in active interplay with individual psychodynamics makes sense, given the failure of psychological commentaries to uncover anything in the childhood of Harris and Klebold, or the structure of their family life, that would help illuminate the horrors of Columbine. No outstanding history of trauma or abuse has been reported that would help explain their violent actions at the age of seventeen. The extremes acted out at Columbine may not match extreme childhood states but they do seem to resonate with the extreme states of mind that Harris and Klebold found themselves in, which, I suggest, were a result of their engagement with the new technologies. While it is generally true that adolescents have always rooted out and discovered the extremes in culture, one assumption of this paper is that the revolution in information technologies has eroded the barrier between adolescents and the shadows of our cultural life.

The interplay between these newly emerging cultural practices and the adolescent process of maturation is not something that can be seen in abstraction. A purely sociological analysis fails to take into account the individual–cultural dyad that shapes the forward movement of the adolescent psyche. The particularities of the lives of Harris and Klebold offer us a rare glimpse of this interface between adolescent maturation and cultural responsiveness. Following Winnicott's emphasis on transitional phenomena and the discovery of the real that re-emerges during adolescence, I address the individual–cultural dyad by thinking through the psychic restructuring of adolescence in terms of the re-negotiation of the border between fantasy and reality. I read the case of Harris and Klebold and this developmental struggle through the contemporary cultural practices that are shifting the ways this very border is lived.

Because Winnicott's main emphasis is upon acknowledging the authenticity of the troubling and distressing psychological states that emerge during this period of life, he offers a fundamental reorientation for adolescent psychotherapy. Seeing an aspect of its pathologies as inherent to adolescence itself, rather than as a deprivation from the past, changes the way we meet and hear the symptom. Clinically, we are then led to consider how we meet the challenge of these adolescent states of mind, finding ways to engage and contain them, rather than attempting to cure what is essentially a normal developmental process. It is in his particular understanding of the nature of containment that we see the potential of Winnicottian theory to enrich the psychoanalytic accounts of adolescence by giving centrality to this profound confluence of psyche and culture that I am describing as the space in which adolescents live.

Containing the violent potential of adolescence

In "Struggling through the doldrums", Winnicott proposes that until recently, preparing adolescents to fight and engage in warfare was one method society had for containing their disruptive energy. Reflecting upon its absence in contemporary society, he observes: "Adolescence now has to contain itself, to contain itself in a way it has never had to do before, and we have to reckon that adolescence has pretty violent potential" (Winnicott, 1961, p. 83).

In light of Winnicott's reflection, I want to look at the massacre at Columbine High School as exemplifying the potential for violence in adolescence and question contemporary attempts to contain adolescent aggression in the post-industrial west, a world without wars, and a culture devoid of formal rites of initiation.

To read the events of Columbine High School as a desperate attempt at self-initiation, where Harris and Klebold took it upon themselves to create their own initiatory rites unsupervised by the civilizing forces in the culture, is to wonder whether there is something about our contemporary attempts to contain the storm of adolescence that fuels acts of such extreme violence and terror.

Winnicott stressed the need for an environmental response to adolescent experimentation. Adolescents, he believed, cannot wholly contain themselves, and thus he spoke of the importance of the adult's being there, holding the line, in the face of the antisocial, destructive behaviour that gives expression to adolescent rage. In today's world, given adolescents' engagement with the current information technologies, adults have a much more difficult time holding the line in the face of such provocation. One consequence of the digital revolution is that for the first time in history adolescents have immediate access to the most profoundly disturbing shadows of our culture through a medium that exists almost entirely outside the purview of parents and community. Parents' lack of technological sophistication increases the common adolescent projection that they are stupid, inept, and easily fooled; and since adolescents are usually more proficient in these new media, their on-line life is almost totally bereft of adult involvement. This was clear in the shocking realization, in the aftermath of so many of the recent school shooting tragedies, that what parents thought of as a safe haven—involvement with computers—was actually a home base from which to call forth and engage, at the level of virtual reality, a whole host of ultra-violent, destructive fantasies.

When we combine the fact that new technologies have always been used as a quick fix to long-standing political, social and economic problems, with the adolescent's attraction to the mercurial nature of a life immersed in digital technology, there is a way in which our culture unwittingly ends up promoting "virtuality" in its attempt to contain the aggression and acting-out endemic to adolescence. There are tremendous benefits for parents, schools, law enforcement, etc. when adolescents can engage in simulated acts of violence or sexuality, as opposed to acting them out in the world, where there are real consequences for their behaviour. We need only to think here of all of the parents of adolescents who take great satisfaction in the fact that their children are no longer on the streets involved in petty crime, drugs, or promiscuity, but safe at home, tucked away in their bedrooms, occupied with their televisions, stereos and computers, having discovered a virtual outlet for their antisocial, aggressive and sexual fantasies. Virtual reality has great appeal for the modern parent in that it provides a "safe" medium in which the most extreme parts of the adolescent psyche can find engagement, all within the safety of the home. The adolescent is no longer a disruption, he or she disappears into the horizon of family life.

With so many of our social institutions in a state of crisis, the adolescent's attraction to cyberspace can be understood in terms of the need for a holding environment. The World Wide Web tantalizes the adolescent with the illusion of being held in an environment that readily makes available the stability, safety and continuity that can no longer be found in many families, schools, or communities. Yet, the adequacy of cyberspace as a holding environment can be questioned, for even when things externally look better with some adolescents, that is, they are not in the community causing trouble, many parents are not clued into what is being constellated at the level of fantasy-images for the adolescent who comes home from school and spends the next seven hours immersed in cyberspace.

The greatest difficulty in parenting an adolescent is staying actively involved in the life of one's child while at the same time allowing her some level of privacy in order that she may experiment with her newly-gained freedom to move about in the world in adult-like ways. In this regard, Winnicott speaks of the parent's role in managing the adolescent's negotiation of the world outside of the family.

> In practice you can watch your adolescents graduating from one grouping to another, all the time widening the circle, all the time embracing new and more and more strange phenomena that society throws up. Parents are very much needed in the management of their own adolescent children who are exploring one social circle after another, because of their ability to see better than their children can when this progression from the limited social circle towards the unlimited social circle is too rapid... [Winnicott, 1963a, p. 92]

Parents are in danger of buying into the pro-social rhetoric promoting the new medias for the developing child and adolescent without recognizing that the necessity of helping their children negotiate the progression outward into an ever-expanding social universe is ever more acute in today's world. The video entertainment industry, the music industry, and the information superhighway represent the "unlimited" in terms of a child's access to highly potent and graphic sites and sounds that can amplify a child's personal fantasy life in ways whose sheer power and magnitude were, until recent times, inconceivable. Adolescents have always searched for outlets to feed their imagination in their struggles with sexuality and aggression, but given the speed and access offered by the new media the potential danger is of moving too rapidly toward the unlimited. Perhaps the world in small doses holds true in its own way for the developing adolescent as it does for the small child.

In the case of Eric Harris and Dylan Klebold, it is clear from the police reports that their parents had little awareness of the nature and extent of their participation in the "unlimited" world of cyberspace. In what follows I want briefly to outline their involvement.

Harris and Klebold were avid players of two popular computer games, "Doom" and "Quake", in which players stalk their opponents through dungeon-like environments and try to kill them with high-powered weapons. Known as first-person shooter games, they make the player the gun whose barrel manoeuvres through increasingly difficult levels. According to Colonel David Grossman, a former West Point Professor of Behavioral Sciences, "When you actually play the point-and-shoot games you are learning the motor skills to kill. You are being reinforced, you are being rewarded, not to passively accept the violence of others, but to inflict violence yourself" (Barry, 1991). Both these games are used by the American military to keep soldiers battle-ready. It is reported that both Harris and Klebold played "Doom" and "Quake", on average, three to four hours every day after school.

Harris also spent a lot of time on his own web site, where he created and displayed eerie drawings of shotgun and knife-toting monsters standing on a pile of skulls. Downloaded instructions for making the very pipe bombs that he eventually used to try to blow up Columbine were also found there. Both young men were fascinated with Hitler. They wore swastikas on their boots and their books and jackets were covered with Nazi symbols. The Internet gave them immediate access to neo-Nazi hate groups.

It is startling to realize that no one in their environment had any inkling of the extent to which their fantasy lives were so completely dominated by neo-Nazi images of hate and rage, bombs and explosions, semi-automatic assault rifles and games of slaughter. A case could be made that lying, cheating, stealing and shape-shifting are the basic fare of adolescent life, for adolescents depend on a kind of hermetic consciousness to keep parents at bay, so that they can protect and nurture what is still in potential, not yet ready for exposure. Winnicott speaks of this as the defence against being found before being there to be found (1963b). But the question we are now faced with is: how does a culture wholly saturated with simulation unleash the darker sides of adolescent concealment? What happens when adolescents make use of the virtual world as a place in which to disappear, becoming invisible to their parents and those around them? One of the most disturbing aspects of this case is how Harris and Klebold were able, for the span of one year, to immerse themselves so deeply in this fantasied act of destruction while carrying on with their everyday lives, undetected by everyone around them, including parents and teachers and friends.

It seems fairly clear from their comments and actions that, although undetected, they were seeking to contain this rage-filled world that dominated their lives through some kind of confrontation. In a videotape made a few weeks before the shooting, they spoke repeatedly of the times when they were almost caught. Harris spoke of the day an employee of Green Mountain Guns called his house and his father answered the phone. "Hey, your [gun] clips are in", the clerk said. His father replied that he hadn't ordered any clips and, as Harris retells it, did not ask whether the clerk had dialled the right number. "If either one had asked just one question," says Harris, "we would've been fucked." Adds Klebold, "We wouldn't be able to do what we're going to do" (Gibbs and Roche, 1999).

Klebold recounts the time his parents walked in on him when he was trying on his black leather trench coat, with his sawed-off shotgun hidden underneath: "They didn't even know it was there." Once, Harris recalls, his mother saw him carrying a gym bag with a gun handle sticking out of the zipper. She assumed it was a BB gun (*ibid*).

In school, Harris completed an assignment in which he was to write about an inanimate object by imagining himself as a shotgun shell and the massive destruction he would cause. The teacher was worried about the essay and wanted to discuss its violent content with Harris's father, but, after learning that Mr. Harris was a retired Air Force officer and that his son hoped to enlist in the military, she concluded that "the essay was consistent with his future career aspirations" (Gibbs, 1999).

The two tested the future Columbine bombs in Harris's garage. Neighbours heard the explosions, but said nothing about it. Harris states: "People fell for every lie. I could convince them that I'm going to climb Mount Everest, or I have a twin brother growing out of my back. I can make you believe anything" (Gibbs and Roche, 1999).

Both Harris and Klebold completed an eleven-month diversion programme for first-time juvenile offenders, after their arrest for breaking into a van and stealing a car stereo. In addition to community service, they successfully completed an anger management course. The following reports of the two counsellors involved in this programme provide testimony to Harris's chilling words: "I can make you believe anything" (Gibbs, 1999).

> Harris is a very bright young man who is likely to succeed in life. He is intelligent enough to achieve lofty goals as long as he stays on task and remains motivated. Klebold is a bright young man with a great deal of potential. If he is able to tap his potential and become self-motivated, he should do well in life. [*ibid.*]

Let us now compare this failure of the environment to take notice, make visible, and respond, with Winnicott's notion of the necessity of confrontation for the developing adolescent. He writes:

> In brief, it is exciting that adolescence has become vocal and active, but the adolescent striving that makes itself felt over the whole world today needs to be met, needs to be given reality by an act of confrontation. Confrontation must be personal. Adults are needed if adolescents are to have life and liveliness. Confrontation belongs to containment that is non-retaliatory, without vindictiveness, but having its own strength. [1968a, p. 150]

Following Winnicott, we note the inability of the adult world to give reality to the rage and alienation Harris and Klebold were feeling through some kind of personal confrontation. Anger management and community service only served to deepen their sense of alienation. There was a fundamental failure on the part of the parents, school and their local community to help them contain the rage and destructiveness which, in their fantasy life, seemingly knew no bounds.

The struggle to find the real

Winnicott points to the adolescent's struggle to feel real when he observes that adolescents often display a fierce and stubborn morality that urges them toward authenticity in their experience and makes them steadfastly refuse false solutions (Winnicott, 1961). In the twenty-first century, the struggle to feel real may well be recontextualized as the struggle to find the real. In his *Harper's Magazine* article, "The gun fire dialogues: notes on the reality of virtuality", Thomas de Zengotita, a teacher at the Dalton School in New York, brings together Nietzsche's sensitivity to the impact of culture on the human psyche with what it means to live in an increasingly simulated world He writes:

> Think of [the impact of culture on the human psyche] as do followers of Nietzsche among French intellectuals. The brain and its structures, the body and its desires, meet culture directly. Inclinations and thresholds are built into our neurochemistry, and stimulating content and forms of behavior are imposed by technologies of communication and the administration of daily life in routines of work and play. The more enveloping and penetrating the stimulations and routines, the more uniform and centerless the settings of our lives—and what else should we expect but occasional psychotic eruptions on a vast plain of disengagements sustained by an economy devoted to simulations? [De Zengotita, 1999]

Consider the experience of playing Doom three to four hours each and every day, where, as a first-person shooter, in an intensely graphic medium, one is encouraged to mow down one's enemies violently with a high power assault rifle; consider immersing oneself in neo-Nazi racist hatred, utilizing its style of language to attack on one's personal web page the individuals or groups that have become the objects of one's rage. At the same time as being immersed in this cyberworld of hate and destruction, Harris and Klebold followed the day-to-day existence of a high school life filled with drama clubs, bowling, proms, and parties. In the background is the world of adults who become easy targets of manipulation.

What is described here is a state of double consciousness which dramatically impacts upon the ability to maintain the boundary between what is real and what is not, a boundary already called into question by the transitional nature of adolescence, and further aggravated by the impact of the new technologies on the everyday sense of reality. As De Zengotita points out:

> These new technologies have as their explicit purpose making representations more and more realistic (think computer graphics

and animations) and making reality more and more representational (think Times Square and sanctioned graffiti). [*ibid.*]

To be in the transformational state of adolescence, no longer a child, not yet an adult, awakening to an upsurge of instinctuality that urges a flesh and blood encounter with the concrete reality of the world, but finding oneself in a post-literate world where simulated images envelop everything and everyone, can blur the distinction between fact and fantasy so that the awakening of adolescence can take place in a blur of unreality.

A sense of unreality was evident in the reactions of the students at Columbine who witnessed the commencement of Harris and Klebold's rampage. When the shooting began, many took it to be a game of paintball (an American military-style game where opposing teams shoot bullets of paint at each other). Others figured a movie was being filmed and wondered if they could play a part. It took a few long moments before it dawned upon these innocent bystanders that this was not a simulated act of violence: real guns were being used to shoot and kill real people.

Making contact with something real can become a key problem for the adolescent growing up in an environment where large portions of everyday life are spent engaging in simulated experiences that may call forth a disengaged and detached style of consciousness. With this in mind, we can consider that the actual attack on the school and its students may have been, at some level, a misguided attempt to break through into something real. In other words, I am proposing that, when looked at teleologically, Harris and Klebold's violent and bloody enactment can be seen as their desperate attempt to resolve what they experienced as a maddening split between the simulated world of games, guns, and explosions, and the actuality of their existence as embodied emotional beings.

Winnicott's essay "The use of an object and relating through identifications" explores the role of aggression in the transition from subjective omnipotence to the discovery of objective reality in early infancy (Winnicott, 1968b). The infant, in a state of subjective omnipotence, uses his mother "ruthlessly". Winnicott describes her as a subjective object, wholly under the infant's mental control. A transition occurs when frustration at maternal failure reaches a certain pitch, and the infant, in unconscious fantasy, damages his internal image of mother by attacking her. The mother's task is to hold the situation over time so that the infant can see, on a moment-to-moment basis, that she is different from the internal mother who is being unconsciously attacked. When the object is destroyed internally, in fantasy, and yet survives outside, the infant comes to the recognition that the object is not subject to his mental control. A new state emerges, what Winnicott refers to as "object usage", which revolves around the infant's dawning awareness of the limitations of his all-out destructive attacks, and the creation of a new mode for discovering the externality of the world and the use of its objects. What is at stake developmentally is the infant's opportunity to break out of a state of omnipotent fantasy, where the world is magically under his control, in order to encounter the actuality of the real.

At adolescence, the discovery of externality, the confrontation with the real, returns as a central dynamic. For Harris and Klebold, the fantasies surrounding guns, bombs and explosions which dominated their internal life, expressed the omnipotence they felt in unleashing their destructive rage against the world. The ferocity of this rage is particular to adolescence. "How shall each adolescent deal with something that really is new, the power to destroy and even to kill, a power which did not complicate the feelings of hatred that were experienced at the toddler age?" (Winnicott, 1961, p. 80).

When Winnicott speaks of the adolescent's need for a personal confrontation in response to this rage that is non-retaliatory and non-vindictive, yet possesses its own strength, I believe him to be indicating how the adolescent progresses beyond this period of the subjective object, where his own internal fantasies of omnipotent destructiveness create a dangerous fusion of fantasy and reality. For Harris and Klebold, to break free from this realm of omnipotent fantasy would be to see the difference between their destructiveness in fantasy, and the actual limits of their all-out destructive attacks. In writing of "the adolescent characteristic by which the good is not that which is handed down by parental benignity but that which is forced into being by adolescent destructiveness", Winnicott (1968c, p. 239) suggests that the use of an object is renegotiated in adolescence, such that adolescent aggression is what allows for the transition from subjective omnipotence (object-relating) to the discovery of the real (object-usage). From this perspective, we can now deepen our original inquiry about the effects of virtuality on the adolescent psyche by considering the adolescent's renegotiation of this developmental struggle in the context of a culture where the line between representation and reality is increasingly blurred. The push toward virtuality can have the unintended consequence of plunging the adolescent deeper into the realm of omnipotent fantasy, thus inhibiting the re-emergence from it that is the developmental task of this stage of life.

What happened to Harris and Klebold speaks to the vulnerability of the contemporary adolescent. It is not that exposure to cyberspace causes all adolescents to become mass murderers, but rather, that the extremity of Harris and Klebold's actions testify to how this separation between fantasy and the actual placing of objects outside the area of projection (*ibid.*) has become increasingly difficult. Immersion in the medium of virtuality, where anything and everything goes (no boundaries, no limits, total exposure) such that one's most primordial sexual and aggressive impulses are given "virtual" free rein, can be a real threat, perverting what Winnicott spoke of as the survival of the object, and staving off a personal confrontation where anger and feelings of destructiveness can be met, encountered, and made real. Such an element was wholly lacking in Harris and Klebold's relationships with the adult world. "If anyone had asked just one question," says Harris, "we would've been fucked" (Gibbs and Roche, 1999).

The fate of imagination in a virtual age

In the wake of the recent epidemic of school shootings, a crisis is underway in schoolrooms across America when children and adolescents, who are routinely given assignments involving the creation of stories and pictures, respond with narratives reflecting a fantasied expression of violence toward other people (murdering another student, teacher or parent), or violence toward property (blowing up the school, setting fire to their home). School officials, post-Columbine, no longer rest assured in the distinction between the exploration of such wishes in fantasy and a literal intention to enact them. The fate of the imagination in a virtual age denotes this crisis of symbolization at the border between fact and fantasy, the real and the imaginable.

Were Eric Harris to have seen a therapist, he would have had the space to describe his anger toward the school jocks who taunted and teased him, to admit to being obsessed with fantasies of bombing the school and shooting his classmates. The symbolization of these fantasies, their being given shape and form though suggestions about painting or drawing them, keeping an ongoing journal of what was most troubling to him, creating stories based upon his internal imagery of destructive explosions, or using video to tell the tale of blowing up the school and shooting his classmates, all could ultimately have provided the sort of act of containment that would mitigate the need for literal action. But what is so compelling about the case of Harris and Klebold is that without the prompting of a therapist, each of them did try, in precisely these ways, to give form and expression to their chaotic feelings. Harris was a prolific diarist, who kept an almost daily record of his thoughts and fantasies about the massacre. Five secret videotapes were made where the young men expressed the ferocity of the rage they felt in planning the massacre, as well as their empathic imaginings about the potential feelings of their parents and closest friends in the aftermath of the shootings. Also, as mentioned earlier, Harris had entered into the perspective of a shotgun shell, and envisioned the havoc he would wreak, in the short story written for English class. Finally, and most dramatically, they made a tape for their video-production course in which they filmed the story of the Columbine High School massacre.

Of course, engaging these fantasies in the space of a therapeutic relationship is very different from engaging them on one's own, but, even so, in the light of these events, my interest is in thinking about the possible effects that living in a virtual age may have upon the adolescent's capacity for symbolization. With adolescence comes an increased capacity and appetite for entering into larger-than-life narratives through books, movies or music that symbolize unconscious ideas, conflicts and wishes. By immersing themselves imaginatively in these symbolically laden narratives and vicariously experiencing the events therein, a catharsis, in the Aristotelian sense of purging, occurs. Symbolization in adolescence is linked to this. Psychoanalytically speaking, it is a kind of abreaction in which unconscious conflicts are discharged, thus moderating the compulsion literally to act out one's deepest fantasies. In this sense, the cathartic function, in which the symbolic and imaginative dimensions of the mind offer a means for releasing powerful impulses and affects, serves as a crucial substitute for action.

This link between symbolization and catharsis is pathologically affected in the present because, potentially, the adolescent imagination can become saturated with images of a virtual world: Game Boys, Nintendos, web site chat rooms, music videos, that can encourage the collapse of potential space in the life of the adolescent, such that dream-space, as a province of inner reality, can no longer perform its containing function. When this happens, as Masud Khan points out, there is a greater tendency for individuals to exploit social space to act out their dreams and fantasies (Khan, 1974). *The Columbine High School Massacre Story*, written, directed and produced by Harris and Klebold, was not a viable mode for symbolizing their rageful fantasy, and the question arises as to why, in their case, it was further enacted with real guns, real blood and real death.

In order to probe further the impact of simulation on the inner world of the adolescent, let us turn to Freud and listen to his cautionary statements concerning the hallucinatory revival of instinctual wishes expressed in dreams, as if they were cautionary statements about virtual reality. For Freud, the dream-work, which he considers to be the essence of the dream, consists of a series of mental operations (condensation, displacement, and symbolization) which constitute the primary processes. These unconscious mental operations, governed by the pleasure principle, work to reduce the unpleasure of instinctual tension by hallucinatory wish fulfilment. "Dreams are things which get rid of (psychical stimuli) disturbing sleep, by the method of hallucinatory satisfaction" (Freud, 1915–1916, p. 136).

Ricoeur contends that what Freud (1900) was wrestling with in his famous chapter seven of *The Interpretation of Dreams* was the indestructibility of the primary system. "Regression, of which dreams are the witness and model" (Ricoeur, 1970, p. 113), reveals man's inability to go beyond this principle completely.

> That this is indeed the most basic intention of the "psychology" is confirmed by the place given to repression in the final pages. The place is not an indifferent one. Freud's final analysis of repression

comes immediately after his pessimistic remarks about the belated appearance of the secondary system as compared with the primary system: repression is the ordinary operational mode of a psychism condemned to making a late appearance and being prey to the infantile, the indestructible. [Ricoeur, pp. 112–113]

Freud describes the dream as a compromise structure in which primitive impulses are given hallucinatory satisfaction, the dreamer remains sleeping, and the censor is always on the alert. Because the psyche is prey to the infantile and the indestructible, Freud approaches the dream with great caution, and a sense of restraint, as if this whole compromise structure could easily become undone, thus setting free the regression brought upon by the dream freely to wreak havoc in our psychic lives. The regressive movement in dreams is animated by a longing for the primitive stage of hallucinatory wishing, where our most primordial desires find satisfaction. Freud describes the wishes that give rise to the dream:

> One can only say that they are invariably of a reprehensible nature, repulsive from the ethical, aesthetic and social point of view—matters which one does not venture to think at all or thinks only with disgust. These wishes, which are censored and given a distorted expression in dreams, are first and foremost manifestations of an unbridled and ruthless egoism...
>
> The ego, freed from all ethical bonds, also finds itself at one with all the demands of sexual desire, even those which have long been condemned by our aesthetic upbringing and those which contradict all the requirements of moral restraint. The desire for pleasure—the "libido" as we call it—chooses its objects without inhibition. [Freud, 1915–1916, p. 142]

Freud further characterizes these wishes as rages without restraint, expressing powerful hatred. Whenever someone gets in the way, the dream is ready to kill that person (think here of Harris and Klebold's manhunt during the rampage to kill the jocks who wronged them). Freud also describes wishes for revenge and death that are directed against those with whom one is most intimately involved in waking life (think of 16-year-old Kip Kingel, another recent perpetrator of school violence, who, in cold blood, murdered his mother and father as a prelude to his shooting rampage at high school).

Freud attunes us to an important dimension of dream life through his description of the dream as a defensive compromise in which instinctual desire finds expression in a quasi-worldly frame of time and space. Dreaming evokes a period of functioning when wish becomes reality through hallucination, or what, for Freud, is the originary experience of wishful satisfaction, when the object no longer appeared but was hallucinated. Thus, the medium of the dream, in its plasticity and fluidity, is unique in its ability to make possible the enactment of our most primordial stirrings of omnipotence, rage, sexuality and destructiveness, in a context where reality and fantasy are nearly indistinguishable (Freud, 1900).

I am proposing that virtual reality, in its world-creating capacity, could also give access to the unleashing of the very same impulses to which Freud refers. We can think of virtual reality as appearing to hold open a space which compels us to enact, in "real time", the essence of the primary process, that is, instantaneous wish fulfilment. Yet, because it is a "virtual" satisfaction of a wish, where the object does not appear, but is hallucinated, the very border between the real and the imaginary, fact and fantasy, waking and dreaming, is severely distorted. If this be the case, an adolescent's immersion in a virtual world could be a narcotic nightmare.

Winnicott offers a further elaboration of the regressive dimensions of the imaginary through his distinction between "fantasying" and "fantasy" (Winnicott, 1971). Winnicott does not assume that all fantasy productions have equal value, or that fantasy is always to be valued as an end in itself. He designates the term "fantasying" for an activity whose aim is not to restore psychic balance but to inhibit it, to use one's inner life as a retreat to deny the world. He reserves the term "fantasy" for the creative expression of the imagination, which, in its containing and vitalizing function, enriches, enlivens and animates our sense of the real.

Winnicott traces the fantasy/fantasying divide to early impingements upon the infant–mother dyad. I am proposing that the relationship to the regressive dimensions of the imaginary comes to the fore again in adolescence. When virtuality becomes the environmental provision for this adolescent renegotiation, its tendency toward detachment, passivity, and derealization can promote a relationship to one's inner world more closely aligned with fantasying than with a connection to what is real. When wishes demanding satisfaction find hallucinatory fulfilment in virtual reality, fantasy loses contact with the real, and no longer functions as a container for instinctual desire. Fantasy, disjoined from its instinctual roots, is partially incapacitated; the capacity to produce images is still there, but when fantasy is prevented from transforming into imagination, its containing and vitalizing function in relation to these images is blocked.

In this regard the internal world of intense hatred and ultra-violence in which Harris and Klebold found themselves was a secret world, well hidden from parents, teachers and friends. So secret, in fact, that we earlier described them as living in a state of double consciousness, in which a barrier kept what was happening in the life of fantasy cordoned off from what was happening to them in the course of their everyday life. This barrier was evidenced by their ability to be completely immersed in the intense world of homicidal and suicidal fantasies that led up to executing the attack, at the same time as Klebold visited, applied for, and was enrolled in a college for the following fall, and Harris had plans to enter the military. A dissociation holds fantasy and reality apart.

Overexposure to the world of cyberspace, disengaged as it is from the flesh and blood reality of bodily life, strengthens the hold of fantasying (in Winnicott's sense) on the personality. Virtuality partially disables the imagination by entrapping it in the bodiless world of images, ultimately creating a state of emptiness and unfulfilment which compulsively seeks gratification by ingesting ever more images. For Harris and Klebold, an intensified hunger for ever more highly graphic and charged imagery, a ravenousness for the image, results in an apotheosis of Hitler, the KKK, images of bombs, explosions and pyrotechnics.

Conclusion: the yearning for catharsis

In their many attempts to symbolize their feelings of anger and hatred, rather than enact them, Harris and Klebold may have struggled with the reality of their feelings of rage and their fantasies of omnipotence. In turning to how the Columbine tragedy ended, we take note of Harris and Klebold's shocking discovery of the difference between the expression of their destructive rage in fantasy, and its actual enactment in shooting and killing other human beings. Their original scheme did not work. They had planned to come in after a huge explosion, having placed bombs all around the school, so that their own shootings would merely complement the destruction and death caused by the bombs. But the bombs did not go off, and what started, with giddiness and glee, as a manic shooting rampage, ended much sooner than planned. The rampage could have continued for two more hours before SWAT teams arrived, but after forty-five minutes, Harris and Klebold returned to the school library where it all began. In reading the detective's report that describes their last moments, we can sense the despair that overcame them as they realized that the explosions and killings that had just taken place could never match the intensity of destruction, havoc and mayhem that took place in fantasy.

> The gunmen fired a few more rounds out the window at cops and medics below. Then Klebold placed one final Molotov cocktail, made from a Frapuccino bottle, on a table. As it fizzled and smoked, Harris shot himself, falling to the floor. Klebold shot himself, seconds later. [Gibbs and Roche, 1999]

Part of the tragedy of Columbine is the yearning for catharsis in the lives of Harris and Klebold. Not even the unleashing of primitive rage against their fellow classmates with semi-automatic weapons and pipe bombs could bring about an experience of cathartic release. These last moments read like a dream: When the final Molotov cocktail fizzles rather than explodes, Harris and Klebold shoot themselves. As if suicide were the ultimate grasping after catharsis, a catharsis that did not come in the wake of a one-year immersion in fantasies of omnipotent destruction, or in forty-five minutes of enacting them at the level of reality.

Harris and Klebold were searching to make contact with something real, something substantial, that would free them from the psychotic world of omnipotent fantasy. In one of their more grandiose moments, they detailed their plan, in the aftermath of the massacre, to hi-jack a plane, crash it into New York City, thus causing the city itself to blow up. Once again, we can understand this as a desire to break through into something vital and real: as if the bombs and the shooting were not enough, the destruction of New York City would be the final guarantor of a catharsis.

The absence of a grounded connection to the real, which for Winnicott is a normal aspect of adolescent development, corresponds to the feelings of unreality associated with psychotic depression (Winnicott, 1961). This is exacerbated by our contemporary struggle to differentiate what is virtual and what is real. In its most extreme form, we need only to recall the state of derealization that accompanied Harris and Klebold's shooting, at point blank range, their fellow classmates, as if they were no different from the bloodless characters populating the video screen.

Such reflections encourage a sensitivity to the predicament of the contemporary adolescent who is immersed in a culture of simulation, where the balance between image, instinct and world has been radically transformed. Being trapped in a simulated world of fantasying intensifies the struggle to make emotional contact with what feels alive and real. Fantasying offers the illusion of liveliness and vitality, yet one remains passive, untouched and unchanged by such engagement. Fantasy-images at the level of virtuality lose their power for cathartic transformation.

Let us compare Winnicott's notion that the destructive forces inherent to the infant's fantasy life are what allows it to break out of the world of subjective objects and make contact with the real, to the practice of puberty rites in traditional cultures. In such rites, physical tests of endurance, as well as circumcisions, knocking out a tooth, or scarring the body, enact a symbolizing process whereby penetration or modification of the child's body brings forth a new awareness of life (Bettelheim, 1962). In both cases, it is a shattering of the self-enclosed, solipsistic world of fantasy that releases an imagination which is in touch with a far greater reality.

If we understand Harris and Klebold's actions of blowing up their school, killing their classmates, and killing themselves as an unconscious desire to break free from the world of omnipotent fantasy and make contact with the real, can we then further hypothesize that the greater the need to get at what is real, the more extreme the act? In this context, we may well read the violent and bloody enactments currently scattered across the landscape of America as the adolescent's urge to break free from entrapment in virtual reality by concretizing the destructive forces inherent to fantasy life. In other words, it may be seen as an attempt to free the imagination from its fixation on the images of a virtual world. In the end, does it take an encounter with real blood and real bodies to finally force upon them the meaning of the real?

Winnicott asks whether society has the health to meet adolescence and help to contain it (Winnicott, 1961). The current epidemic of adolescent violence leads me to conclude that in contemporary times the answer is no. If the recent spate of school shootings may be seen as an expression of how adolescents in our culture experience the shadows of a virtual age, then careful study of the adolescent psyche could provide us with clues to where, as a culture, we are most conflicted, most ill. In being a witness to this suffering we cannot help but uncover those parts of our own psyche that are most anaesthetized to the impact of the massive technological, social and political changes of our current era, and thus, the fate of the adolescent becomes the fate of ourselves.

Note

1. That this cultural unconscious is also a potent, potentially exploitable reservoir of energy is also recognized by the advertising industry, which employs "cool hunters" to track down what is happening with today's teenager and uses this knowledge to set standards for the fashion, music and television industries. See Gladwell, M. "The Coolhunt", *The New Yorker*, 17 March 1977.

CHAPTER NINE

"I like my life, I just like my life": narratives of children of latency years

Amal Treacher

Aspects of contemporary cultural theory focus on biography and autobiography, in terms both of collecting oral histories and of the production of the life story. Alongside these documentations lie theorizations of life histories and autobiographical narratives. Both the telling of lives and their theorizations, however, centre on adults and their fantasies, memories and confessions, on how adults make sense of their past and present. A common assumption in this work is that childhood is the raw material for adult life; it is that which is reworked, understood, and, retrospectively, narrativized. The implication is that children themselves do not develop autobiographical narratives culled and reworked from the fantasies and memories of their families and from available cultural accounts.

I am interested in challenging this, in collecting children's autobiographies through documenting and theorizing their narratives of themselves, others, family life, and their relation to the social and cultural worlds they inhabit. I use social and cultural theory and an object relations view of psychoanalysis as theoretical points of reference. My interest is in how children speak about and imagine their lives, and thus give voice to their own developing autobiographies. I explore the emotional and social dynamics that come to bear on their subjectivity. The work that forms the basis for this article comes from interviews with children aged between seven and eleven, an age group that has been largely neglected theoretically and about which there is little detailed knowledge. The children come from a newly built school with approximately two hundred pupils. The classes for the seven- and eight-year-olds have had the same cohort of pupils throughout, while the class for the nine-year-olds has a history of continually taking in new pupils, frequently refugees. These pupils were very aware of this. In this section of the study I interviewed eight children, four boys and four girls, of different ethnic groupings. Each was interviewed on three separate occasions. The first session was based on documenting their family stories; in the second I used a story stem as the basis for their own elaboration of a family day; in the third I listened to them finish off a story about a baby searching for a family. Crayons, pencils, paper and plasticine were on the table throughout; some children drew at length, others did not.

Narrative theory—Cavarero and Winnicott

Winnicott did not theorize a self that narrates, or the place of narratives in self-identity, but I am extrapolating from his work to draw out possible interpretations of latency-aged children and the place of narrative in their lives. Winnicott was concerned, however, with the conditions necessary for the true self to find spontaneous expression. Health and the capacity to know and find expression for the creative self depend upon being in touch with the core of that self. An essential aspect of the healthy individual is the capacity to make spontaneous gestures that can be perceived and received by another human being. Part of the purpose of speaking one's narrative is to reach out to others and to express connections with them. In doing so, there is some expression of the true self, but the individual has to have a capacity to enter and make use of a transitional space to allow this. Winnicott recognizes the necessary dependence of persons on others, and sees the self as constituted in relationship with and through others. All involved contribute to and participate in the creation of the authentic narrative spoken.

The transitional space between self and other is necessary for the individual to find itself, a discovery that can only occur when the person can move away from and still be in touch with the first other, the mother.

Seven-year-old Jenny declared with verve during her interview, "I like my life; I just like my life. I don't know what to say except that I like it!" The contemporary Italian philosopher, Adriana Cavarero, asserts, and perhaps Winnicott would have concurred, that stories are there because life is full and rich with events, thoughts, feelings and meanings. There are theoretical similarities between Winnicott and Cavarero on the self, other and narration (Cavarero, 2000), especially in the use Cavarero makes of the work of the German philosopher, Hannah Arendt. Arendt was concerned with issues of freedom, with individuals' moral culpability, and with the importance of acting on, and agency in, the public arena. Arendt and Winnicott were both preoccupied with, and passionate about matters of life and living. Arendt, writes Kristeva, was caught up in a passion "in which *life* and *thought* are one and the same, her varied yet profoundly coherent intellectual odyssey never ceased to place *life*—in and of itself, and as a concept to be elucidated—at the centre" (2001, p. 3). It is the life of the mind that is essential to Arendt's conceptualizations, fundamental to which is a self that "is an embodied self" (Jacobitti, 1997, p. 203).

Winnicott argued throughout his work that the self is situated critically through its relationships with others and this is the theoretical and ethical belief that Cavarero pursues with such vigour in her explorations of the "narratable self". The "narratable self" is a self that is exposed to and formed from the beginning "within the interactive scene of the world" (Kottman, 2000, p. ix). Because of this interactive and deeply social context the self is "exposed to, and narratable by, another" (Kottman, 2000, p. xvii). It is not just that we are vulnerable to the other's stories of us, but that the self and a sense of self-identity is utterly dependent on the other for its existence.

Cavarero (2000) argues that as human beings we need the other person both to give us back our story and to tell us our narrative: we are nothing without the other. It has been often repeated that Winnicott believes there is no such thing as a baby, a statement through which he argues for the centrality of relationships between self and other. He and Cavarero thus share an emphasis on the idea of a human being as requiring the other, either to tell us our story (Cavarero) or to witness our being (Winnicott). From different theoretical positions and interests they insist upon the other as crucial for the discovery and sustenance of the self. The self and narrative are understood as profoundly social.

It has become a commonplace within the social sciences to argue "that the activity of being human is intricately tied to the activity of telling and listening to stories" (Andrews, 2000, p. 77), that is, that human beings are "storied selves". We understand the world we inhabit through the narratives told; we *are* the narratives we tell. In one theoretical framework, it is not that we use stories to express ourselves, but rather that narratives speak through us. From a social constructionist viewpoint, Bruner argues that "we *become* the autobiographical narratives by which we 'tell about' our lives" (Bruner, 1987, p. 15). Linguistic and cultural conventions not only determine how we tell our narratives and what is emphasized, but more that these narratives form the essence of who we are, and what we experience and perceive.

With a different emphasis Lévi-Strauss argues that the narratives that form the basis of myth are social and function to bind groups of people together. They constitute a form of imaginative living that assists us in coming to terms with the social world (Levi-Strauss, 1994). Myths are held in people's minds and, while they are not necessarily aware of them, their narratives provide a means to express individual dilemmas through social language and belief systems.

Both these theoretical perspectives share the view of narrative as social. First, we derive the stuff of our own narratives from the society and the cultural period that we inhabit, and the family history that we inherit. Second, narratives themselves involve reaching out to others to connect to them and express our attachments to them. For Cavarero, and for seven-year-old Jenny, telling and listening to our own stories and those of others happens because life is lively and there is a wish to celebrate, know and understand the very uniqueness of others and ourselves.

While for some narrative theorists the life as lived coincides with the life as told (Seale, 1998), for others who draw on psychoanalysis to conceptualize subjectivity, the relationship of narrative and lived experience is more complex (Craib, 2000). For the latter:

[N]arratives come in many kinds; they are contradictory and fragmented; there is no such thing as a coherent story. There is also, in the aftermath of grand "narratives" of the social and political order, and in a time of identifications rather than identities, no entirely firm sociocultural ground from which to tell stories. [Andrews, 2000, p. 8]

This coincides with a more general psychoanalytic viewpoint that asserts that "human subjectivity itself is diverse and fragmented, and carries within it the pushes and pulls of various available narratives" (Andrews, 2000, p. 9).

Bollas (1995) describes health as based on two major capacities: being able to move across temporal zones, and being able to disseminate experience. Through the capacities for movement across temporality, fantasy, thought and feeling, and the potential they offer for the dissemination of experience, the narrative/s can convey both what Bollas (1986) has termed "the idiom of the individual", and what Winnicott sees as the expression of what is spontaneous and creative. Day Sclater attributes to Winnicott the view that meanings are "emotional and relational", they are "never fixed or unified, but [are] fluid, shifting and multiple" (Sclater, 1998). Such an emphasis on the human subject implies a particular account of narrative because of its consideration of the unconscious and its place in subjective life. It acknowledges a gap between the narrative of the life and the life as lived. It is not that the narrative represents a "false self", but that it is contingent both on what is available from social and cultural positioning and from the fraught psychic processes within.

Most theoretical work on children of mid-school years conceptualizes them as in the process of consolidating cognitive capacities, perceptions and affects. Both psychoanalytic accounts and those of developmental psychology suggest that little of interest is going on within the minds of children of this age group. For example, for Margot Waddell (1998) latency is a place and space between the turbulence and "primitive" state of mind of infancy and early childhood and the sexually troublesome challenges and difficulties of pubescence and adolescence. This time of life is a period when children are moving across from the family into the outside world and exploring the world beyond the family from a place of security.[1]

Winnicott wrote little specifically on the period of latency, describing it as a stage in life in which:

> the development of instinct ceases, so that for the time being the child is left with an instinctual life based on what has been built up in the earlier period... Whatever else may be said about the latency period, it seems fairly clear that there are big defences organized and maintained. [Winnicott, 1958, p. 118]

In his writings more generally, however, a view of the latency child as developing into an individual who is able to play, create and explore the world outside of the family from the secure base of home can be discerned. Children of this age group are likely to be moving from dependency on the family to wanting more independence, exploring school, friendships and creating a life outside (Winnicott, 1963a). They are increasingly aware of the environment; many become vegetarian, concerned with the welfare of animals, others are concerned with people more materially deprived than themselves. For Winnicott, maturity involves the capacity to attend to personal needs without being antisocial, "independence is never absolute. The healthy individual does not become isolated, but becomes related to the environment in such a way that the individual and the environment can be said to be interdependent" (1963a, p. 84).

One of the main emotional processes of this period is coming to terms with the necessity of relatedness and relationships with others. Since this entails understanding another's personal, separate existence, it may only reluctantly be worked towards. Initially it is the Oedipus complex that entails discovering and coming to terms with the complexity of living (Bollas, 1993). This is not only a matter of having to accept parental passion and an inevitable exclusion from an aspect of the parents' relationship; it involves the child's discovery that s/he has a mind and that others have one too. For Bollas, maturity has to involve the movement from being in a dilemma (two-person relationship) to inhabiting a life that is complex (many relationships). This process is consolidated during the latency period through an increasing knowledge of the me/not-me boundary.

Developmental psychology, with its emphasis on the unfolding mechanisms of cognition, language and perception, assumes the smooth progression from the "immaturity" of childhood to the "maturity" of adulthood. There is no such smooth progression in psychoanalytic theory since fantasy, affect, and relationships with others all contribute to its account of the formation of subjectivity. In psychoanalysis, latency is thought of both as a stage in development and a mental state, which share characteristics and processes. Meltzer (1973) describes latency less as a stage in life, and more as a possible state of mind distinguished by the following characteristics: the need to master; the need to be in control; the wish to be challenged and stretched through the acquisition of knowledge. Here, latency is perceived as a time of balance and a space dominated by a quest for "joined-up writing", where "joined-up writing" can be interpreted both as an actual wish for adult writing, and as a metaphor for an internal self that can be linked and coherent.

Children and narrative—stories held and stories told

The children I interviewed were completely engaged in speaking their stories and talking about their experiences, friendships and relationships with their siblings. They spoke energetically and seemed to desire the act of narration and the pleasure of telling stories, especially the girls. They interspersed their narratives with asides: eight-year-old Jason spoke about the excitement of pretending to be someone else, adding, "it can be spooky". They wanted fun and pursued it purposefully. Part of their pleasure in being interviewed or in the interview itself seemed to derive from being singled out for special treatment although they were also pleased to avoid part of the relentless timetable of school. None of the girls spoke directly about being or feeling special but two boys did: one about feeling he had been chosen by God, who always answered his prayers, the other because I had chosen him to be interviewed.

At this time of life, school is increasingly a space where children can explore how they and others fit in and build up an awareness of groups and how they function. Children will talk at length with friends, as they did with me, about other children, teachers and adults. But they also expressed their independence from parents and teachers, thereby marking a different phase of life with different needs and desires. These moves towards independence can also evoke anxiety, as the child negotiates and comes to terms with the challenges of school, clubs and friendships (Waddell, 1998). Along with a growing awareness of the world they live in, this age group is also struggling with difference, so that the forming and sustaining of friendships requires the support, though not necessarily the active intervention, of adults. Rachael spoke about her teacher's advice as being supportive in helping her to gain some space from her best friend and enabling the friendship to continue without too many disagreements. Alex appreciated his parent's interventions with his rather bossy but younger sister.

In these interviews, the peer group and siblings were the central reference. For two boys and for all the girls, it was friends who were important; the family was barely mentioned. For example, Alex described the pleasures of being with his tight-knit friendship group. It was clear that his investment in James Bond films was only partly because of his own delight in watching them; the films and computer games also gave him a point of contact with other boys. He spoke with commitment about enacting scenes from the films or playing the computer games with them. The girls talked about joys and difficulties with friends; Rachael described how she has to walk away from her best friend to "get some air and to calm down". She saw this as necessary to sustain the friendship.

The concern with their peer group, with maintaining friendships and with their siblings was the most notable area of these interviews and it represents a very different emphasis from that of Walkerdine's work on stories in girls' magazines, undertaken in the early 1980s. There she identifies the preoccupation with the family and a continual concern with the other, whether boys, friends or family. She notes that mothers in particular had to be persistently attended to and kept in mind and that the girls had to suppress their aggression. Two characteristics stand out in her account of these written stories: being selfless, and being good and nice. Walkerdine sees these stories as preparing the way for future family life by shifting the girl's desires towards it (Walkerdine, 1990).

There was no sense of this in the narratives of my interviewees. Rather, they show that these children are preoccupied with and invest in their *current* lives, specifically with friends at school and outside it. There is no mention of future family life. Current family life is focused on siblings who generated much talk and feelings ranging from affection to annoyance. Three children did talk about the family as a valuable source of comfort and seemed to take it for granted, but the siblings generated the real energy in their stories. When Alex drew his sister first in his family map, she appeared as a rather large figure dominating the page. When he began to draw his father he was much smaller. Alex commented on this and started again, and his father was again the much smaller figure. Alex, who was skilled at drawing, commented that here he could not get the perspective right. But at another level he was quite accurate about his relationship with and his feeling towards his sibling.

Five of the eight children interviewed spoke about their parents' relationships with their siblings and told family stories about arguments and play between brothers and sisters.

For the third session, when they were asked to construct a family day, they all had their family spend the day outside home and they cast themselves as the motivators and generators of action and excitement. All the girls spoke about the pleasure of movement and the joy of being in their bodies, about the school sports day and about playground activity, about enjoying running, playing "dip-dip-do", dancing, singing and the satisfaction of jumping and playing group games. The boys did not speak directly about this but observation of them in the playground—running and fighting with one another—illustrates their obvious gratification in physical activity.

Although adults were in the background of the narratives, there were crucial differences in how the parents were represented when they were mentioned. Fathers were described as fun and encouraging, and they initiated ideas although they were not present in the action. Mothers were relegated to making suggestions for lunch, dismissed as ineffectual, or were totally absent. It was children of the same age group who solved the danger and near death scenarios in their stories. Rachael, a nine-year-old, did produce a woman who helped the children back to the shore at a very late stage in her narrative of risk. The only other point where an adult had a part in a story of high peril was when I intervened anxiously with a nervous, "Where are the adults?" Eight-year-old Ayisha responded with a half-hearted part sentence as a sop to my fretting, but once this was done, she was off, following her own curiosity and a peer-centred narrative.

The attention to siblings and peer group relationships in these interviews has some similarities to Juliet Mitchell's recent account of the importance of horizontal relationships—for children, siblings and peer groups; in adult life, partners and colleagues (Mitchell, 2000). She argues these relationships should not replace our understanding of parental relationship, but that they too must be considered in an understanding of subjectivity.

The interviews also recognized some of the pain and complexity of their lives, and two children expressed disappointment and frustration with their families, especially their fathers. Jenny, whose parents are separated, spoke openly about feeling neglected: "He forgot my birthday and did not even buy me a present." He "does not behave like a normal Dad, who buys things and comes home from work. He dumped my Mum." She then quoted her mother saying that the father "is selfish". Nine-year-old Kareem told me that when his father plays with him it can turn "rough" but it is difficult to tell his father to try to be gentler. He hoped he would not treat his children like that, but would always love and be responsive towards them. This theme also emerged in the session on a family day out, when two children spoke about families not loving their children enough, of neglecting and abandoning them, and allowing them to wander the countryside, lost and alone. Their accounts were unsentimental and their frankness illustrated them inhabiting life on many different levels, able to verbalize contradictory fantasies and feelings. These children are well aware of the complexity and reality of lived family life and of parental strengths and vulnerabilities. They have a knowledge of reality and move easily across the boundaries within and without the family.

The transformational use of narratives and the other

Winnicott (1996) argues that fantasy serves a twofold purpose: it is a way of imagining a different past or present *and* it is a way of coming to terms with "reality" in all its complexity. Warner (1994) describes the verb "to wonder" as "[it] communicates the receptive state of marvelling as well as the active desire to know, to inquire and as such it defines very well at least two characteristics of the traditional fairy tale: pleasure in the fantastic, curiosity about the real" (p. xvi). She adds that it is through the unreality of the fairy tale that glimpses of other possibilities can occur. This marvelling and wanting to know applied equally to these children's fantasies as they appeared in their narratives. For Warner dreaming "gives pleasure in its own right, but it also represents a practical dimension of the imagination, an aspect of the faculty of thought, and can unlock social and public possibilities" (p. xvi). For example, seven-year-old Jenny told a story about herself and her mother being very very rich, so she could have many pets, cats, dogs, ponies, lots of horses, and live in a grand house with huge grounds so they could comfortably house them all. Then she described her grandparents, who own a shop and struggle to make ends meet. She was very aware and concerned about them, but her disquiet lay alongside her fantasy of material wealth. As Wallace Stevens states, it helps us to see the actual world if we can visualize a fantastic one (quoted in Warner, 1994, p. xvi).

Their stories revealed these children wanting to accept their lives but also wanting to transform them. They spoke about their lives without rancour or disappointment, with pleasure and, at times, with a wry humour. At other times they seemed to express a wish for things to be different. The girls used their narratives to transform the everyday into something quite other. Both the narrative itself and another human being, the interviewer, were used to transform their sense of self and in this way to function as a kind of "transformational object", to use a term of Bollas. He argues that the mother's transformation of the infant's environment by nurturing and attending to its needs is a transformation we seek to re-experience throughout adult life (1986).

The girls and boys approached fantasy and imagination differently, with the girls more able to incorporate violence and destruction into their accounts. Their enjoyment of aggression, thrill, near-death adventures, and murderous fantasies of killing and destruction was missing from the boys' accounts. Perhaps this difference has some relation to socially endorsed values of boys' and girls' behaviour. For girls the aggression in a narrative could be seen as an expression of something felt but not allowed articulation elsewhere, an assertion of longed-for but out-of-reach independence.

The use of the other and the object to identify with, and speak through, seemed to work differently too, so that it seemed easier for the girls to inhabit a character and use the pronoun "I". They seemed more able to get inside their characters and draw out their narratives through the protagonist. For boys the identification was more distanced, for instance, when they relayed blow-by-blow accounts of a film. The girls used names, either of known people or invented characters, whereas the boys avoided this and spoke with a sense of detachment about their family members or their invented characters.

The girls were much more fantastic in their narratives and they seemed to find it easier to play. Like the boys they used popular culture, but they used it differently. They spoke about songs and music, they sang themselves, and one girl danced. The boys did not use song, music or dance. Ayisha put together two different characters from two different soaps so seamlessly that it took me a while to understand what she was doing. The girls' narratives, full of fantasy and excitement, seemed to be imagining something quite other as a way of exploring their personal and social relations. These fantasies illustrated how the girls, at this period of life, wished to be active agents, and represented themselves as the pivot of the narratives.

The school had recently had an outing to Southend and all the girls used this day at the seaside to develop stories that were full of danger, threats and rescue: being stranded at sea; being helped by benign dolphins who turn into malevolent sharks; having an easy time swimming then finding themselves in a terrific and terrifying storm. They transformed an ordinary school outing, and themselves, into something extraordinary, something quite other. In this way, their imaginings enabled them to conceive of themselves as special and different. Their narratives were located in wide interior and exterior vistas, their range of emotions was extensive, and their external landscapes changed rapidly from something recognizable to a space that could be anywhere, anytime. These girls' narratives used phantasy as that which exceeds the social and as that which cannot be contained by social and cultural constraints (Rose, 1998).[2] The boys did not express their phantasies in the same way at all; through observing them in the playground however, it seemed as if it were through action rather than words, that they asserted themselves and expressed their attachments to their peer group.

As indicated earlier, this is a particular moment in development where children need to forge an adult-free world to attain autonomy and a sense of self. All these narratives separated out self and other, especially them and their parents. There were obviously numerous dynamics in operation and it may be that mothers especially are internalized so profoundly that, paradoxically, they are not worthy of mention precisely because of their importance for identity. In conjunction with the assertion of independence and aggression, there was much emphasis on concern; for example, Rachael spoke about not being too loud at social events as she should look after others, and Alex spoke about wanting to give money to a friend of his who was much poorer.

The children were involved in recounting their attachments and connections with others even as they were caught up with the act of narration itself. They seemed to want both the story itself and their enthusiasm for telling it to be witnessed. They were quite assertive about their right to choose to speak about which topic and when, and they protected their privacy. One seven-year-old boy frequently replied, "I do not know", which I understood belatedly as his way of safeguarding his private space. I was reminded of Winnicott's assertion that there is a part of all of us that does not want to be known or found.

For Cavarero and Arendt the self is elusive and cannot be known, while for Winnicott the catastrophe is both that we will never be known and/or that we will be discovered and known before we are ready. As Adam Phillips puts it, Winnicott's core catastrophe is "the annihilation of the core self by intrusion, a failure of the holding environment" (1988, p. 149). Children as well as adults have contradictory needs to be known and to be private. Simultaneously with the profound need to avoid intrusion from the other, the other is needed to reflect back our self and also to sustain our very self—"a sophisticated game of hide-and-seek in which *it is joy to be hidden but disaster not to be found*" (Winnicott, 1963b p. 186, italics in original).

For the other is also used for the self to appear—for both Cavarero and Winnicott the self can paradoxically only appear in the gaze of others. As Cavarero argues, the self is always in a constitutive relation *with* the other (2000, p. 88). It is not just that the self is formed through the constitutive relationship with the other; it is that "the relation with the other is necessary for her very self-designation as unique" (Cavarero, 2000, p. 89). This is no homage to interiority but, as with Winnicott, an attention to the reciprocity between human beings. For Arendt, our promises to others are essential to our sense of self-identity, for if "we were isolated selves, capable only of self-reflection, we would become lost in the confusion of our inner experiences—of conflicting feelings, motives, capacities, thoughts, needs and projects" (Jacobitti, 1997, p. 209). For the children in these specific interviews, the necessary reciprocal relationships were centred on their peer group and friendships.

Cavarero argues that we all desire our own story and simultaneously use others, both to hear their stories and thereby locate our own. Whether adults or children, we use narrative and others in order to locate ourselves and to assert our uniqueness. In this account, other human beings and narrative are used to assert and to transform life. Simultaneously with this, there is the wish for relatedness and reparation (emphasized by Waddell (1998) as characteristic of mid-childhood). Children use themselves for creativity, connections and sustaining good things such as relationships with others and internal good objects. Throughout these very enjoyable interviews, the children expressed their capacities to identity with others, to communicate, and to struggle with understanding themselves and others. For example, Kareem knew that he could find his father overwhelming, and he drew on his experience to make sense of it. He claimed that "it's the way he was brought up"; he also knew that he could struggle to do it differently.

The narratives told by these children—fantastic or not—can be seen as a means by which the children find order through disorder. Their narratives share a characteristic with adult narratives: a need to find coherence out of the confusion of living. As Jeffrey Prager, following Charles Taylor, puts it, "the self is ever seeking to order memory, perception, and reason so as to generate an experience of wholeness" (1998, p. 182). Further, the attempt to put a life into a story, to articulate a narrative, is frequently an attempt to reconcile much that is inarticulate, confusing and ill understood—a packaging of the mess of living and being. These children knew about the complexity of living and the intricacy of human relatedness, about the push-and-pull realities of wanting to assert the self against others while knowing their limitations and those of others. But, over and above these realities, there was their continuous emphasis on their pleasure in living and being, in stretching their physical and emotional muscles, and in acknowledging the importance of other human beings. As Jenny said, speaking for all of them, "I like my life, I just like my life."

Notes

1. The conceptualizations of latency-aged children derive from a number of sources, including the Tavistock Clinic series *Understanding Your Child* (Tavistock Clinic and Rosendale Press), and *Childhood* by Steinberg and Meyer (1995).
2. The different spellings of phantasy and fantasy indicate different usages and theoretical inclinations. The Kleinians use the spelling 'phantasy' to distinguish between an unconscious processes and the semi-conscious daydreams that can be referred to as fantasies. In this article I use 'fantasy' to indicate the conscious expression of narratives, while Rose uses 'phantasy' to express the continual unconscious elements of psychic life.

CHAPTER TEN

Winnicott and music*

Nicholas Spice

Perhaps the title of this paper should not be "Winnicott and music" but "Winnicott and music: why he had nothing to say about it". For though Winnicott loved music, he rarely mentions it in his writings and then only in passing. When, in a talk on "Playing and Culture", he says "what holds for play also holds for the St. Matthew Passion", he is drawing our attention to the relationship between art and play in general (Winnicott, 1968d, pp. 203–206). He is not saying anything particular about music, let alone about Bach's masterpiece. He thinks of the St. Matthew Passion because he is about to go and hear it at the Festival Hall. In this context, any work of art would have served as well. Elsewhere, a throwaway analogy between his own intellectual development and the development of an instrumental musician seems to endorse a rather conventional view of the musician's work: "One could compare my position", he writes in the introduction to *Therapeutic Consultations in Child Psychiatry*, "with that of a cellist who first slogs away at *technique* and then actually becomes able to play

---

*This article was originally given as a paper to the Squiggle series *Original Themes in Winnicott* in June 2001.

music taking the technique for granted" (Winnicott, 1996, p. 6). One of my purposes here will be to suggest that it is precisely this view of musical learning as a process of deferred gratification that we would do well to replace with a more "Winnicottian" model.

Like most intellectuals, psychoanalysts do not commonly illustrate their wider cultural speculations with discussions of music. For example, none of the contributors to a recent Squiggle collection, *Art, Creativity, Living* (Caldwell, 2000), chose to deal with music. Here art means literature (Shakespeare) and the visual arts (Rembrandt); this sits comfortably in an intellectual tradition that, at the outset, famously applied itself to *Hamlet* and Leonardo Da Vinci.

At the same time, as far as I am aware, there has been nothing in music criticism by way of the application of psychoanalytic ideas, comparable in explanatory power to Harold Bloom's theory of the anxiety of influence in the history of literature or Adrian Stokes's analysis of works of visual art in terms of the good and the bad breast. The reason for this will be thought to be self-evident. Music is not representational. Its subject matter, if it has one, cannot easily be agreed upon. It is not about people. There is no obvious way back from the notes to the person who wrote them. From *Salome* or *Rosenkavalier* you would scarcely guess the trouble Frau Strauss had getting Richard into bed, and the asperities of Bartók's string quartets rather effectively hide their creator's rumoured partiality for feathers: it has been said that Bartók liked his wife to dress up as a duck when they made love.

The common argument that music is not talked about because it cannot be talked about is, I suspect, an evasion. All art communicates meanings that cannot be paraphrased. That is one of the reasons we think of it as art. The ineffableness of poems and paintings has not stopped us talking about them. We take it for granted that this talk brings us closer to the incommunicable content of our experience of them. Description and discussion help us to develop a deeper attention to the objects of our gaze. Were someone to be quite unable to say anything about a poem or a painting they claimed to like, we might reasonably think their experience of it had been rather vague. But where music is concerned this muteness is the rule, a rule that the exceptions have done little to challenge [Adorno's writing on Berg (1992) or Mahler (1991) and Robin Holloway on Haydn (1998) are just a couple of inspiring examples that come to mind]. Most intelligent people who love music remain inarticulate about music. And the reason is simple: they just don't know anything much about it.

This ignorance of ours about music fits oddly with the high respect in which we evidently hold it. Music has a special place in our lives. We are not happy with our ignorance about it. We regret that we did not learn music when we were children. We wish our parents had not allowed us to give it up. We want our children to have what we did not have. We send them for music lessons and exhort them to practise. Yet whether we would have been much better off had we never given up the piano or the violin, and whether our children, if they persevere, will end up much less musically illiterate than we are, is open to doubt, since what mostly counts as learning music seems to be designed to tell us very little about it. Ignorance about music is almost as common among people who took music lessons as among those who did not.

I see this in myself. Indeed, it is my enduring interest in my own musical illiteracy that has led me to these reflections. In a sense, every point that I raise here takes its origin from my experience of learning music as a child: particularly, my brief experience of composing music in contrast to my much more extended experience of performing it.

My enthusiasm for music broke into a passion for it when I was around ten years old. I was learning the piano and my favourite composer was Chopin. When, one Sunday evening, my teacher played me Chopin's Aflat major Waltz, Op. 42, I was enraptured by it and went home determined to write such music myself. My *Valse Chromatique* was the first of the little pieces for piano that I wrote in response to Chopin's Aflat major Waltz. Then I started writing songs. My mother looked out poems for me, which I set to music and sang to my own accompaniment: A. E. Houseman's "Bredon Hill", John Donne's "The Bait" ("Come live with me and be my love") and an odd fragment by Edith Sitwell, "We are the children in the heat of the day". Nearly forty years later, I remember these compositions almost as though I had written them yesterday. For all their primitive musical fumblings, I am still proud of them. I can still remember how I felt about them when I was a boy: how I felt that they were mine, because I had made them; how—though I could not have put it this way at the time—they defined me to myself. I can now see that what these attempts at composition gave me was the experience of authorship, and through authorship, authenticity.

Around the onset of puberty I stopped composing and devoted all my spare time and energy to becoming a performer. Performing music became the way I defined myself to the outside world, my way of securing status and approval. At twelve years old I had vowed to become a composer. At seventeen years old I had forgotten that vow and was on the way to becoming a professional instrumentalist. I went to a music academy but left after a year, and then it was only a matter of time before I had effectively given up music altogether. My reasons for stopping music belong to a story I have not yet written for myself. Perhaps this article belongs to that story, for I can now see that part of the reason I gave up training as a performer was my frustration at how little I seemed to be getting to know about music. By the age of eighteen, I had devoted enough hours of my life to music to expect to have acquired a fairly deep knowledge of it. Yet if someone had asked me to justify my enthusiasm for Chopin, to defend my annoyance with the Alberti bass, to say why I liked some passages in Mozart more than others, to expand on the key structure of a Beethoven quartet, to discuss the acoustics of brass instruments, to write or play a pastiche in a chosen style, let alone to play my own compositions, I would have been stumped. All I could do was to play the music through. All I could do was to perform. Where my childhood compositions had given me an intimate knowledge of music, my adolescent performances left me feeling curiously on the outside, only half in the picture.

Reflecting on these experiences, and, without doubt, projecting a personal fracture onto the world at large, I have come to see the character of Western musical culture (by which I mean the culture of Western art music) in terms of the pronounced difference between what one does when one composes and what one does when one performs. I believe that performance values predominate over compositional values in our contemporary musical culture, and that this can account for some of the worst distortions in that culture. Chiefly, the marginalization of the contemporary composer, the breakdown in understanding between composers and their audience, and—itself partly the cause of these last two effects—the illiteracy and muteness I have spoken of, whether among performing musicians, the listening public, or the intelligentsia. This illiteracy leads us alternately to overvalue and then undervalue music, in the concert hall treating it as the object of a quasi-religious veneration, and out of the concert hall treating it as wallpaper, a pleasant backdrop to our work and play.

I want to spend most of the rest of this paper thinking about music lessons. There are two advantages to this approach. Firstly, it locates the larger issues in a manageable context, focussing attention on an institution which most of us know something about, either because at one time in our lives we received music lessons ourselves, or because we have considered music lessons for our children and perhaps watched how they have responded to them. Secondly, music lessons share quite striking features with sessions in psychotherapy or psychoanalysis. Thoughts about music lessons can, therefore, draw on psychoanalytic ideas without resorting too much to generalization or metaphor. If, as I believe, Winnicott's generous and gentle characterization of what nurtures a happy and productive human being can illuminate a future for our musical culture, then we shall want to show this through concrete examples. The traditional instrumental music lesson offers this opportunity.

In Britain there is a well defined ladder that leads from first instrumental music lessons to the concert platform. A child who shows special ability for learning to play and perform pieces of music may be identified as gifted. Once this word has been spoken, the possibility, however faint and remote, of a career as a professional performer will enter the minds of teacher and parent as a fantasy about the child's future. The child will likely be happy to share in this fantasy, and she will begin to recognize each little performance she gives as preparation for the day when she takes her place among the great ones. She progresses quickly through the graded examinations, acquiring plaudits and distinctions on the royal road to Grade 8, from which eminence she will survey the promised land of professional music: music college just inside the gates, the hectic mirage of the concert platform shimmering in the distance.

The child who is not singled out as gifted will continue her music lessons with only half her mind on the job. Progress will be slow, falter, or come to a stop. A series of laboured, if not straightforwardly atrocious performances will be the unheeded signposts to a showdown. The child begins to avoid practising. The teacher urges her to practise and then grows indifferent. The parent urges her to practise and then gets angry. A battleground is staked out. Since money is involved, sooner or later the child wins the battle and the music lessons stop. Later, when the child has grown up and has children herself, she finds she regrets having given up music as a child, she wishes her parents had made her continue with the lessons, and she looks around for a music teacher for her own children. And so it goes on.

Children who avoid practising usually say it is because they are bored. This is taken by the teacher and the parent to mean either that they are not talented or that they are just not interested in music. If the child were talented, how could he be bored? If he were interested in music why wouldn't he practise? The parents often already have the answer to these questions, since one of the benefits they see in getting their children to learn musical instruments is that this will teach them the discipline of deferred gratification, teach them that if they want to play music tomorrow they must, in Winnicott's unWinnicottian phrase, "slog away at technique" today. In so far as they think this, the parents know in advance that their children will be bored by music lessons—that's part of the point. And they are right, since, as occupations go, preparing pieces of music for performance can be pretty boring, especially when the pieces don't amount to much as music. Franz Liszt advised pianists to read books while they were practising and invented a sort of arm support called the chiroplast to help them do so. Here is Sviatoslav Richter describing how he practised a new piece:

> I adopt a purely repetitive method whenever I've got to learn a new piece; I identify all the really fiddly bits and study them first, practising them mechanically. I take a page at a time, go over it as often as I need to and don't move on to the next until the first is under my belt. And only when I've finished the second one do I move on to the third. However difficult it may be, there isn't a passage that doesn't become easy if practised a hundred times... Purely repetitive work of this kind may appear stupid, and I admit that it comes close to being so. [Richter, 2001, p. 139]

Children often find it tedious to repeat the same piece over and over again. To them it may indeed appear stupid. Moreover, they may resent the targeting of this activity on a performance, an occasion which looks suspiciously like a public display of good behaviour, and they may be uneasy at the linkage of musical learning to adult approval: parents, school teachers, the wider world.

The child who learns a musical instrument may be thought of as serving the needs of two related constituencies: on the one hand, parents, family, school; on the other, the dominant musical culture which demands a continuous supply of well-trained and conservative performing musicians to take over custody of the canonic musical texts. In this situation, the child has only two options: to contract to give what is required in exchange for certain rewards, or to head for the door. In terms of the child's relationship with music, the price of both responses is high. Refusing to comply may be the healthiest strategy for the child, since defiance is an act of self-definition, but the cost is nonetheless the temporary or permanent loss of art music as an expressive resource, a refuge, a source of meaning and pleasure. For the child who embraces music lessons the outcome is more ambiguous. Her feelings about music—her love of music—will be complicated and perhaps compromised by her compliance with her parents' wishes and the demands of the big wide world. For the musical success of a child is taken as an outward sign of the success of the child *qua* child, of successful parenting, of the success of the family, of the success of her school. Ultimately, it will even be taken as a sign of the success of her country.

Learning the language of music is a means to a number of different ends of which performing music is just one. I suppose we could go on performing the existing repertoire until the end of time, but a musical culture that stopped producing new music would be a dying culture. Composition should surely be the first reason for learning the language of music. And the second reason, I suggest, should be to acquire musical knowledge, where to know music is defined as understanding it in relation to oneself or understanding oneself in relation to it. Exploration and composition; the exercise of curiosity and creativity; finding out and making new. These are limitless fields of play that the instrumental music lesson, fixated as it is on performance, leaves neglected and uncultivated.

"Play" and "Compliance", are not exactly opposites in the Winnicottian lexicon, but they are effectively mutually exclusive.

When you play you do not comply. Where you comply you are not really playing. If playing music turns out to be complying with it and with a lot of other things besides, then something must be wrong. To anyone familiar with Winnicott's ideas, my characterization of the typical instrumental music lesson will have prompted a flood of antithetical responses. For if this characterization is roughly accurate, then the instrumental music lesson runs directly counter to the spirit of everything Winnicott came to believe as a result of his observations of babies, children and adults. And I think we only need to imagine a music lesson conducted according to Winnicottian principles to realize how oddly restricted and one-sided what we take for granted as musical education has become.

The Winnicottian music lesson would work against and seek to dismantle the structures of compliance that hold the traditional music lesson in place. The first and most subversive step in this direction would be to depose performance as the governing principle of the music lesson and enthrone play in its stead. Music lessons conducted under the principle of play would promise no results. With no promise of return, the ownership of the music lesson by the parental and music cultural constituencies would cease to be worth anything very definite. The music lesson would be handed back to the child.

In this radical and insurgent manoeuvre the music teacher would necessarily play a vital role. For now, inverting the order of things, the music teacher would be there not to deliver results to the parent or to the music business but to protect the child from the demands of both these authorities. As such the Winnicottian music teacher would recognize with an acute sensitivity the nature of what was at stake for the child. As things currently stand, it often seems as though parents think of music lessons much as they might think of tennis lessons: there's a technique to be learnt and a professional to impart it, and that's that. But music lessons are much closer to sessions of psychotherapy than to a course of tennis coaching.

In most cases, taking music lessons is the only chance the child gets of a regular one-to-one meeting in private with an adult professional, usually for between half and hour and an hour, at least once a week, and sometimes over an extended period of time, even several years. The purpose of this encounter is not psychotherapy, but it is to teach the child how to make individual use of an expressive medium with a rich if elusive relationship to emotional, psychological and somatic states of being. Music is highly charged stuff. In Winnicottian terminology, music is a world of transitional objects and the music lesson is a transitional space of a sort, a holding environment in which the child can take time to find music in herself and to find herself in music. The Winnicottian music teacher will be aware that in defining herself through music and in making music her own, the child will be laying open aspects of herself that are deep and private. To open herself to music and through music, the child must feel safe, much as the patient in psychotherapy must feel safe in Winnicott's account. To feel safe, the child must be able to trust that what goes on in the music lesson is confidential. The music teacher must not seem to be on the parent's side. Unless the child chooses to bring the parents into the picture—unless the child herself decides it is time to show what she has been doing—what goes on in the music lesson remains between the teacher and the child. And the teacher must firmly close the door of the music room to the parent's anxious enquiries.

The other condition for the growth of the child's individual relationship with music is time. The Winnicottian virtues of patience, a willingness to wait, a reluctance to dictate or to rush to solutions, a happy tolerance of nonsense and deadends, will be essential virtues of the Winnicottian music teacher. The child must feel that he has all the time in the world to find himself in music. So there will be no deadlines, no exams (unless the child wants to work that way), no performances as objectives, and above all no pre-emptive body of dogma about how things have to be done to be correct.

Within this private space, held by the attentive presence of the teacher, the child will begin to encounter music, the infinite resource of made and possible objects in sound, exploring it and searching it for things that he can make use of, that he can make his own. He will begin to play with music. Granted that music is a cultural resource, an artificial man-made resource, pleasurable play will only take place where the child has some understanding. Music lessons are about giving the pupil enough musical understanding to enjoy meaningful play with music. The more detailed and various the child's knowledge of the language of music—the more he understands how to articulate musical thoughts and the more fluent he becomes at translating musical utterances into sound—the more complex will be the forms of musical play available to him. But understanding and play start with the very first music lesson, gratification is not deferred, interest is immediate. To play every note on the piano with one finger, to strike a set of percussion instruments with a variety of different beaters, to take the piano apart and see how it is made, to listen to a Tchaikovsky symphony while watching the digital clock on the hi-fi system to track just how much happens in the first twenty-five seconds, to draw a bow across an open string, to fill ten beer bottles with different amounts of water and then play a tune on them with a spoon, to do a thousand different simple things in your first music lesson is to start to understand the language of music, to begin to orientate yourself in this infinite world of timbres, tones, colours, combinations of sound. How many ways can you play a single note? The experience of authorship and through authorship, authenticity can begin in the simplest possible of ways.

And when it comes to Mozart—if it comes to Mozart—the possibilities for play are not to be restrained by a sense of respect for a holy text. Respect that is not earned is a hollow kind of thing and demeans the object of respect. "Ayez respecte pour la musique, Florence!", barked the very nice father of a young French girl of my acquaintance, as we drove in his car with a Haydn quartet on the radio that Florence was interrupting with her mischievous and excitable chatter. "Have respect for the music, Florence!" Nothing, I thought, could be more likely to excite her contempt. To the child learning Mozart, Mozart must prove that he deserves respect, which means that the child must be granted free access to the body of Mozart to do with it what she will. To learn respect for Mozart is to be free to pull Mozart to pieces so as to see how Mozart is made and where Mozart is well made and where less well made. It is to pull and push and stretch and bite Mozart, to rail against him and say you are bored by him, to love him and hate him, to test him (if necessary to the limits of destruction), to burlesque him and alter him, to steal from him and make him your own. To learn to respect Mozart is to discover that nothing you do to Mozart will change him. That he survives. It is to treat Mozart as a body of human knowledge and not as a collection of religious texts. To use Mozart as a springboard for something new. To encounter him as one composer to another.

When you prepare a piece of music for performance you enter a narrowing perspective, with the performance itself situated at the vanishing point where an impossible perfection is achieved. When you explore a piece of music as a composer, as a philosopher with a curiosity for knowledge and a desire to be interested and an eye for what you can use for yourself (and it is as all these things that a child can encounter music in his or her very first music lesson), you enter an open perspective that widens to infinity. It is not difficult to see which of these activities harmonizes with the Winnicottian vision, nor to identify which is "guilt driven labour" and which the exercise of "ruthless original virtue".

There is an obvious sense in which this should be directed at music teachers rather than at the psychoanalytic community, since it offers a critique of musical institutions not psychoanalytical ones. But if anything that I have said resonates with your own experience of music as a praxis, then I will perhaps have succeeded in suggesting once again how quietly powerful Winnicott's ideas can be when applied in other than psychotherapeutic contexts. For I am quite sure that Winnicott's ideas could revolutionize the culture of Western art music. All the serious work remains to be done. At the theoretical level there is much to be written about the psychodynamics of the music lesson: about how it fits into the oedipal relations between boys and girls and their parents, about the startling contrast in psychological terms between what we are doing when we compose and what we are doing when we practise in order to perform, about what is at stake in our fear for the integrity and preservation of the musical canon, and so on. My own hunch is that the culture of instrumental performance attracts and is sustained by a certain kind of obsessive–compulsive behaviour, a sort of higher head banging, enormously rewarding to the head banger (such as Sviatoslav Richter) but recognized as mad by large numbers of children. Reflecting on my own youth spent at the keyboard, I wonder about the extent to which practising a musical instrument up to six or seven hours a day isn't perhaps some sort of defence, some kind of trance of suspended animation, a version of what Winnicott identified as "fantasying". Then again, it occurs to me that the preparation of a piece for performance satisfies a need to repair something, to make safe through reparation, and so I think of Klein and the depressive position. Meanwhile, composition, with its strategies of smash and grab, seems to speak to Winnicott's ideas of the self forged on the anvil of destructiveness and plunder. When I reflect on what goes into the production of a musical performance, I remember Winnicott's notion that the child whose ruthless original virtue, met with a blank by the depressed mother, is compelled then to devote his energies to revivifying her: to make his living, as Adam Phillips puts it, by bringing the mother to life. Is the professional performer condemned to make his living perhaps by repeatedly bringing back to life the maternal corpse of the musical canon? While the composer is engaged in testing the mother's holding capacity to destruction and finding that she survives?

At the practical level, at the level of what we can do now, I find the idea of applying Winnicott's ideal of the psychotherapeutic environment to the traditional instrumental musical lesson utterly subversive because it would redress the balance in a product-orientated culture away from performance towards purposeless knowledge, towards composition and towards discourse—the breaking of that muteness about music which I began with. The much bemoaned fractures in our contemporary musical culture are almost always blamed on the composers. If only they wrote intelligible music everything would be alright. It's all the fault of Stockhausen or the Darmstadt School, and, even, it's all the fault of Schoenberg. But composers are just composers. They get up in the morning and compose. They are driven by a need to keep things interesting at all costs. As the American composer George Perle put it, "if it's secondhand it's boring" (1995, p. 305). Waking to a world increasingly clogged up by secondhand musical objects, composers tack off to the margin. Berating composers is a deadend strategy. If we want change, it will not come from the top down but from the bottom up, through the education of a listening and playing public for whom music is not a substitute for religion but a vital part of the way they define themselves to themselves.

REFERENCES

Andrews, M. (2000). Introduction to life history. In: M. Andrews *et al.* (Eds), *Lines of Narrative* (pp. 1–10). London & New York: Routledge.
Adorno, T. W. (1992). *Mahler: A Musical Physiognomy*. Chicago: University of Chicago Press.
Adorno, T. W. (1991). *Alban Berg*. Cambridge: Cambridge University Press.
Balint, M. (1968). *The Basic Fault*. London: Tavistock Publications.
Berry, E. (1999). Games feared as violent youths' basic training. *Boston Globe*, 29th April.
Bettelheim, B. (1962). *Symbolic Wounds: Puberty Rites and the Envious Male*. New York: Collier Books.
Bick, E. (1964). Notes on infant observation in psychoanalytic training. *International Journal of Psychoanalysis*, 45: 558–566.
Blos, P. (1967). The second individuation process of adolescence. *The Psychoanalytic Study of the Child*, 22: 162–186.
Boas, G. (1966). *The Cult of Childhood*. London: The Warburg Institute.
Bollas, C. (1986). The transformational object. In: G. Kohon (Ed.), *The British School of Psychoanalysis: The Independent Tradition*. London: Free Association Press.
Bollas, C. (1993). Why Oedipus. In: *Being a Character* (pp. 47–65). London: Routledge.

Bollas, C. (1995). The functions of history. In: *Cracking Up* (pp. 103–145). London: Routledge.
Bowlby, J. (1944). Forty-four juvenile thieves: their character and home life. *International Journal of Psycho-Analysis*, 25: 1–57 and 207–228.
Bowlby, J. (1953). *Child Care and the Growth of Maternal Love*. London: Penguin.
Bowlby, J. (1969). *Attachment and Loss, Volume 1: Attachment*. Harmondsworth: Penguin.
Bowlby, J. (1973). *Attachment and Loss, Volume 2: Separation: Anxiety and Anger*. Harmondsworth: Penguin.
Bowlby, J. (1980). *Attachment and Loss, Volume 3: Loss: Sadness and Depression*. Harmondsworth, Penguin.
Bowlby, J. (1988). *A Secure Base. Clinical Applications of Attachment Theory*. London: Routledge.
Bradley J. (1993). *Understanding Your 10 Year Old*. London: Rosendale Press.
Brafman, A. H. (1988). Infant observation. *International Revue Psychoanalysis*, 15: 45–59.
Brierley, M. (1937). Affects in theory and practice. *Trends in Psycho-Analysis* (pp. 43–56). London: Hogarth Press, 1951.
Britton, R. (1998). *Belief and Imagination*. London: Routledge.
Bruner, J. (1987). Life as narrative. *Social Research*, 54(1): 11–32.
Caldwell, L. (1986). Review of Denise Riley. *War in the Nursery: Theories of the child and the mother* in *M/F*, 10–11: 89–94
Caldwell, L. (2000). *Art, Creativity, Living*. London: Karnac Books.
Cavarero, A. (2000). *Relating Narratives: Storytelling and Selfhood*. London & New York: Routledge.
Craib, I. (2000). Narratives as bad faith. In: M. Andrews *et al.* (Eds.), *Lines of Narrative* (pp. 64–74). London & New York: Routledge.
Davids, J. (2000). The Family in the Child's Mind, unpublished paper given at The Anna Freud Centre International Colloquium.
De Zengotita, T. (1999). The gunfire dialogues: notes on the reality of virtuality. *Harpers Magazine*, July Issue.
Dolto, F. (1968). Le complexe d'Oedipe, ses étapes structurantes, et leurs accidents. In: *Au Jeu du Désir. Essais Cliniques*. Paris: Seuil, 1981.
Fairbairn, W. R. D. (1952). *Psychoanalytic Studies of the Personality*. London: Tavistock Publications.
Feldman, M. (1989). The Oedipus Complex: manifestations in the Inner World and the Therapeutic Situation. In: *The Oedipus Complex Today*. London: Karnac Books.

Ferenczi, S. (1913a). Stages in the development of the sense of reality. In: *First Contributions to Psycho-Analysis* (pp. 213–239). London: Hogarth Press, 1952.

Ferenczi, S. (1913b). Le développement du sens de la réalité et ses stades. In: *Œuvres Complètes, Tome II: 1913–1919, Psychanalyse II*. Paris: Payot, 1970.

Ferenczi, S. (1926). The problem of acceptance of unpleasant ideas—advances in knowledge of the sense of reality. In: *Further Contributions to the Theory and Technique of Psycho-Analysis* (pp. 366–379). London: Hogarth Press, 1969.

Ferenczi, S. (1930). The principles of relaxation and neocatharsis. In: *Final Contributions to the Problems and Methods of Psycho-Analysis* (pp. 108–125). London: Maresfield Reprints, 1980.

Ferenczi, S. (1931). Child-analysis in the analysis of adults. In: *Final Contributions to the Problems and Methods of Psycho-Analysis* (pp. 126–142). London: Maresfield Reprints, 1980.

Ferenczi, S. (1933). Confusion of tongues between adults and the child. In: *Final Contributions to the Problems and Methods of Psycho-Analysis* (pp. 156–167). London: Maresfield Reprints, 1980.

Ferro, A. (1999). *The Bi-Personal Field: Experiences in Child Analysis*, New Library of Psychoanalysis. London: Routledge.

Fonagy, P., & Target, M. (1996). Playing with reality. *International Journal of Psychoanalysis, 77*(2 & 3).

Frankel, R. (1998). *The Adolescent Psyche: Jungian and Winnicottian Perspectives*. London and New York: Routledge.

Freud, A. (1958). Adolescence. *The Psychoanalytic Study of the Child, 13*: 255–278.

Freud, A. (1966). *The Writings of Anna Freud, Volume II: The Ego and the Mechanisms of Defense* [rev. ed.]. New York: International Universities Press.

Freud, A. (1969). *Normality and Pathology in Childhood*. London: Hogarth Press.

Freud, S. (1900). *The Interpretation of Dreams*. In: *The Standard Edition of the Complete Psychological Works of Sigmund Freud*, 4 and 5.

Freud, S. (1905). *Three Essays on the Theory of Sexuality*, S.E., 7.

Freud, S. (1909). Analysis of a phobia in a five-year-old boy. S.E., 10.

Freud, S. (1910). The psycho-analytic view of psychogenic disturbance of vision. S.E., 11.

Freud, S. (1911a). Formulations on the two principles of mental functioning. S.E., 12.

Freud, S. (1911b). Psycho-analytic notes on an autobiographical account of a case of paranoia. S.E., 12.
Freud, S. (1912). On the universal tendency to debasement in the sphere of love. S.E., 11.
Freud, S. (1913a). The disposition to obsessional neurosis. S.E., 12.
Freud, S. (1913b). *Totem and Taboo*. S.E., 13.
Freud, S. (1914). On Narcissism: an Introduction. S.E., 14.
Freud, S., (1915a). Instincts and Their Vicissitudes. S.E., 14.
Freud, S. (1915b). The phases of development of the sexual organisation. In: *Three Essays On The Theory Of Sexuality*. S.E., 7.
Freud, S. (1915c). Overview of the transference neuroses. In: I. Grubrich-Simitis (Ed.), *A Phylogenetic Fantasy, Overview of the Transference Neuroses*. Cambridge, MA and London, England: The Belknap Press of Harvard University Press, 1987.
Freud, S. (1915–16). *Introductory Lectures on Psycho-Analysis*. S.E., 15.
Freud, S. (1917). *Mourning and Melancholia*. S.E., 14.
Freud, S. (1920). *Beyond the Pleasure Principle*. S.E., 18.
Freud, S. (1927). *The Future of an Illusion*. S.E., 21.
Freymann, J. R. (1992). *Les Parures de l'Oralité*. Paris: Springer-Verlag.
Fromm, M. G. (1989). Winnicott's work in relation to classical psychoanalysis and ego psychology. In: M. G. Fromm & B. L. Smith (Eds.), *The Facilitating Environment: Clinical Applications of Winnicott's Theory* (pp. 3–26). Madison, CT: International Universities Press.
Fromm, M. G., & Smith, B. L. *Winnicott and Self Psychology*, op. cit., pp. 52–87.
Gibbs, N. (1999). Special Report: The Littleton Massacre. *Time*, 3rd May.
Gibbs, N., & Roche, T. (1999). The Columbine Tapes. *Time*, 20th December.
Gregory, R. (1998). Brainy mind. *British Medical Journal*, 19–26 December: 1693–1695.
Green, A. (2000). Clinical and observational psychoanalytical research: Roots of a controversy. In: J. Sandler (Ed.). London: Karnac Books.
Greenberg, J., & Mitchell, S. (1983). *Object Relations in Psychoanalytic Theory*. Cambridge, MA: Harvard University Press.
Grubrich-Simitis, I. Overview of the transference neuroses. In: I. Grubrich-Simitis (Ed.), *A Phylogenetic Fantasy, Overview of the Transference Neuroses*. Cambridge, MA and London, England: The Belknap Press of Harvard University Press, 1987.
Grosskurth, P. (1986). *Melanie Klein. Her World and Work*. London: Karnac Books.

Hegel, G. W. E. (1807). *La Phénomènologie del'Esprit.* J. Hippolyte (Trans.). Paris: Aubier, 1941.
Heimann, P. (1950). *International Journal of Psycho-Analysis,* 31: 329–334.
Holloway, R. (1998). Haydn: the musician's musician. In: W. Dean Sutcliffe (Ed.), *Haydn Studies* (pp. 321–334). Cambridge: Cambridge University Press.
Holmes, J. (1993). *John Bowlby and Attachment Theory.* London: Routledge.
Jacobitti, S. (1997). Thinking about the self. In: L. May & J. Kohn (Eds.), *Hannah Arendt: Twenty Years Later* (pp. 199–220). Massachusetts & London: The MIT Press.
Jones, E. (1922). Some problems of adolescence. In: *Collected Papers.* London: Maresfield Reprints, 1948.
Kestenberg, J. S. (1977). Psychoanalytical observation of children. *International Review of Psychoanalysis,* 4: 393–407.
Khan, M. (1974). *The Privacy of the Self.* Madison: International Universities Press.
King, P. (1978). Affective response of the analyst to the patient's communications. *International Journal of Psycho-Analysis,* 59: 329–334.
Klaus, M. H., & Kennell, J. H. (1976). *Maternal–Infant Bonding.* St Louis: The C.V. Mosby Co.
Klein, M. (1937). *The Psycho-Analysis of Children* [Preface] (pp. 9–12). London: Hogarth Press.
Klein, M. (1952). On observing the behaviour of young infants. In: *Developments in Psycho-Analysis.* London: Hogarth Press.
Kottman, P. (2000). Introduction to Cavarero, *Relating Narratives* (pp. vii–xxxi). London & New York: Routledge.
Kristeva, J. (1980). Motherhood according to Giovanni Bellini. In: *Desire in Language* (pp. 237–270). Oxford: Basil Blackwell.
Kristeva, J. (1987). *Stabat mater.* In: *Tales of Love* (pp. 234–264). New York: Columbia University Press.
Kristeva, J. (2001). *Hannah Arendt, Life is a Narrative.* Toronto: University of Toronto Press.
Lacan, J. (1953–1954). *Les Écrits Techniques de Freud, Le Séminaire, Livre I,* J.-A. Miller (Ed.). Paris: Seuil, 1975.
Lacan, J. (1958). *Ecrits.* London: Tavistock Publications, 1977.
Lacan, J. (1967). Discours de clôture. In: *Enfance Aliénée.* Paris: Denoël, 1984.
Lacan, J. (1969–1970). *L'envers de la Psychanalyse, Le Séminaire, Livre XVII* (text established by J.-A. Miller). Paris: Seuil, 1991.

Lacan, J. (1970). Radiophonie. In: *Scilicet*, no. 2/3. Paris: Seuil.
Lacan, J. (1974). *L'éveil du Printemps de Frank Wedekind* [Preface]. Paris: Gallimard.
Lacan, J. (1975). Le symptôme (conference in Geneva). In: *Le Bloc-Note de la Psychanalyse*. Geneva, 1985, no. 5.
Lanyado, M. (1997). Memories in the making: the experience of moving from fostering to adoption for a five-year-old boy. *Journal of the British Association of Psychotherapists*, 3(34/1).
Lanyado, M. (1999). It's just an ordinary pain: Thoughts on joy and heartache in puberty and early adolescence. In: D. Hindle & M. Vaciago-Smith (Eds.), *Personality Development as a Psychoanalytic Perspective*. London: Routledge.
Lee, G. (1997). Alone among three—the father and the Oedipus Complex. In: *Fathers and Families*, Winnicott Studies Monograph. London: Karnac Books.
Levi-Strauss, C. (1994). *The Raw and the Cooked: Introduction to the Science of Mythology*. London: Pimlico.
Lush, D. (1993). *Understanding Your 9 Year Old*. London: Rosendale Press.
Marcus, S. (1984). *Freud and the Culture of Psycho-analysis*. New York: Norton and company.
Mannoni, M. (1970). *The Child, His Illness and The Others*. London: Karnac Books.
Meltzer, D. (1973). *Sexual States of Mind*. Strathclyde: Clunie Press.
Miller, L. (1993). *Understanding Your 8 Year Old*. London: Rosendale Press.
Mitchell, J. (2000). *Mad Men and Medusas, Reclaiming Hysteria and the Effects of Sibling Relations on the Human Condition*. London: Penguin Books.
Ogden, T. (1993). On potential space. In: Dodi Goldman (Ed.), *In One's Bones*. London: Jason Aronson.
Parkes, C. M. (1972). *Bereavement: Studies in Grief in Adult Life*. Harmondsworth: Pelican.
Perle, G. (1995). *The Right Notes* (p. 305). Stuyvesant, NY: Pendragon Press.
Perrier, F. (1968). Sur la clinique, le transfert et le temps. In: *Chaussée d'Antin*. Paris: Albin Michel, 1994.
Phillips, A. (1988). *Winnicott*. London: Fontana Press.
Pontalis, J.-B. (1977). *Entre le Rêve et la Douleur*, Gallimard (Ed.).
Prager, J. (1998). *Presenting the Past: Psychoanalysis and the Sociology of Remembering*. Cambridge, MA & London: Harvard University Press.

Rassial, J.-J. (1990). *L'Adolescent et le Psychanalyste*. Paris: Rivages.
Richter, S. (2001). *Notebooks and Conversations* (p. 139), Bruno Monsaingeon (Ed.). Princeton: Princeton University Press.
Ricoeur, P. (1970). *Freud and Philosophy: An Essay on Interpretation*. New Haven & London: Yale University Press.
Rickman, J. (1951). Number and the human sciences. In: *Selected Contributions to Psycho-Analysis* (pp. 218–223). London: Hogarth Press, 1957.
Rodman, F. R. (Ed.) (1987). *The Spontaneous Gesture, Selected Letters of D. W. Winnicott*. Cambridge, MA: Harvard University Press.
Rose, J. (1984). *The Case of Peter Pan*. London: Macmillan.
Rose, J. (1998). *States of Fantasy* Oxford: Clarendon Press.
Rose, N. (1982). Review of E. Badinter. *The Myth of Motherhood*, Souvenir Press (1981) in *M/F*, 7: 82–86.
Rose, N. (1990). *Governing the Soul*. London: Routledge.
St-Exupéry, A. (1955 trans.). *Wind, Sand, And Stars*. Toronto: Heinemann.
Sarnoff, C. (1987). *Psychotherapeutic Strategies in Latency Years*. NY: Jason Aronson.
Sclater Day, S. (1998). Creating the self: stories as transitional phenomena. In: *Auto/Biography*, 6: 85–92.
Seale, C. (1998). *Constructing Death* Cambridge: Cambridge University Press.
Seligman, D. M. H. (1993). Infant observation and psychoanalytic theory. *Psychoanalytic Quarterly*, 62: 274–278.
Sellin, B. (1994). *Une Âme Prisonnière*, P. Schmidt (Trans.). Paris: Robert Laffont.
Spitz, R. (1950). Anxiety in infancy: a study of its manifestations in the first year of life. *IJPA*, 31: 138–143.
Steinberg, L., & Meyer, R. (1995). *Childhood*. New York: McGraw Hill.
Stern, D. (1985). *The Interpersonal World of the Infant*. New York: Basic Books.
Tyson, P. (1996). Introduction to discussion of P. H. Wolff's paper. *Journal of the American Psycho-Analytical Association*, 44(2): 392–396.
Van Heeswyk, P. (1997). *Analysing Adolescence*. London: Sheldon Press.
Vanier, A. (1998a). *Lexique de Psychanalyse*. Paris: Armand Colin.
Vanier, A. (1998b). *Lacan*. Susan Fairfield (Trans.). New York: Other Press, 2000.
Waddell, M. (1998). *Inside Lives: Psychoanalysis and the Growth of the Personality*. London: Duckworth.
Walkerdine, V. (1990). Some day my prince will come. In: *Schoolgirl Fictions* (pp. 87–106). London: Verso.

Warner, M. (1994). *From the Beast to the Blonde.* London: Chatto & Windus.
Winnicott, C., Shepherd R., & Davis, M. (1989). *D. W. Winnicott. Psychoanalytical Explorations.* Cambridge: Harvard University Press.
Winnicott, D. W. (1941). The observation of infants in a set situation. In: *Collected Papers: Through Paediatrics to Psycho-analysis* (pp. 52–69).
Winnicott, D. W. (1945). Primitive emotional development. In: *Collected Papers: Through Paediatrics to Psycho-analysis* (pp. 145–156). New York: Basic Books, 1975.
Winnicott, D. W. (1949). Mind and its relation to the psyche-soma. In: *Collected Papers: Through Paediatrics to Psycho-analysis* (pp. 243–254).
Winnicott, D. W. (1950). Aggression in relation to emotional development. In: *Collected Papers. Through Paediatrics to Psychoanalysis* (pp. 204–218). London: Tavistock Publications.
Winnicott, D. W. (1951). Transitional objects and transitional phenomena. In: *Collected Papers: Through Paediatrics to Psychoanalysis* (pp. 229–242). London: Tavistock Publications.
Winnicott, D. W. (1954). The depressive position in normal emotional development. In: *Collected Papers: Through Paediatrics to Psycho-analysis* (pp. 262–277).
Winnicott, D. W. (1956a). Primary maternal preoccupation. In: *Collected Papers: Through Paediatrics to Psychoanalysis* (pp. 300–305). London: Tavistock Publications.
Winnicott, D. W. (1956b). The antisocial tendency. In: *Collected Papers* (pp. 306–315). London: Tavistock Publications.
Winnicott, D. W. (1958a). The capacity to be alone. In: *The Maturational Process and the Facilitating Environment* (pp. 29–36). London: Karnac Books, 1990.
Winnicott, D. W. (1958b). Child analysis in the latency period. In: *The Maturational Process and the Facilitating Environment* (pp. 115–123). London: Karnac Books, 1990.
Winnicott, D. W. (1960a). Ego distortion in terms of true and false self. In: *The Maturational Processes and the Facilitating Environment* (pp. 140–152). London: Hogarth Press, 1965.
Winnicott, D. W. (1960b). The theory of the parent–infant relationship. In: *The Maturational Processes and the Facilitating Environment (1965)* (pp. 37–55). London: Hogarth Press and the Institute of Psycho-Analysis.
Winnicott, D. W. (1961). Adolescence: struggling through the doldrums. In: *The Family and Individual Development.* London: Routledge, 1989.

Winnicott, D. W. (1962a). Providing for the child in health and in crisis. In: *The Maturational Processes and the Facilitating Environment* (pp. 64–72). London: Hogarth Press, 1965.

Winnicott, D. W. (1962b). A personal view of the Kleinian contribution. In: *The Maturational Process and the Facilitating Environment* (pp. 171–178). London: Hogarth, 1965.

Winnicott, D. W. (1962c). Ego integration in child development. In: *The Maturational Processes and the Facilitating Environment* (pp. 56–63). London: Hogarth Press, 1965.

Winnicott, D. W. (1963a). From dependence towards independence in the development of the individual. In: *The Maturational Processes and the Facilitating Environment* (pp. 83–92). London: Hogarth Press, 1965.

Winnicott, D. W. (1963b). Communicating and not communicating leading to a study of certain opposites. In: *The Maturational Processes and the Facilitating Environment* (pp. 179–192). London: Hogarth Press, 1965.

Winnicott, D. W. (1963c). The development of the capacity for concern. In: *The Maturational Process and the Facilitating Environment* (pp. 73–82).

Winnicott, D. W. (1939/1964). Aggression and its roots. In: *Deprivation and Delinquency* (pp. 84–99). London: Tavistock Publications, 1984.

Winnicott, D. W. (1964). What do we mean by a normal child. In: *The Child, the Family and the Outside World*. London: Pelican.

Winnicott, D. W. (1965). The price of disregarding psychoanalytic research. In: *Home is Where We Start From* (pp. 172–182). New York & London: W. W. Norton & Company, 1986.

Winnicott, D. W. (1967). Postscript: D.W.W. on D.W.W. In: C. Winnicott, R. Shepherd & M. Davis (Eds.), *Psycho-Analytic Explorations* (pp. 569–584), Cambridge: Harvard University Press, 1989.

Winnicott, D. W. (1967a). The location of cultural experience. In: *Playing and Reality* (pp. 95–103). London: Routledge.

Winnicott, D. W. (1968a). Contemporary concepts of adolescent development and their implications for higher education. In: *Playing and Reality* (pp. 138–150). London: Routledge.

Winnicott, D. W. (1968b). The use of an object and relating through identifications. In: *Playing and Reality* (pp. 84–99). London: Routledge, 1991.

Winnicott, D. W. (1968c). Comments on my paper "The use of an object". In: C. Winnicott, R. Shepherd & M. Davis (Eds.), *Psycho-Analytic Explorations* (pp. 238–239). Cambridge: Harvard University Press, 1989.

Winnicott, D. W. (1968d). Playing and culture. In: R. Shepherd, C. Winnicott & M. Davis (Eds.), *Psycho-Analytic Explorations* (pp. 203–206). London: Karnac Books.

Winnicott, D. W. (1968–1969). III. Answer to comments, In: C. Winnicott, R. Shepherd & M. Davis (Eds.), *Psychoanalytical Exploration* (pp. 189–192).

Winnicott, D. W. (1969). The use of an object in the context of *Moses and the Monotheism*. In: *Psychoanalytical Explorations* (pp. 240–246).

Winnicott, D. W. (1970). On the basis for self in body. In: C. Winnicott, R. Shepherd & M. Davis (Eds.). *Psycho-Analytic Explorations* (pp. 261–283). Cambridge: Harvard University Press, 1989.

Winnicott, D. W. (1971). *Playing and Reality*. London: Tavistock Publications & Harmondsworth: Pelican Books, 1974.

Winnicott, D. W. (1971a). Transitional objects and transitional phenomena. In: *Playing and Reality* (pp. 1–25). London: Tavistock Publications.

Winnicott, D. W. (1971b). Dreaming, fantasying and living: a case history describing a primary dissociation. In: *Playing and Reality* (pp. 26–37). London: Tavistock Publications.

Winnicott, D. W. (1971c). Playing: a theoretical statement. In: *Playing and Reality* (pp. 38–52). London: Tavistock Publications.

Winnicott, D. W. (1971d). Playing: creative activity and the search for the self. In: *Playing and Reality* (pp. 53–64). London: Tavistock Publications.

Winnicott, D. W. (1971e). Creativity and its origins. In: *Playing and Reality* (pp. 65–85). London: Tavistock Publications.

Winnicott, D. W. (1971f). The location of cultural experience. In: *Playing and Reality* (pp. 95–103) London: Tavistock Publications.

Winnicott, D. W. (1971g). Le corps et le self. In: *Lieux du Corps*. Nouvelle Revue de Psychanalyse, Numéro 3, Printemps, 1971.

Winnicott, D. W. (1971h). *Therapeutic Consultations in Child Psychiatry* [Introduction]. London: The Hogarth Press and The Institute of Psycho-Analysis, 1971.

Winnicott, D. W. (1991). The defensive position. In: *Human Nature*. New York: Bruner/Mazel.

Winnicott, D. W. (1996). *Therapeutic Consultations in Child Psychiatry*. London: Karnac Books.

Wise, I. (Ed.) (2000). *Adolescence*. London: Institute of Psycho-Analysis.

Wolff, P. H. (1966). The irrelevance of infant observations for psychoanalysis. *Journal of American Psycho-Analytical Association*, 44(2): 369–392.

INDEX

Abraham, K., 47, 48
abuse, child, 1, 55, 102, 106, 157
acting out, 12, 135, 139, 141–143, 152, 159
adolescence, 133–152
   and time, 134–147
   and sexual drive, 133, 134
   imagination, 167–172
   parenting of adolescents, 160–162
   struggle to find the real, 163–167
   violent potential of, 158–163
   see also puberty
adoption, 11, 84, 86, 93–112
Andrews, M., 180, 181
antisocial tendency, 56, 101, 156, 158, 159, 182
Arendt, H., 179, 189, 190
art, 193, 194, 196, 199, 203
attachment theory, 94, 100–112, 126, 188, 189

Balint, M., 48, 126
Bettelheim, B., 174

Bick, E.:
   infant observation, 59, 61
Bion, W., 65, 123
Blos, P., 61, 150, 155
Boas, G., 2
Bollas, C., 181, 182, 187
Bowlby, J., 16, 60
   attachment theory, 94, 100–102, 105
Brafman, A., 10
   infant observation, 59–70
breast, 9, 19, 23, 49–51, 194
   absent, 123
   see also mother
Brierley, M., 48
Britton, R., 114, 125
Bruner, J., 180

Caldwell, L., 1–14, 194
catharsis, 168, 169
   yearning to find, 172–175
Cavarero, A., 189, 190
   narrative theory, 178–183

215

child:
    images of, 6–9
    Kim Phuc, 7
    of dreams, 21–25
    of metapsychological synthesis,
        34–37
    of prehistory, 31–34
    of psychosis, 25–31
    of trauma, 37–41
    premature, 71–80
    psychoanalysis of, 113–132
    universal, 2
Columbine school massacre,
    153–176
Cordié, A., 82
culture, 1–5, 8, 17, 33, 53, 67, 125,
    153, 188
    cultural theory, 177–181
    family, 116
    impact of, 136, 149, 154–159, 161,
        164, 167, 174, 175
    individual–, 154, 156, 157
    musical, 193–204

Darwin(ism), 18, 19
Davids, J., 10, 126
    on Vanier, 149–152
death-drive, 12, 136, 137, 140, 148
defects:
    of inscription in language, 71–92
defence, 155, 182
    emotional, 100–112
    mechanisms, 48, 56, 161, 203
development:
    early emotional, 45–58
    of imagination, 167–172
    struggle to find the real, 163–167
developmental psychology, 181, 182
De Zengotita, T., 164
doldrums, 137, 142, 151, 155, 158
Dolto, F., 134, 135, 137, 138, 146, 150
Drapeau, P., 4, 9
    mythical children, 15–44
dream(s), 90, 91, 126, 147, 191
    Freud on, 19, 31, 169, 170
        child of, 21–25

dream-work, 169–171
The Interpretation of Dreams,
    169

Ego, 3, 9, 23–37, 41–43, 45–54, 56,
    127, 139, 155, 156, 170
    development of, 20
    drives, 21
    instincts, 21–24, 27, 35, 42, 43, 45
    pleasure-, 23, 35–37
    psychology, 15, 16
    reality-, 23, 35–37
    -relatedness, 28, 49, 52–54
    -subject, 20, 34, 35
epistemophilic drive, 83
Ernaux, A., 90

Fairbairn, W., 16, 17, 48, 49, 56, 57
false self, 30, 31, 40, 42, 50, 53–56,
    181
family, 3, 5, 6, 72, 79, 88, 120, 122,
    126, 129, 150, 155, 157, 159, 160,
    177, 178, 181, 182, 184–186, 188,
    189
    history, 11, 12, 89, 115–117, 178,
        180
    new, 11
    observation, 63, 66
    see also adoption; fostering
fantasy, 4, 7, 9, 11, 13, 20, 23, 33,
    36–40, 82, 140, 148, 149
    in adolescence, 157, 159–163,
        165–174
    mythical, 15–44
    narratives of, 177–192
    psychoanalytical theory of,
        122–126
    transformational use of, 186–191
    unconscious, 40, 136, 165
Feldman, M., 125
Ferenczi, S.:
    early emotional development,
        45–58
    omnipotence, 34
Ferro, A., 115, 119, 120
Fonagy, P., 114, 125, 126

fostering, 11, 93–107
    to adoption, 107–112
    see also attachment theory
Frankel, R., 12
    an American tragedy
        (Columbine), 153–176
Freud, A., 16, 61, 54, 65
    adolescence, 155
    preadolescence, 150
Freud, S., 3, 4, 9, 81, 123
    Beyond the Pleasure Principle,
        37–41
    early emotional development,
        45–47, 51
    "Formulations on the two
        principles of psychic
        functioning", 45
    "fort–da", 60, 145
    infant observation, 61, 64
    Instincts and their Vicissitudes,
        34–37
    jouissance, 148
    mythical children, 15–44
    puberty (adolescence), 133, 146,
        155, 169
    scientific psychology, 18, 19
    structural theory, 18
    "The Interpretation of Dreams",
        169–171
    "Three Essays on the Theory of
        Sexuality", 83, 133
Freyman, J., 144

Gibbs, N., 162, 163, 167, 173
Glover, E., 48
Green, A., 16, 65
Gregory, R., 65
Grossman, D., 161

hallucination/hallucinatory, 9, 20,
    22, 23, 46, 49, 50, 123, 148, 169,
    170–172
Harding, J.:
    images of children, 7
Hegel, G., 144
Heimann, P., 57

Holmes, J., 94, 101, 102
Human Sciences, 2, 4

Id, 18, 24, 42, 49, 53, 155, 156
identification, 21, 29–32, 42, 51, 79,
    151, 155, 188
    primary, 19, 29, 30, 37
    projective, 66
images, 123, 125, 161, 169, 172
    fantasy-, 160, 174
    of children, 4, 6–9
    simulated, 165
imagination, 113, 114, 117, 123, 125,
    126, 130, 140, 160, 167–174, 187
imaginative fantasy, 115, 123, 130
infant observation, 10, 28, 38, 50, 53,
    56, 146, 200
    curricular discipline, 61–64
    history of, 59–61
    potential for learning, 66–68
    research, 64–66
information technology, 157
integration, 26, 28, 37, 49, 122, 125,
    130, 149

Jacobitti, S., 179, 190
Jones, E., 48, 155
jouissance, 82, 83, 85, 86, 91, 134,
    145, 146, 148
Joyce, A., 10–12
    psychoanalysis of a child,
        113–132
    response to Mathelin, 91, 92

Kestenberg, J., 65
Khan, M., 169
King, P., 57
Klein, M., 3, 15–17, 61
    depressive position, 204
    infant observation, 64–66
    Kleinian concepts, 38, 40
    object relations, 48
    on phantasy/fantasy, 191
    Psycho-Analysis of Children, 47
Kottman, P., 179
Kristeva, J., 6, 7, 179

Lacan, J., 3
  adolescence, 133–152
  jouissance, 148
  knowledge, 83
language, 2, 15, 17, 18, 42, 46, 141, 144, 145, 147–149, 164, 182, 199
  defects of inscription in, 71–92
Lanyado, M., 10–12, 150
  multiple traumatic loss, 93–112
Laplanche, J., 3, 16
latency age, 12, 127, 133, 134, 146, 177–192
Laufer, M., 152
Lee, G., 124, 125
Levi-Strauss, C., 180
libido, 20, 21, 23, 25–27, 33, 34, 134, 136, 150, 170
  see also sexuality
loss, 32, 33, 55, 64, 74, 78, 91, 146, 150, 199
  multiple traumatic loss, 93–112

Mallarmé, S., 80, 87–89
Mannoni, M., 126
Marcus, S., 3
Mathelin, C., 10, 11
  defects of inscription, 71–92
memories, 54, 69, 100, 177
  frozen, 55
metapsychological synthesis, 21, 34–37
Moebius band, 30
mother, 3, 10, 24, 27–29, 33–35, 37–41, 45–56, 62–68, 114, 116, 120–129
  good enough, 37, 50, 51, 124
  of premature baby, 10, 71–80
  narratives of children, 177–192
  see also adoption; breast; fostering
mourning, 73, 78, 105–107, 150
Mozart, A., 44,196, 202
music, 13, 44, 77, 79, 138, 149, 160, 168, 169, 188
  lessons, 197–204
  Winnicott and, 193–204
myth, 4, 33, 145, 180

Name-of-the-Father, 85, 91, 145
narcissism, 19–21, 32–36, 38, 39, 43, 53, 55, 140
  and fantasy, 115–117, 120
  in children, 25–31
  primary, 7, 48
  secondary, 48
narrative theory, 178–183
neglect, 1, 7, 37, 45, 95, 102, 103, 106, 186
neurosis, 33
  adult, 6
  and dreams, 19, 21
  in children, 21–25
  obsessional, 47
  psycho, 18

object, 3, 13, 17–43, 46, 48–57, 65, 76, 82, 83, 91, 92, 97, 116, 117, 119, 124, 128, 129, 136, 144, 145, 148, 150, 165, 166, 167, 170, 171, 174, 190, 201
  love-, 25, 41
  primary, 123
  relation, 19, 22, 30, 48, 54, 57
  transitional, 20, 52, 53, 97, 98, 100
  transformational, 187
objet a, 82, 85
oedipal:
  conflict, 31, 138, 150
  impulses, 134, 155
  parents, 152
  situation, 114, 129, 203
  space, 116, 117, 124, 125, 129, 131
Oedipus complex, 124, 133, 134, 145, 146, 182
Ogden, T., 124
one-body psychology, 47, 48, 50, 51, 53, 54
Other, the, 82, 85, 86, 143, 147, 148

paradox(ical), 94, 96, 98, 114, 124, 128, 129, 151, 189
  Lacanian, 136
  status, 20

Winnicottian, 38, 39, 100, 123–125, 142, 189
parent(ing), 3, 5, 9, 11, 13, 30, 32, 62, 67, 69, 90, 91, 99, 115, 116, 121, 126, 128, 129, 184–186, 189
  adoptive, 11, 80, 83–87, 89, 91–96, 100–112
  and music lessons, 195, 197–204
  fantasies of, 12, 30, 31, 197
  foster, 93–96, 100–112
  idealized, 42
  –infant relationship, 21
  of adolescents, 135–141, 150–154, 159–162
  of premature babies, 73–80
  parental discourse, 126
  separation from, 47, 60, 101–112, 146, 182, 183
  see also adolescence; adoption; fostering; mother
Parkes, C., 105
paternal metaphor, 133, 145, 146
peer group, 150, 184, 186, 188, 190
Perrier, F., 147
phantasy, 22, 36, 124, 188, 191
  see also fantasy
Phillips, A., 189, 204
play, 13, 22, 30, 33, 38, 40, 41, 53, 104, 182, 184–186, 188
  in adolescence, 155, 161, 164
  in therapy, 109–111, 114–120, 127, 128, 130, 131
  transitions and, 98–100
pleasure principle, 21, 22, 37–41, 45, 148, 169
Pontalis, J., 16, 30
Prager, J., 190
prehistory, 92
  child of, 21, 31–34
premature birth, 71–80
primary maternal preoccupation, 37, 78
psychic reality, 17, 42, 49, 114, 122, 123, 125, 126, 130
psychosis, 19, 23, 41, 50, 85, 135, 145
  child of, 21, 25–31

puberty, 12, 133–136, 138, 146, 149, 150, 174, 196
  see also adolescence

rage, 8, 51, 115, 120, 129, 158, 161–164, 166, 168, 171–173
  see also violent
Rassial, J.-J., 142, 143
Real, the, 24, 82, 90, 92, 142, 146–149, 157, 163–167, 171, 172, 174, 175, 187
reality:
  -ego, 23, 35–37
  principle, 21, 22, 33, 36, 38–40, 45, 51
recapitulation, theory of, 155
rejection, 96, 103, 105
Richter, S., 198, 203
Rickman, J., 47
Ricoeur, P., 169, 170
Roche, T., 162, 167, 173
Rodman, F., 15, 17, 18
Rose, J., 2, 6, 191

Sarnoff, C., 127
Schreber, President:
  Freud's study of, 25, 26, 31, 32
Self, the, 12, 13, 26–30, 37, 42, 46, 50–53, 55, 91, 123, 125, 128, 131, 154, 178–180, 189, 190, 204
  Split, 55
Sellin, B., 143
separation, 94, 95, 97, 100–112, 142, 145, 167
  from mother, 38, 78
  -individuation, 150
sexuality, 2, 3, 12, 16, 83, 133, 136, 148, 149, 151, 160, 171
shame, 90, 107, 116
siblings, 56, 102, 105, 183–186
signification, 8, 9, 145
signifier, 85, 88, 89, 140, 144–146
speech, 67, 79, 90, 92, 135, 148, 149
  rhythm of, 143, 144
  -symbolism, 46, 52

Spice, N., 13
   Winnicott and music, 193–204
Spitz, R., 60
Stern, D., 69
Strachey, J., 18
superego, 18, 31, 42
symbolization, 140, 144, 167–169

Target, M., 114, 125
therapeutic:
   environment, 99, 204
   process, 96, 99
thinking, 113–132
Tonnesmann, M., 9
   early emotional development, 45–58
tragedy:
   Columbine school massacre, 153–176
transitional space, 33, 53, 99, 178, 179, 201
transitions:
   and play, 98–100
   creating, 93–112
   from fostering to adoption, 107–112
trauma, 26, 31, 53, 126, 146, 157
   child of, 21, 37–41
   in childhood, 54, 55–57, 69, 79
   see also multiple traumatic loss
two-body psychology, 50, 51, 54, 57

Van Heeswyk, P., 149
Vanier, A., 10, 12
   on adolescence, 133–152
violent, 1, 55, 103, 114, 115, 117, 129, 136, 157, 165, 174
   potential of adolescence, 158–163
virtual:
   age, 167–172
   cyberspace, 160, 161
   reality, 159–162, 164, 165

Waddell, M., 181, 184, 190
Walkerdine, V., 184
Warner, M., 186, 187
Winnicott, D.
   adolescence, 133–152
   and music, 193–204
   early emotional development, 45–58
   fantasy, 123, 186–189
   good enough mother, 124
   narrative theory, 178–183
   object, 97–100
   paradox, 99, 123–125
   play, 99
   potential space, 123–125
   primary maternal preoccupation, 78
   spatula game, 60
   tragedy, 153–176
writing, 183
   in autism, 143
   problems, 80–92
Wise, I., 149, 152
Wolff, P., 66
World Wide Web, 159